ScottForesman

LITERATURE
AND INTEGRATED STUDIES

Grade Eight

Reading, Writing &
Grammar SkillBook

ScottForesman

Editorial Offices: Glenview, Illinois
Regional Offices: San Jose, California • Tucker, Georgia • Glenview,
Illinois • Oakland, New Jersey • Dallas, Texas

Visit ScottForesman's Home Page at http://www.scottforesman.com

Acknowledgments
Cover art (detail): Sam Adoquei, "Portrait of Rockney C.," 1992, Collection of the artist.

Copyright © 1997
Scott, Foresman
and Company
Glenview, Illinois.
All Rights Reserved. Printed in the United States of America.

ISBN: 0-673-32435-4
These blackline masters may be used for making duplicating masters or for photocopying for classroom use by schools without written permission. Reproduction of this material by any other means or for purposes other than classroom use is prohibited without prior written permission from ScottForesman,
1900 East Lake Avenue,
Glenview, Illinois 60025.

Contents

Vocabulary Skills		
	Context	1
	Direct and Indirect Context Clues	3
	More Context Clues	5
	Clues in Longer Contexts	7
	Using Your Common Sense	9
	Understanding Word Structure	11
	Compound Words	13
	Recognizing Root Words	15
	Using Prefixes	17
	Negative Prefixes	19
	More About Prefixes	21
	Using Suffixes	23

Reading Skills		
	Adjusting Rate and Method to Purpose	25
	Using Patterns to Help You Read	29
	Making a Survey	33
	Intensive Reading	35
	Putting Your Reading Skills to Work	39
	What Is Imagery?	41
	Recognizing Imagery	43
	Responding to Imagery	45
	Visualizing What Happens	47
	Reviewing the Use of Imagery	51
	What Is Figurative Language?	53
	Making Sense of Figurative Language	57
	Understanding Figurative Comparisons	59
	Reviewing Figurative Language	63
	Making Inferences	65
	Identifying Clues	67
	Inferences About Time and Place	70
	Inferences About Characters	72
	Inferences About Fantasy	76
	Reviewing Inferences	78
	Finding the Direct Statement of Main Idea	80
	Identifying the Implied Main Idea	82
	Evaluating Details	84
	Reviewing Main Idea	86
	What Are Judgments?	88
	Fact and Opinion	90
	Mixed Statements	92
	Valid and Objective Opinions	94
	Words with Emotional Effect	96
	Appeal in Advertising	98

Writing Skills		
	Main Idea in a Paragraph	100
	Topic Sentences	102
	Writing a Narrative Paragraph	104
	Plot	106
	Character and Dialogue	108
	Classifying	110
	Arranging Details in Spatial Order	112
	Writing a Descriptive Paragraph	114
	Comparing and Contrasting	116
	Writing a Compare/Contrast Description	118
	Writing an Explanatory Paragraph	120
	Cause and Effect	122
	Writing a Cause-and-Effect Paragraph	124
	Writing a Persuasive Paragraph	126
	Writing a Summary Paragraph	128
	Research: Choosing a Topic	130
	Research: Using Reference Sources	132
	Research: Taking Notes	134
	Research: Organizing Information	137
	Research: Outlining	139

Grammar, Usage, and Mechanics Skills		
	Kinds of Sentences	141
	Subjects and Predicates	143
	Simple and Compound Sentences	145
	Sentence Fragments and Run-Ons	147
	Combining Subjects, Predicates, and Sentences	149
	Varying Sentence Structure	151
	Direct Objects and Subject Complements	153
	Indirect Objects	155
	Independent and Dependent Clauses	157
	Complex Sentences	159
	Compound-Complex Sentences	161
	Adjective and Adverb Clauses	163
	Combining Sentences with Clauses	165
	Improving Sentences	167
	Expanding Sentences	169
	Appositives	171
	Identifying Nouns	173
	Kinds of Nouns	175
	Plural Nouns	177
	Possessive Nouns	179
	Plural or Possessive	181
	Personal Pronouns	183

Possessive Pronouns	185
Interrogative, Relative, and Demonstrative Pronouns	187
Reflexive and Intensive Pronouns	189
Indefinite Pronouns	191
Subject and Object Pronouns	193
Pronouns as Subject Complements	195
Pronouns in Comparisons	197
Using *who* and *whom*	199
Pronoun Agreement	201
Identifying Verbs	203
Action or Linking Verb	205
Verb Phrases	207
Simple Tenses	209
Principal Parts of Verbs	211
Perfect Tense	213
Transitive and Intransitive Verbs	215
Principal Parts of Irregular Verbs	217
Forms of *be*, *have*, and *do*	221
Troublesome Verb Pairs	224
Active and Passive Verbs	227
Consistent Verb Tenses	229
Subject-Verb Agreement	231
Subjects Separated from Verbs	233
Sentences in Inverted Order	235
Agreement with Special Subjects	237
Agreement with Indefinite Pronouns	239
Identifying Adjectives	241
Comparative Forms of Adjectives	243
Identifying Adverbs	245
Functions of Adverbs	247
Comparative Forms of Adverbs	249
Adjective or Adverb	251
Good, *well*, *bad*, and *badly*	253
This, *that*, *these*, and *those*	255
Using Negative Words	257
Placement of Modifiers	259
Participles and Participial Phrases	261
Gerunds and Gerund Phrases	264
Infinitives and Infinitive Phrases	267
Placement of Participial Phrases	269
Prepositions and Prepositional Phrases	271
Preposition, Adverb, or Infinitive	273
Adjective and Adverb Prepositional Phrases	275
Two Kinds of Conjunctions	278
Identifying Interjections	280
Combining Sentences with Modifiers	281
Capitalizing Proper Nouns and Adjectives	283
Capitalizing Titles	287
Commas in Sentences	289
Other Uses of Commas	291
Semicolons and Colons	293
Quotation Marks	295
Other Punctuation Marks	297
Answer Key	299

Acknowledgments

VOCABULARY

From "After the Blast" by Allen Bonenko. Copyright ©1980 by the National Wildlife Federation. Reprinted by permission from the October-November 1980 issue of NATIONAL WILDLIFE Magazine.

Adapted from pp. 8-11 in *Dove* by Robin Lee Graham, with Derek L. T. Gill Copyright © 1972 by Robin Lee Graham and Derek L. T. Gill. Reprinted by permission of Harper & Row, Publishers, Inc. and Angus and Robertson Publishers, Sydney, Australia.

READING

Adapted from GREAT LATIN SPORTS FIGURES by Jerry Izenberg. Copyright © 1976 by Jerry Izenberg. Reprinted by permission of William Morris Agency, Inc. on behalf of the author.

"The First Wonder of the World" by Edward L. Lee from CHILD LIFE. Copyright © 1980 by Children's Better Health Institute, Benjamin Franklin Literary & Medical Society, Inc., Indianapolis, Indiana. Used by permission.

From BOOK SIX, HEALTH AND GROWTH by Julius B. Richmond, et al. Copyright © 1974, 1971 Scott, Foresman and Company.

Adaptation from "Houses That Grew" by Marguerite Z. Mudge in RANGER RICK'S NATURE MAGAZINE, August 1978. Copyright ©1978 by the National Wildlife Federation. Reprinted by permission.

Adapted from "The Age of Dirigibles" by Lynn Hartsell in BOYS' LIFE, April 1980. Reprinted by permission of the author.

Laurence Yep, *Dragonwings*. New York: Harper & Row, Publishers, 1975, p. 223.

Madeleine L'Engle, *A Wrinkle in Time*. New York: Dell Publishing Co., Inc., 1962, p. 38.

Excerpts from *Earthquakes* by Patricia Lauber. Reprinted by permission of the author.

From *Sleep in Thunder* by Ed Lacy, copyright © 1964 by Ed Lacy. Reprinted by permission of Grosset & Dunlap, Inc.

Adaptation of pp. 71-72 from *I Would Rather Be a Turnip* by Vera and Bill Cleaver. (J. B. Lippincott Co.) Copyright © 1971 by Vera and William J. Cleaver. Reprinted by permission of Harper & Row, Publishers, Inc. and Hamish Hamilton Ltd.

"Dreams" from *The Dream Keeper and Other Poems* by Langston Hughes. Copyright 1932 by Alfred A. Knopf, Inc. and renewed 1960 by Langston Hughes. Reprinted by permission of the publisher.

"Motor Cars" from *Songs from Around a Toadstool Table* by Rowena Bennett. Copyright © 1967 by Rowena Bennett. Used by permission of Follett Publishing Company.

"Gathering Leaves" from *The Poetry of Robert Frost* edited by Edward Connery Lathem. Copyright 1951 by Robert Frost. Copyright 1923, © 1969 by Henry Holt and Co., Inc. Reprinted by permission.

James Forman, *The Survivor*. New York: Farrar, Straus and Giroux, Inc., 1976.

From "Letters You'd Better Get Over With" by Peg Bracken. Reprinted with permission from *The Saturday Evening Post* (January 12, 1957). © 1957 The Curtis Publishing Company.

From "Mountain-Road Blowout" in *Mysteries for Crimebusters* by the Editors of Read Magazine. Copyright © 1978 by Xerox Corporation. Reprinted by permission of Grosset & Dunlap, Inc.

Excerpts from *Runway Zero-Eight* (British title: *Flight Into Danger*) by Arthur Hailey and John Castle. Copyright © 1958 by Arthur Hailey, Ronald Payne, and John Garrod. Reprinted by permission of Doubleday & Company, Inc. and Souvenir Press of London.

P. A. Engerbrecht, *Under the Haystack*. New York: Dell Publishing Co., Inc., 1973, pp. 132-133.

Arlene Hale, "West of the Mississippi." South Nashville, Tennessee: The Methodist Publishing House, 1956.

E. L. Konigsburg, *From the Mixed-up Files of Mrs. Basil E. Frankweiler*. New York: Dell Publishing Co., Inc., 1967, pp. 5-6.

From *Run Far, Run Fast* by Walt Morey. Reprinted by permission.

Adapted from "The Choice" by W. Hilton-Young from *Punch*. © Punch (Rothco). Reprinted by permission of Rothco Cartoons Inc.

Abridged from *Leap Into Danger*, English translation ©1959 by the University of London Press, Ltd. and Leif Hamre. Reprinted by permission of Harcourt Brace Jovanovich, Inc.

Excerpt from "Tenacious Termites" by Judith Fisher from *Science 81*, May 1981.

"Soup" from *Smoke and Steel* by Carl Sandburg, copyright 1920 by Harcourt Brace Jovanovich, Inc.; renewed 1948 by Carl Sandburg. Reprinted by permission of the publisher.

From "The Male Dancer" by Walter Terry in THE SATURDAY REVIEW, May 1981. Copyright © 1981 by Saturday Review Magazine Co. Reprinted by permission.

From "Junior Olympians" by Jody Shields, reprinted from *Seventeen* ® Magazine, July 1980. Copyright © 1980 by Triangle Communications Inc. All rights reserved.

WRITING

From "Oh Broom, Get to Work" by Yoshiko Uchida. Copyright © 1977 by Yoshiko Uchida. Reprinted by permission of the author.

From *Harriet Tubman: Conductor on the Underground Railroad* by Ann Petry. Copyright © 1955, renewed 1983 by Ann Petry. Reprinted by permission of Russell & Volkening, Inc. as agents for the author.

Sir Arthur Conan Doyle, *The Hound of the Baskervilles*. London: John Murray, Ltd.

"The Drummer Boy of Shiloh" by Ray Bradbury. Copyright © 1960 by Ray Bradbury. Reprinted by permission of Don Congdon Associates, Inc.

Adapted from *The Dark Child* by Camara Laye. Copyright © 1954 by Camara Laye. Reprinted by permission of Farrar, Straus and Giroux, Inc. and William Collins, Sons & Company Limited.

Willa Cather, *My Antonia*. Boston: Houghton Mifflin Company, 1918, 1926, p. 11.

Gloria Gonzalez, *Gaucho*. New York: Alfred A. Knopf, Inc., 1977, pp. 8-9.

Jamake Highwater, *Legend Days*. New York: Harper & Row, Publishers, Inc., 1984, p. 66.

From *The Founding of the Republic* by Richard B. Morris. Revised edition copyright © 1985 by Lerner Publications Company. Reprinted by permission of Lerner Publications, 241 First Avenue North, Minneapolis, Minnesota, 55401.

Lesson 1
Context

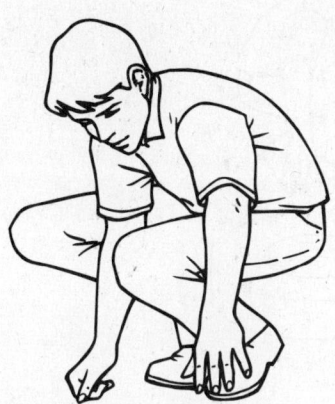

What is this boy doing?

You can see he is squatting down. He seems to be reaching for something, but what and why? What is going on here?

Actually, the boy belongs in a larger picture. Look at the picture on the next page. Imagine him in it, like a piece from a jigsaw puzzle put into place. His actions become quite clear when you see him as part of a larger picture.

You also have to look for the "larger picture" when you read. Look at the word below. What does it mean?

SCALE
Is it part of the skin of a fish?
Is it an instrument for weighing something?
Is it a series of musical notes?

You could not really tell what the boy is doing until you saw him in place in the larger picture of which he is a part. In the same way, the word *scale* has no exact meaning unless it is part of a sentence. The other words that surround a particular word in the sentence or paragraph of which it is a part are its **context**. The context of a word often contains clues to the word's meaning. What does *scale* mean in the following context?

By piling the wooden boxes on top of each other and climbing to the top of the stack, Frank was able to *scale* the high stone wall.

In the picture on the next page, the jack, the wrench, the hubcap, and the tires are clues that help you understand what the picture is about. There are clues in the sentence, too—context clues—in the words that surround *scale*. Underline the words or groups of words in the sentence that help you understand the meaning of *scale*.

The picture is a context because it gives you information about what the boy is doing. The sentence is also a context because it gives you information about what scale *means*.

Grade Eight SkillBook, Vocabulary

Even familiar words like *scale* can cause problems when you read. Since some words can have many different meanings, you must know which meaning the writer intends. Context clues can help you solve this problem.

Exercise
Read the following sentences and write a meaning for each of the italicized words on the line below each sentence.

1. The facts brought out in the case were enough to *clear* the man so he was able to leave the courtroom free and happy.

   _____

2. June will not leave her *post* at the door without permission.

   _____

3. The man was sentenced for two *counts* of burglary.

   _____

4. The company used a lie detector as a *screen* for applicants before hiring.

   _____

5. When Ron ran over the nail, he was out of luck; he didn't have a *spare* tire.

   _____

Grade Eight SkillBook, Vocabulary

Lesson 2
Direct and Indirect Context Clues

Circle the words in the following two sentences that tell you what the italicized words mean.

A. During the past hundred years, wonderful *frescoes*, or wall paintings, have been discovered in caves in France and Spain.

B. The first finds were *polychrome* (multicolored) paintings of bison and other animals at Altamira, in Spain.

In sentences A and B the writer indicates exactly what is meant by the words *frescoes* and *polychrome*. This information is set off, in the first case with commas, in the second with parentheses. An explanation of this kind is called a **direct context clue**. It often follows the unfamiliar word it explains very closely and is usually set off with punctuation such as commas, parentheses, or dashes.

Often, however, there may not be a word or phrase that gives the exact meaning of an unfamiliar word. Read the following sentences and then write the meaning of each of the italicized words on the line below.

C. Ancient artists used red and black *pigments* made from clay and soot to do their paintings.

Pigments means _____

D. Some of the paintings are in almost *inaccessible* spots; to reach them a visitor may have to wriggle through long, narrow, wet passages.

Inaccessible means _____

In sentences C and D the italicized words are not directly defined. But the general information in the sentences gives **indirect context clues**.

Sentence C doesn't tell you exactly what *pigments* are. But it does tell you who used them ("ancient artists"), what colors they were ("red and black"), what they were made from ("clay and soot"), and what they were used for ("paintings"). Using these indirect context clues, you should be able to figure out that *pigments* are paints.

Sentence D doesn't tell you exactly what *inaccessible* means. But it does tell you that the word has something to do with how hard it is for visitors to reach some of the paintings. Therefore, a good guess would be that *inaccessible* means something like "hard to reach."

Exercise

Use both direct and indirect context clues to figure out the meaning of each of the italicized words in the sentences below.

_____ 1. The most *celebrated* of these caves is Lascaux (las kô´), in southern France, famous for its beautiful paintings of bison, horses, and other animals.
   a. unknown
   b. well known
   c. ugly

_____ 2. The *archaeologists* who study these caves date the paintings from 10,000 to 30,000 years ago.
   a. cave people
   b. scientists
   c. tourists

_____ 3. In some of the caves a variety of *implements*—from needles to harpoons—have been found along with the paintings.
   a. baskets
   b. statues
   c. tools

_____ 4. The cave artists also did engravings, and their *burins*, the cutting tools they used, have also been found.
   a. engraving tools
   b. spear points
   c. needles

_____ 5. The fact that the paintings were often placed where it was very unlikely that anyone would see their beauty suggests that their purpose was not *aesthetic* but magical.
   a. silly
   b. artistic
   c. scientific

_____ 6. The wooly rhinoceros, an extinct Ice Age mammal, appears in paintings on the walls of *Font-de-Gaume* in the southwestern region of France.
   a. a cathedral
   b. a cave
   c. a building

Lesson 3
More Context Clues

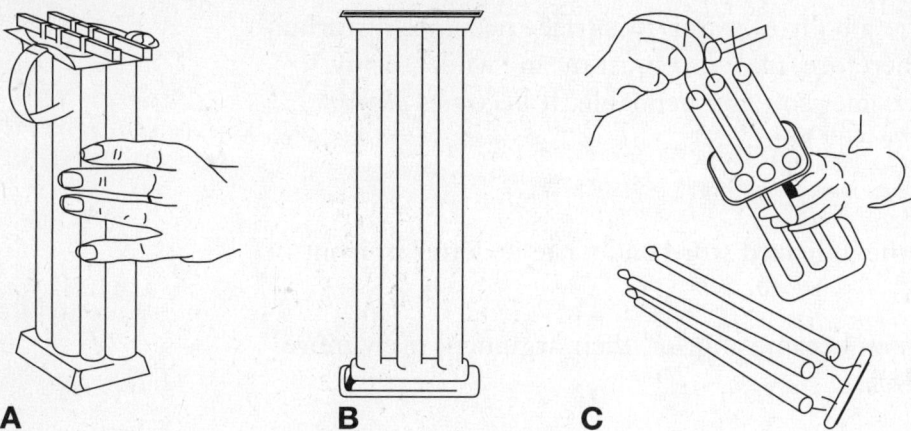

Which picture tells you most about the object shown?

_____ Picture A, because it shows the size of the object.

_____ Picture B, because it shows the outline of the object.

_____ Picture C, because it shows the object in use.

Seeing how an object is used probably gives you the best clues to what it is. Similarly, knowing the way a word is used in a sentence can give you clues to the meaning of the word. In the sentences below, see if you can figure out the meaning of the italicized words.

The old barn leaned to one side, had holes in the roof, and was badly in need of paint; the farmhouse was equally *dilapidated*.

J. P. Morgan was a rich and powerful man; Andrew Carnegie was another *magnate*.

In both of these sentences, the italicized word is being used in a comparison. The barn is in bad shape and the farmhouse is like it. It, too, is *dilapidated*. Therefore, *dilapidated* must mean "run down, falling apart." J. P. Morgan was rich and powerful, and Andrew Carnegie was like him. He was also a *magnate*. Therefore, a *magnate* must be "a rich and powerful person."

The older girl sat quietly and paid attention to the movie, but the younger one was very *unruly*.

One of the dogs was very brave, but the other was quite *timorous*.

In these two sentences, the italicized words are being used to show contrast. The older girl was quiet and attentive, but the younger one was not. She was *unruly*. Therefore, *unruly* must mean "disorderly, unmanageable." One dog was brave, but the other was not. This dog was *timorous*. Therefore, *timorous* must mean "cowardly, fearful."

Grade Eight SkillBook, Vocabulary

The wind began to blow very hard, and the lake became *turbulent*.

The heat of the sun made the wax very *pliable*.

In these two sentences, the italicized words are being used to show effects. When wind blows very hard on a body of water, its surface becomes disturbed, wavy. It becomes *turbulent*. Therefore, *turbulent* must mean "wild, stormy." When the sun heats wax, it becomes soft and bendable. It becomes *pliable*. Therefore, *pliable* must mean "easily bent."

Exercise

Choose the best meaning for the italicized word and write its letter in front of the sentence.

_____ 1. As the two women became angrier, their argument grew more and more *vociferous*.
   a. polite
   b. loud
   c. cheerful

_____ 2. Jenna really likes rock climbing, and Ami is nearly as *ardent*.
   a. tall
   b. tanned
   c. eager

_____ 3. The world looked *nebulous* through the mist-covered window.
   a. hazy
   b. familiar
   c. clear

_____ 4. Emily Dickinson published little while she was alive, most of her poems appearing *posthumously*.
   a. frequently
   b. quietly
   c. after death

_____ 5. His career took off like a rocket and came down just as *precipitously*.
   a. rapidly
   b. comfortably
   c. slowly

Lesson 4
Clues in Longer Contexts

(a) Over a period of twenty-five years, English scholar Sir Arthur Evans *excavated* the ruins of the palace of King Minos on the island of Crete. (b) In the process he dug up thousands of clay tablets covered with the letters of an unknown language. (c) For many years neither Evans nor anyone else could read the *inscriptions* on the tablets.

Exercise A
Write the letter of the answer in the blank next to the question.

_____ 1. Which sentence contains a good clue to the meaning of *excavated*?

_____ 2. What is the best meaning for *excavated*?
   a. removed
   b. rebuilt
   c. uncovered

_____ 3. Which sentence gives a good clue to the meaning of *inscriptions*?

_____ 4. What is the best meaning for *inscriptions*?
   a. writings
   b. addresses
   c. stains

(a) Then in 1935 Evans gave a lecture attended by a thirteen-year-old schoolboy named Michael Ventris who was interested in codes.
(b) Listening to Evans talk about the tablets, the amateur *cryptographer* discovered what was to be the most important *objective* of his life. (c) Young Ventris decided that his goal would be to discover the meaning of the unknown writings.

_____ 5. Which sentences contain a good clue to the meaning of *cryptographer*?

_____ 6. What is the best meaning for *cryptographer*?
   a. cave explorer
   b. code expert
   c. film maker

_____ 7. Which sentence contains a good clue to the meaning of *objective*?

_____ 8. What is the best meaning for *objective*?
   a. aim
   b. error
   c. friendship

(a) Ventris had finished school, served in England's Royal Air Force, and became an architect before he was able to return to his job of discovering the meaning of Linear B (as Evans had called the unknown writings). (b) Still, Ventris was only thirty-one when the announcement of his *decipherment* of Linear B in 1953 made his name known to scholars all over the world.

_____ 9. Which sentence contains a good clue to the meaning of *decipherment*?

_____ 10. What is the best meaning for *decipherment*?
   a. enjoyment
   b. figuring out
   c. collection

When the sentence in which an unfamiliar word appears doesn't contain enough context clues to help you figure out the word's meaning, look for clues in the material that comes closely before or after it.

Exercise B
Read the following paragraphs, and then choose the best meaning for each of the italicized words from the list below on the right. Put the letter of that meaning on the blank in front of the word.

The damage done to the animal populations and the places where they lived by the eruptions of Mount St. Helens was enormous but not *incalculable*. Even before the volcano at least temporarily stopped belching ash and mud, scientists were estimating the loss of animals and their *habitats*.

The eruptions *obliterated* a huge area of forest. They completely destroyed 240 miles of prime woodland, both banks of the Toutle River, and more than 150 miles of *adjacent* streams. Another 1,000 miles of streams at a greater distance became impossible to reach because the roads leading to them were gone. The ash from the volcano is *devastating* to wildlife. Scientists believe that at least 1.5 million game birds and animals could eventually be lost in the state of Washington alone.

_____ 1. incalculable   a. rapid
_____ 2. habitats   b. nearby
_____ 3. obliterated   c. improved
_____ 4. adjacent   d. living places
_____ 5. devastating   e. very harmful
                                f. wiped out
                                g. uncountable

Lesson 5
Using Your Common Sense

Read the following paragraphs and look for context clues to the meanings of the italicized words.

    They came into a part of the cave with weird and beautiful rock shapes everywhere. Connie pointed her flashlight around the cave's walls and the shadows danced. It looked as if the *stalactites* and *stalagmites* themselves were moving about.

    "This is quite a young cave," she said, shining her light on a spear of rock that hung down to within inches of her face. Water dripped slowly from its tip. "Most of these formations—like this stalactite—are still 'alive.' Minerals dissolved in the water dripping from the cave roof form all these shapes."

    "I didn't know we had a *spelunker* with us!" Alice said.

    Connie laughed. "You sure have! I used to poke around in caves with my mother and father every chance I'd get. Come on, let's look in there. Don't trip over these stalagmites."

Exercise A

Study the context clues and then decide which of the explanations below for each italicized word makes the most sense. Circle its letter.

1. *stalactites*
    a. The stalactites appear to be moving. One comes to within inches of Connie's face. They must be some sort of cave-dwelling animal that flies about, like a bat.
    b. The stalactites are formed by dripping water. They must be underground streams.
    c. Stalactites are formed by minerals dissolved in water. One hangs down in front of Connie. Stalactites must be rock formations hanging down from the roof of a cave.

2. *stalagmites*
    a. Like stalactites, stalagmites are formed by minerals dissolved in water. Connie warns Alice not to trip over them. Stalagmites must be rock formations growing up from the floor of a cave.
    b. Connie warns Alice not to trip over the stalagmites. A stalagmite must be a piece of equipment that is used in exploring caves.
    c. Connie warns Alice not to trip over the stalagmites. A stalagmite must be a cave-dwelling animal that crawls about.

3. *spelunker*
    a. Connie and Alice are exploring a cave. A spelunker must be a piece of equipment that is used in exploring caves.

b. Alice says that she didn't know they had a spelunker with them. A spelunker must be a kind of cave-dwelling animal whose coloring makes it very hard to see.
c. Connie says that she has always enjoyed exploring caves. A spelunker must be someone who explores caves.

Exercise B
Read the following paragraph and then choose from the list below the *two* words that best fit the context of each of the numbered blanks. Write the letters of the two words on the blanks.

　　Last Saturday my family went to a museum downtown. When we arrived at the museum, we bought a 1. _____ to help us find our way around. My little brother wanted to see the skeletons of the dinosaurs and other 2. _____ animals first. At noon we had lunch in the 3. _____ . In the afternoon we saw some Tibetan 4. _____ that would make those who wore them look like ghosts or devils. My little brother was so 5. _____ that he fell asleep on the way home.

1. a. poster
　b. guidebook
　c. post card
　d. map
　e. newspaper

2. a. circus
　b. ancient
　c. imaginary
　d. pet
　e. extinct

3. a. restaurant
　b. lobby
　c. theater
　d. cafeteria
　e. store

4. a. belts
　b. masks
　c. gloves
　d. shoes
　e. costumes

5. a. hungry
　b. tired
　c. frightened
　d. weary
　e. angry

Name _____ Class _____ Date _____

Lesson 6
Understanding Word Structure

1. Charlie Chaplin was a famous comedian and **actor** in silent films.

2. He also made sound films, such as *The Great Dictator*, in which he **enacted** the role of a comic dictator.

3. He made a few more films after that, but was generally **inactive** in his old age.

When you come across an unfamiliar word, you should look at it closely. Look for word parts that you already know. For example, look at the words in dark type in the sentences above. Each has a familiar root, *act*. By looking at the parts added to the root, you may be able to figure out the word's meaning.

This is called analyzing a word by using **structure**.

Exercise A
Here is a list of words that may be unfamiliar to you. Try to break them down into their parts. Separate these parts by slashes (/). Example: *annoyance:* annoy / ance.

1. disprove _____
2. masklike _____
3. likable _____
4. unusual _____
5. sorrowful _____

As you can see, when unfamiliar words are broken into smaller pieces, it is easier to pronounce them.

Read the article that follows. Study the italicized words.

The French call it "dent-de-lion" (lion's tooth) because of its *irregular* leaves. Dandelions are found in most *backyards*. You may think of them as weeds, but don't use a *herbicide*. Eat them instead. Dandelions are *nutritional* and loaded with vitamins.

The leaves can be added to any *saladlike* dish. The roots can be ground up to make a *caffeine-free* coffee substitute. The blossoms are used to make jelly, wine, and tea.

Enjoy your dandelions!

Now look at the italicized words. Some may be unfamiliar to you. But many of these words probably have parts that you already know. You can use these word parts to help you both pronounce and understand the words.

Grade Eight SkillBook, Vocabulary

Name _____ Class _____ Date _____

Exercise B
Here are the words from the article on the previous page. Fill in the blanks by writing the missing word parts.

1. _____ regular

2. _____ yards

3. herb _____

4. nutrition _____

5. salad _____

6. caffeine- _____

When you can break down unfamiliar words by structure—that is, separating their word parts, saying them, then pronouncing the whole word together—you have taken a big step toward understanding and pronouncing such words.

Lesson 7
Compound Words

Do you ever find yourself drifting off during the day and dreaming about being somewhere else? Do you ever have *daydreams*? *Daydream* is a **compound word**. A compound is made of two or more words that combine to form one word with a single meaning.

Read the paragraph that follows. Pay attention to the words that are italicized.

> Traveling along a highway in Michigan, you may notice a strange thing. There are not any discarded beverage cans or *no-deposit* bottles littering the *roadside*. This is because Michigan has a *Bottle Law*. That means all buyers of beverages must pay a deposit on the beverage container. Because of this, and because there are many people who will collect empty containers to claim the deposit (usually about ten or twenty cents), it is rare to see an empty can or bottle lying about.

1. Which compound is spelled with a hyphen?
2. Which compound is written as two separate words?
3. Which compound consists of two words written together as one?

As you see, compound words can be written three different ways. They can be written with hyphens *(no-deposit)*, as two or more separate words *(Bottle Law)*, or as one word *(roadside)*. No matter how they are written, compound words are always considered one word in meaning.

Some compounds mean exactly what you think they mean. *No-deposit* is easy to figure out, since *no* and *deposit* explain themselves. The same applies to a compound like *roadside*. By taking each word and joining them in meaning, you have the meaning of the compound.

Other compounds are not so easy to understand. You may need context clues and even a dictionary to help you. The meaning of *hotbed* cannot be understood merely by combining the meanings of the two words. If you look in a dictionary, you will find that *hotbed* means a bed of earth covered with glass and heated in order to grow plants.

Exercise
Read each sentence. Choose the best meaning for the italicized compound word and circle the letter.

1. Peggy used a large brass key as a *paperweight* on her desk.
   a. object to hold down papers
   b. weight made of paper

2. The tactics of the new ruler were those used in a *police state*.
   a. prison tower
   b. country where life is strictly controlled

Grade Eight SkillBook, Vocabulary

3. Our *up-to-date* home computer has a CD-ROM.
   a. modern
   b. purchased on credit

4. Ms. Kay was hired to write the *screenplay* for the movie.
   a. a folding screen
   b. motion picture script

5. Billy had to get a *part-time* job after school to earn money.
   a. extra
   b. not full time

6. Stephen King's book was on the *best-seller* list.
   a. expensive
   b. popular

7. Ellen bought the *paperback* version of the play.
   a. book with soft cover
   b. book wrapped in paper

8. The *warehouse* was filled with cartons of furniture and electronics.
   a. a place to store things
   b. a worn out building

9. Call the *toll free* number for information.
   a. telephone
   b. no cost

10. Aunt Irene suffers from *heartburn*.
    a. a serious heart attack
    b. a chest pain caused by eating certain foods.

Grade Eight SkillBook, Vocabulary

Name _____ Class _____ Date _____

Lesson 8
Recognizing Root Words

```
        read | er
un | read
        read | able
re | read
```

Look at the words in the figure above. You will notice that they are all based on the same word, *read*. This word is called a **root word**. Most roots have one general meaning, which can be changed when other word parts are added to it. Word parts may be added before or after the root.

Word parts added to a root are called **affixes**. A word made of affixes and a root is called a **derivative**.

Exercise A
Use the derivatives found in the figure above to complete the sentences.

1. Jamie was an avid _____ of poetry.

2. For months after the magazine arrived, it remained _____.

3. Some people find newspapers more _____ than books.

4. Karen had to _____ the difficult lesson three times.

When you discover a word with several parts, try to separate the parts in your mind. Look for the root word. Use common sense to find the root word, and don't separate anything that is not a familiar word part.

Exercise B
Study the list of derivatives below. Find the root word in each and write it beside the derivative.

1. friendly _____

2. drainage _____

3. revisit _____

4. preview _____

5. submarine _____

6. mouthful _____

7. dampness _____

8. misprint _____

Grade Eight SkillBook, Vocabulary

Name _____ Class _____ Date _____

9. interstate _____

10. unbeatable _____

Exercise C
Find the root of each word in the list by referring to the four roots below. Write the letter of the proper root beside each word.

   a. hear
   b. heart
   c. ear
   d. earth

1. unearthly _____
2. heartless _____
3. earthy _____
4. dishearten _____
5. earful _____
6. unheard _____
7. earthen _____
8. overhear _____
9. earlike _____
10. hearer _____

Exercise D
Some of the words below are derivatives and some are root words. Circle the derivatives. Do nothing to the roots.

1. imagine
2. personal
3. disharmony
4. refinish
5. measurement
6. journey
7. careless
8. superfine
9. regularize
10. cheer

Lesson 9
Using Prefixes

In Sheldon, Connecticut, school officials were so *unhappy* with the number of students absent from school without permission that the officials *rewrote* the rules. Now, parents of such students are being arrested.

Note the italicized words in the news article. They both have word parts added to the beginnings of root words. These parts are called **prefixes**.

1. Find the root word in *unhappy*. Then find the prefix.
2. What does the prefix do to the root?

By studying *unhappy* you can see how a prefix can change the meaning of a root word. To understand what such prefixes do to the root, you must know the meaning of the prefix. In the word *rewrote*, used above, the prefix *re-* means "do again" or "do over." If you know this you can figure out that *rewrote* means "wrote over" or "wrote again."

Here is a short list of some prefixes commonly used in the English language. Study their meanings and spellings.

SOME COMMON PREFIXES
anti- = against; opposed to; not
dis- = opposite of; reverse of
inter- = together; between; among
mis- = bad; badly; wrong; wrongly
pre- = before in time, place, order
re- = again; anew; back
sub- = under; below; down
trans- = across; over; through
un- = not; the opposite of
semi- = half; partly; twice

Exercise A
Use the prefixes above to complete the sentences. Use context to help you choose the appropriate prefix.

1. The students were about to _____ enter the school after the fire drill.

2. Doctors sometimes _____ agree about the way to treat a patient.

3. The visitors took the _____ way downtown to the museum.

4. We found the old lumber was warped and _____ even and not usable.

Grade Eight SkillBook, Vocabulary

Name _____ Class _____ Date _____

5. The club held _____ monthly meetings in the church basement.

6. The _____ gravity machine helped the astronauts prepare for their journey.

7. Bella attended a _____ view of the new television show.

8. Jesse wouldn't allow anyone to _____ treat his little brother Rab.

9. We used _____ state highways all the way to Los Angeles.

10. Mr. Gomez decided to _____ plant the tomatoes to a sunny spot.

Exercise B
Think of other words that begin with each of the 10 prefixes listed on the previous page. Write them below. If you have difficulty, think about the meaning of the prefix or use a dictionary.

1. anti _____
2. dis _____
3. inter _____
4. mis _____
5. pre _____
6. re _____
7. sub _____
8. trans _____
9. un _____
10. semi _____

Lesson 10
Negative Prefixes

In 1912, *incomplete* fragments of a human skull were shown to a gathering of scientists in London. The fragments were said to have been discovered near Piltdown, a town in England. The skull was supposed to have come from a previously *unknown* type of early man. For years scientists would *disagree* about whether the fragments were real or not.

Then in 1953, two scientists announced a discovery. After putting the skull pieces through a number of new tests, the scientists found that some parts were *nonhuman*. The skull was a fake. Piltdown Man had never existed.

Look at the words in italics. What do they have in common? All the words are derivatives with **negative prefixes.** Other negative prefixes are *mis-*, *im-*, *il-*, and *ir-*. You will find them in many words. But be careful not to mistake any similar combinations of letters for these prefixes. Example: *in-* is not a prefix in *ink-blot*, *mis-* is not a prefix in *miser*.

Exercise A
Read the rest of the article. Find the derivatives with negative prefixes; there are five such words. Write them on the blanks and circle the prefixes.

When the Piltdown skull fragments were shown to the scientists in 1912, many of the experts expressed their mistrust of the illogical apelike jaw. It looked suspiciously like a modern ape's jaw, and a key piece was missing. Yet for forty years the skull was accepted, by and large, as evidence of a new human ancestor.

Then in the late 1940s, J. S. Weiner, a lecturer at Oxford University, decided to put the imperfect skull through the latest tests. Together with two other scientists, he found that the skull had been artificially stained to look old, and the jaw was mismatched. It was really that of an ape, with the teeth filed down to look human. Though the skull was proven to be a fake, it was impossible to accuse its "discoverer" Charles Dawson, an amateur archaeologist; he had been dead for thirty-five years.

1. _____
2. _____
3. _____
4. _____
5. _____

Name _____ Class _____ Date _____

Exercise B
Look at each of the prefixes you have circled in Exercise A. Now, think of another word that begins with the same prefix. Write the words in the blanks below.

1. _____
2. _____
3. _____
4. _____
5. _____

Lesson 11
More About Prefixes

Illustration of Alice by Sir John Tenniel

Caption: *In Lewis Carroll's story*, Alice in Wonderland, *Alice finds a bottle that says "Drink Me" outside. She does so. Suddenly she begins to grow and* outgrows *her clothing*.

Read the caption above. Two of the words in the caption above, *outside* and *outgrows*, have the same prefix. But it changes meaning in each word. The prefix *out-* in *outside* means "outer." In *outgrows*, the prefix means "beyond."

The meanings of some prefixes change according to the root word they are added to. For example, *sub-* means "under" in *submarine* and *subzero*. But in *subtopic* and *subdivision* it means "resulting from further division of something."

Sometimes it is hard to understand exactly what the prefix does to the root word. The prefix *out-* in the word *outworn* does not mean that a thing is worn outside, but that it is "outgrown" or "worn out." Turn to your dictionary when you are unsure of a prefix's meaning.

Grade Eight SkillBook, Vocabulary

Name _____ Class _____ Date _____

Exercise
Read each example sentence, studying the use of the prefix in the italicized word. Then read the next sentence and choose the definition that fits the italicized word. Write the letter of the correct definition in the blank.

1. An *extraterrestrial* is someone who comes from beyond the earth.

    Extraordinary feats are deeds _____ the ordinary.
    a. within
    b. outside
    c. under

2. If you are *overcharged* for an item, you are billed too much.

    A child that is *overactive* is _____ active.
    a. not
    b. slightly
    c. too

3. An athlete who *outshines* his or her competitors is better than they.

    An *outstanding* achievement is something _____ than usual.
    a. no different
    b. more
    c. less

4. *Coauthors* of a book work together to write it.

    The *copilot* of a plane _____ the pilot fly the plane.
    a. hinders
    b. instructs
    c. helps

5. *Midyear* exams take place in the middle of the year.

    If you make a *midair* flip off a diving board, you make a turn in the

    _____ of the air.
    a. top
    b. middle
    c. lower part

Lesson 12
Using Suffixes

Read the following paragraph.

    Robin Lee Graham was an adventure fifteen when he and two friends set sail from Honolulu to Lanai in a boat they made themselves. "We started happy," he wrote, "unaware that a veteran sail never makes a depart on Friday, and so much in a hurry we overlooked the small-craft warning." The weather, peace at first, became storm, and the waves became danger. Before they could know what was happening, bits of shredded canvas flew ribbon through the air.

    What's wrong with the paragraph? Clearly, no one would write the way it is printed above. Here is the paragraph with the words written normally.

    Robin Lee Graham was an *adventurous* fifteen when he and two friends set sail from Honolulu to Lanai in a boat they made themselves. "We started *happily*," he wrote, "unaware that a veteran *sailor* never makes a *departure* on Friday, and so much in a hurry we overlooked the small-craft warning." The weather, *peaceful* at first, became *stormy* and the waves became *dangerous*. Before they could know what was happening, bits of shredded canvas flew *ribbonlike* through the air.

Exercise A

1. Compare the italicized words with the words in the first version. What parts of the words in the second paragraph have been added?

   _____

2. Underline the parts of the italicized words that have been added.

3. In which two italicized words have the spellings of the original words been changed when the endings were added?

   _____

    The endings that were added to the original words are called **suffixes**. A suffix is a word part added to the end of a root word. Words with one or more suffixes are called **derivatives**.

    Sometimes the spelling of a root word changes when a suffix is added. The three most common spelling changes are:

1. Final *e* is dropped . . . . ice + y = icy

2. *y* changed to *i* . . . . happy + ly = happily

3. Final consonant doubled . . . . run + er = runner

Grade Eight SkillBook, Vocabulary

Exercise B
Choose the derivative from the list at the left that best completes each sentence. Pronounce each derivative to yourself. The first is done for you.

darkly
darken
darkness

careless
carelessness
carelessly

1. As the sky began to <u>darken</u>, the twins began to worry about being lost.

2. Complete _____ brought more worries, but a bright moon seemed to help them find their way.

3. In spite of their _____ in getting lost, the twins were sure they would get home.

4. They promised that they would never again _____ go for a walk without telling someone where they were going.

Prefixes and suffixes change or add to the meaning of a root word. A suffix can also change the way the word is used in a sentence.

Exercise C
Answer the questions that follow. Think about the meanings of the suffixes.

1. Would a mountain climber be likely to be *careful* or *careless* when going up a dangerous slope?

2. If you were stung by a mosquito, would that cause an *irritant* or an *irritation*?

3. Would a good lecture on proper English be *educational* or would it be *educatable*?

4. Did the fans at the baseball game find the game *enjoyable* or *enjoyment*?

5. When the senators in Congress debated, did they discuss *legislature* or *legislation*?

Lesson 1
Adjusting Rate and Method to Purpose

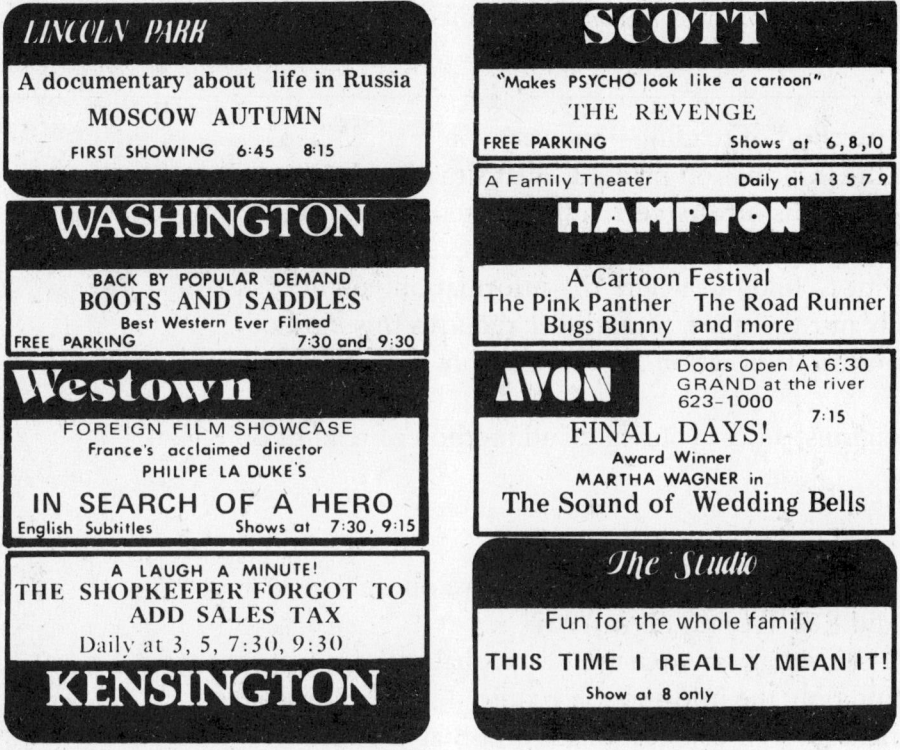

Exercise A

The movie section of a newspaper is printed above. Write answers to the following:

1. It's Saturday night and you're planning to see a movie. You must walk to the theater, and the only one within walking distance is the Avon. As quickly as you can, find the name of the movie playing at the Avon and write it down.

2. There are three theaters that you can get to easily by bus—the Washington, the Studio, and the Kensington. Of the movies playing at these three theaters, which sounds the most interesting?

3. If you go to the movie with an older brother who has a car, you can go to any theater in the area. Choose the film you would most like to see and write the title here.

Grade Eight SkillBook, Reading

4. For which situation—1, 2, or 3—did you read all, or nearly all, of the movie listings?

_____

5. For which were you able to find the information most quickly?

_____

Your purpose affects your **method** of reading—the way you read. When you want or need to know all the information printed, as in situation 3, you read more slowly and carefully. This is **intensive reading,** often necessary in reading assignments for class. When you don't need to know everything, you can glance quickly over the print to find out where the information you need is located, and then read carefully just that part. Situation 1 requires this kind of reading, which is called **skimming.** In situation 2, you probably skimmed three times.

To read with flexibility, you must adjust your rate and method of reading to your purpose.

Exercise B

Your purpose in reading the following article is to answer these questions: A) Who was El Viejo? B) What did Lee Trevino do in 1967?

What method of reading—skimming or intensive—is probably more suitable? Read the article to find only the information required by the purpose. As soon as you find the information, answer questions A and B at the end of the selection.

A GREAT SPORTS FIGURE
by Jerry Izenberg

He was called El Viejo (el vē-ä′hō). When Lee Trevino looks back on the years during which the old man shaped him, it is never *grandfather* that he thinks of. It is always El Viejo—the old man. That is the way Lee Trevino remembers him.

It was in Dallas, Texas. El Viejo was the man who held the small family together. He was a gravedigger, and he worked six days a week for a dollar a day. In the morning, before the dawn broke, Lee Trevino would hear the sounds of El Viejo making coffee and the quiet way in which he closed the door and slipped off into the dew-fresh grass and weeds outside to begin the long walk to the cemetery. After dark, he would return.

The house was little better than a shack. There was no indoor plumbing of any kind, and outside there was no well. Water had to be purchased, and the only place it could be bought was farther down the road to Dallas. Each day from the time he was six or seven, Lee Trevino took an empty bucket and walked into town to get it.

Trevino is a Mexican-American. On the golf course, he grins and calls himself "Super Mex." He tells stories in an exaggerated dialect that is really a put-on. It is the way of people who have known prejudice and who have not been broken under its cruel burden. But deep down he takes his Mexican-American background as a thing of pride.

Lee Trevino's way up was long and hard and lonely. But now he plays in the biggest golf tournaments, and he wins a lot of them. He makes money all over the world.

But he still recalls the country clubs where Mexican-Americans were not welcome to play, the years of hunger, and the fact that unlike so many of the top professional golfers, his road to success was a rocky one.

He caddied, as did so many of golf's superstars. He worked on a driving range. He invented a gimmick which paid off in small bets which he almost always won and which kept him in food. The gimmick was a family-sized soda bottle. Using the bottom of the wide end to putt and the side to hit other shots, he was able to win from most opponents, who played with a full set of clubs.

In 1967, Trevino entered the U.S. Open Golf Tournament for the first time and came in a late finisher. But the next year he won the event, beating Jack Nicklaus by four strokes, and he went on to win tournaments on both sides of the Atlantic.

But then you could expect nothing less. El Viejo was his grandfather.

Answer these questions without looking back at the article.

A. Who was El Viejo?

_____

B. What did Lee Trevino do in 1967?

_____

Exercise C

Your purpose now is to read the article again to understand and remember it in more detail. Choose a method of reading suitable for this purpose and reread the article. Then complete the following statements without looking back.

1. El Viejo kept the Trevino family together by working as a
   a. farmer
   b. golfer
   c. gravedigger

2. Trevino's Mexican-American background is something about which he feels
   a. ashamed
   b. proud
   c. sad

3. As a youngster, Trevino earned money any way he could, including
   a. betting on his ability to play golf with a bottle
   b. playing baseball for a minor-league team
   c. digging graves in a nearby cemetery

4. Trevino won his first big tournament in
   a. 1960
   b. 1967
   c. 1968

5. Trevino beat _____ by four strokes to win the U.S. Open.
   a. Tom Watson
   b. Jack Nicklaus
   c. Arnold Palmer

If you could not answer the questions in part B, you read too quickly for your purpose.

Lesson 2
Using Patterns to Help You Read

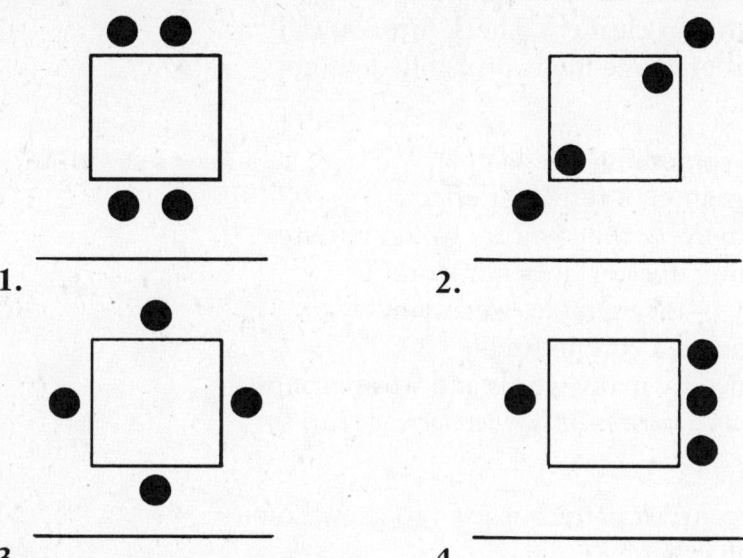

1. _____ 2. _____

3. _____ 4. _____

What do ● and □ mean by themselves? If you said "Not much," you're right. But look at them arranged in different patterns above.

Exercise A
Some labels are listed below. Try to match these labels with the patterns above by writing the letter of the label on the blank under each pattern. You will not use one label.

  a. boxers with their managers
  b. some goldfish in a tank
  c. ping-pong doubles
  d. an expert being questioned by reporters on TV
  e. a card game

Matching the labels with the patterns takes some imagination, but, just by putting the same square and the same four dots into different arrangements or patterns, the meaning is changed.

Ideas and events can be arranged in patterns, too, as you will see in this lesson.

Time order. Thoughts and actions are often presented in time order, the order in which things happen. Most stories are written in the time-order pattern. When you give or follow directions, you are likely to use time order as well; first do this, next do that, then do so-and-so. Time order is an easy pattern to recognize because it is often signaled with clues like dates or words that have to do with time, such as *first, next, then, at last, three months later, finally, for days, before,* and *after.*

Grade Eight SkillBook, Reading

Listing. Another pattern a writer might use takes the form of a simple list. The items in the list could be presented in any order without changing the meaning.

An example is the list a busy person might make of things to do before going on a trip: water plants, pick up clothes at cleaner's, check furnace, call Helen, close windows. In this case, the order of the items probably does not matter.

Cause-effect. When something makes something else happen, we have a cause-effect pattern; that is, a cause brings about a result, or effect.

You use a cause-effect thinking pattern every time you try to figure out why something happened or why something does or does not work. In reading, you use this pattern in many ways—for example, when you try to understand why a character in a story acted in a certain way.

The cause-effect pattern can be signaled by many words and word groups. Some of the most common of these are *since, consequently, therefore, so that, for this reason, because,* and *as a result*.

Comparison-contrast. A comparison-contrast pattern is used to show how two things are alike or different from each other.

Whenever things are compared, and particularly when they are contrasted, each serves to emphasize the other. If a very short person stands beside a very tall one, the height (or lack of it) of each is emphasized. Writers know that they get stronger effects by using the comparison-contrast pattern.

Clue words that frequently signal comparison-contrast patterns include *however, on the contrary, on the one hand / on the other, but, although, yet*.

You can usually get a better understanding of what you are reading if you know the way an author has arranged the information in a sentence or paragraph.

Also, you can adjust your reading to suit each pattern. If you are reading a selection that uses comparison-contrast, you will be on the lookout for how things are alike or different. If the selection uses mainly a cause-effect pattern, you will pay special attention to what causes something to happen or what the results are. If time order is the main pattern, you will try to remember the order in which things happened. In this way, understanding patterns can affect your method of reading.

Name _____ Class _____ Date _____

Exercise B

Read the following article and then answer the questions about patterns.

THE FIRST WONDER OF THE WORLD
by Edward L. Lee, II

(A) The Egyptian pyramids were built almost 4,700 years ago on a rocky plain just a few miles from Cairo. They were tombs in which the pharaohs, or kings, were buried. As a result, a pyramid consisted of two parts. The first part was the burial chamber, which was usually located at the bottom of a shaft cut into the rock. The second part of the pyramid was the superstructure which made up the upper part of the pyramid. After the burial, it was open to visitors. The inner walls of this part were usually painted with scenes from the life of the buried pharaoh. The last painting recorded the pharaoh's death and expressed his wish for the living to pray for him.

(B) Because the early Egyptians believed that life continued, furniture, clothing, weapons, food, and generous amounts of gold and other valuables were buried with the pharaohs. These they would need in the afterworld.

(C) To guard against thieves, the pyramid builders did two things: First, to protect the pharaoh's body and the precious jewelry placed upon him, he was put in several sealed coffins, each inside a larger one. These were finally placed in an even larger stone coffin so heavy that robbers could not easily open it. Second, the actual location of the pharaoh's burial chamber was kept secret. In fact, the pyramids sometimes had two or even three burial chambers to fool thieves. The pharaohs often had only their most trusted servants carry them to the burial chamber in order to keep secret the location of this chamber.

(D) Often referred to as the Great Pyramid, Khufu (kü´fü) is the largest and oldest of the three pyramids at Giza (gē´zə). It is considered to be the greatest single building ever constructed. It covers an area of thirteen acres. Made of limestone and granite, Khufu was built from more than 2 1/2 million blocks of stone, each weighing an average of 2 1/2 tons. Khafre (kä´frā), built somewhat later by King Khafre about 2650 B.C., is only four feet shorter than Khufu. In front of Khafre is the world-famous Sphinx (a huge statue with a man's head and a lion's body), which is thought to have been built at about the same time as this pyramid. The third and smallest pyramid of Giza is Menkaure (men kü´rā), which was built around 2600 B.C. Barely 200 feet high, Menkaure is less than half the size of its towering neighbors.

(E) The pyramids of Giza, the first Wonder of the World, prove the mathematical genius, hard work, artistic splendor, and cleverness of the Egyptians.

Grade Eight SkillBook, Reading

Name _____ Class _____ Date _____

1. What clue words in the third sentence of paragraph A suggest a cause-effect pattern?

   _____

2. What word in the first sentence of paragraph B also suggests a cause-effect pattern?

   _____

3. What burial items are listed in the first sentence of paragraph B?

   _____

4. What pattern do you find in paragraph D?

   _____

5. What pattern is used in paragraph E?

   _____

32   Grade Eight SkillBook, Reading

Name _____ Class _____ Date _____

Lesson 3
Making a Survey

Before you begin to read a selection, you should look at the following features: title, headnote, captions, illustrations, subtitles, and the first and last paragraphs.

Notice the *title* of the article that is printed on the next page. It may cause you to ask certain questions. *What were the health conditions of early times? Who—or what—was the unknown enemy?*

Sometimes stories and articles have *headnotes*—phrases or sentences that are intended to spark your interest in a selection. The headnote accompanying the article on health conditions, which appears above the title, may raise further questions in your mind. *In what ways are conditions different today? What is a communicable disease? Why didn't doctors treat the people affected by the diseases?*

Asking yourself questions based on the title, headnote, captions, and illustrations is part of a process called **making a survey**. Such questions help you set purposes for reading. They give you information before you begin to study and help you to get more out of the selection when you actually do read it.

In addition to the features already discussed, there are several others that you can use as you get ready to read. Articles are sometimes divided into sections that are headed by *subtitles*. Subtitles often provide clues about how the material is organized and usually state the subject matter covered in the section. Look over the subtitles in the article on the next page.

Exercise

1. Around what major thought patterns does the material seem to be organized? Use the subtitles as clues.

   _____

2. Write a question based on one of the subtitles.

   _____
   _____

Another step in making a survey includes reading the first and last paragraphs. The opening paragraph will sometimes state the main idea of the entire selection and will probably hint at the difficulty of the material. The closing paragraph may summarize all the points covered or it may state a conclusion.

3. Write a question based on either the first or last paragraph.

   _____
   _____

Now read the entire article, keeping in mind your questions raised by the survey.

Grade Eight SkillBook, Reading

Health conditions in the U.S. today are very different from those in times when communicable diseases killed thousands of people.

EARLY HEALTH CONDITIONS: FIGHTING AN UNKNOWN ENEMY

Today in the United States there are still health problems to solve. However, people live longer and enjoy better health than ever before. No longer are we at the mercy of such diseases as smallpox, bubonic plague, yellow fever, and typhoid fever. These diseases in the past spread rapidly, killed people by the thousands, and often wiped out whole families and entire villages.

What was it like long ago when little was known or done about public health and sanitation? An examination of conditions in three early communities shows why people could not prevent communicable disease, the kind of disease that is passed from one person to another.

The London plague of 1665

In London, about 1665, a disease known as the Black Death got started. The disease spread like wildfire because of unsanitary conditions. Streets were dirty, many houses were crowded and full of rats, and personal cleanliness was unusual.

Throughout 1665, the death rate mounted with a speed that struck terror into every heart. It is estimated that 43 died in May; 590 in June; 6137 in July; 17,036 in August; 31,159 in September; in all, over 70,000 people before the year ended.

Conditions in colonial times

In 1606 a handful of English colonists settled near the James River in what is now the state of Virginia. The inhabitants of this first settlement, called Jamestown, had health problems so severe that the whole colony was very nearly wiped out.

In the summer of 1607, hot, humid weather fell on Jamestown. Food spoiled and the water became not only unpleasant to the taste but polluted with deadly germs. Sickness spread rapidly. The colonists died at an alarming rate. At the end of the summer only about 50 of the 104 original settlers remained alive.

Microbes—the unknown enemy

People in past years failed in their war against communicable diseases because they did not know the real nature of their enemy.

The enemy, of course, is the *microbe*. Microbes are tiny plants and animals, some so small they can be seen only with a microscope. Many microbes are helpful, but the harmful ones can make people very sick.

Even after the microscope came into use, years of scientific "detective work" were needed to fight communicable diseases. Almost two hundred years passed between the time the first microbe was seen under a microscope and the time the microbe's role in disease began to be understood.

Lesson 4
Intensive Reading

To gain as much information as you can from the following article, you must do an **intensive reading**—a slow, careful one.

Exercise A
First, survey the article, including headnote, title, illustration, subtitles, and first and last paragraphs.

1. What is the general topic of the article?

   _____

2. Based on your survey, what main thought pattern would you expect to find in this material?

   _____

3. How much do you already know about the general topic?

   _____

4. Do the words and sentences seem easy, of average difficulty, or rather hard?

   _____

Exercise B
Read the following article. Stop when you come to a number in parentheses and answer the questions immediately following the article. Answering these questions will help you understand—and remember—what you are reading. Read carefully. There are questions at the end.

How would you like to have lived in a house made of earth?

HOUSES THAT GREW
by Marguerite Z. Mudge

Before the days when trains, trucks, and ships carried building materials to distant places, people made shelters of whatever nature gave them.

Long ago people lived in caves. They found the caves or hollowed them out of the sides of cliffs. The caves protected them from weather and enemies. (1)

In the far north, snow igloos have kept out the bitter cold. On tropical islands, thatches made from palm trees have given shelter. (2)

In rocky lands people have often made walls for their houses out of stone. In forest regions they have built houses of wood. In some places such shelters as this are still in use. (3)

Where nature did not provide caves, snow, rocks, plants, or wood,

Grade Eight SkillBook, Reading

people had to find other building materials. In hot, dry climates they made *adobe* (ə-dō´bē) bricks by drying a mixture of clay and straw in the sun. Adobe houses are cool, even in the heat of noon. (4)

Houses made of sod

Settlers of the Great Plains found little with which to build houses. On the rockless prairies, grasses and wildflowers stretched as far as the eye could see. The only wood the people had was from thin lines of trees along riverbanks. There wasn't much clay, and the climate wasn't hot or dry enough to make adobe bricks. (5)

The settlers turned to the only material around—the earth. The thick prairie soil was held together by matted grass roots. From this sod, also called "Nebraska marble," the settlers made their "soddy" houses. (6)

First they turned over long rows of prairie soil with their plows. Next they cut these into blocks of sod one to three feet wide. They placed these pieces of earth side by side on the ground to form the outline of the house. Then, as if laying bricks, they piled hunks of sod higher and higher. They left spaces for a door and windows. Finally, if they lived near a river they cut some slender trees to make poles to support the roofs of their sod houses. (7)

Blocks of tough earth made prairie sod houses strong but dark.

Soddy houses were usually about sixteen feet wide and twenty feet long. The soddy was cool in summer and warm in winter. It kept out the wind and most of the rain. It did not burn in the fierce fires that sometimes swept across the plains. (8)

However, indoors a soddy was dark. To brighten their rooms, people often plastered the inside walls with light ashes or papers. They put pots of flowers on the dirt windowsills. Also, heavy rains sometimes seeped through the sod roofs. The water formed puddles on the dirt floor and made it hard for the settlers to keep their houses clean. After a storm they often had to shovel more earth on the roof to plug the holes. (9)

Decline of the soddy

Some years after the first soddies were built, railroads brought more people to the Great Plains. Trains also brought such things as lumber, bricks, and other building materials. Old soddies were often fitted with wooden roofs so rain no longer leaked in.

After a while people built wooden houses and left the old soddies to sink back into the prairie. (10)

1. Why did people live in caves?

2. What two building materials are mentioned in the paragraph?

3. What two building materials are mentioned in this paragraph?

4. What is adobe made of?

5. What building materials were lacking on the Great Plains?

6. What is sod?

7. What thought pattern is used to describe the building of a sod house?

8. What were some of the advantages of the soddy?

9. What were two disadvantages of the soddy?

10. What caused the decline of the soddy?

Grade Eight SkillBook, Reading

Name _____ Class _____ Date _____

Exercise C
Now answer the following questions without referring to the article.

1. What are some of the different kinds of houses mentioned at the beginning of the article?
   _____
   _____

2. In what part of the U.S. were sod houses built?
   _____
   _____

3. What steps did the settlers follow to obtain the sod and to build their houses?
   _____
   _____
   _____
   _____

4. What were some of the advantages and disadvantages of the soddy?
   _____
   _____
   _____

5. The development of what means of transportation made lumber, bricks, and other building materials available to the settlers?
   _____
   _____

Lesson 5
Putting Your Reading Skills to Work

Keeping in mind everything that affects the way you read—your purpose, the difficulty of the material, your familiarity with the subject, and the thought pattern the author has used—read the article and answer the questions that follow it. Decide on the best rate and method of reading—but be flexible. Speed up or slow down as the material requires. First survey the article. To guide your reading, think of at least two questions about the article below.

The USS Shenandoah, the first rigid gas-filled airship built in the U.S., took her maiden voyage in 1924. Many believed the giant airship would challenge the airplane for mastery of the skies.

THE AGE OF DIRIGIBLES
by Lynn Hartsell

The sleek, silvery, cigar-shaped airship, longer than two football fields, was on one of her many cross-country flights to demonstrate the airworthiness of dirigibles. This cruise covered more than 9,000 miles around the U.S., and gave millions of people their first look at such an airship.

To many, the graceful *Shenandoah*, which cruised at 60 miles per hour, was a symbol of a new air age. Its future certainly looked better than that of the rickety-winged airplanes that were also trying to set long-distance records.

Development of the dirigible

In both Europe and the U.S., dirigible development continued. The U.S. Navy built the sister ships *Akron* and *Macon*, both 100 feet longer than *Shenandoah*. Each carried five small scout planes, which took off and landed from a trapezelike "sky hook" hanging from the dirigible.

But dirigibles, whose inner framework makes them different from non-rigid gas-filled blimps, were plagued with bad luck. *Shenandoah* was destroyed in a thunderstorm in 1925. *Akron* crashed off the New Jersey coast in 1933. Seventy-three persons were killed. *Macon* went down in a storm in the Pacific Ocean in 1935.

But Germany, whose Zeppelin Company was the world leader in dirigible manufacture, was determined to prove the airships safe and comfortable. The 800-foot long *Graf Zeppelin*, built in 1930, had ten luxurious private rooms, each with an observation window; a brightly decorated lounge; a formal dining room; and an all-electric kitchen. It carried a total of more than 13,000 passengers on trips to four continents, before being retired in 1937.

The German *Hindenburg*

The German dirigible *Hindenburg* was even more luxurious, with 25 private rooms and a dance floor with an aluminum piano. Four 1,100-horsepower diesel engines drove her along at 84 m.p.h. In 1936, the

Hindenburg made ten successful round trips between Germany and the U.S.

The German airship was inflated with 7,300,000 cubic feet of highly flammable hydrogen gas. U.S. dirigibles had used the safer helium, which does not burn.

But helium was more scarce and produced only in the U.S. The American government refused to sell it to other countries—especially Germany, because of the military ambition of the Nazi government.

Then, on her first trans-Atlantic trip of 1937, the *Hindenburg* met disaster. While landing at Lakehurst, New Jersey, the ship suddenly burst into flames. Incredibly, only 36 of the 97 persons aboard died in the blazing crash, but the name *Hindenburg* came to mean "disaster" in many minds.

Whatever doubts people may have had beforehand about dirigibles, the *Hindenburg* disaster was final proof: the golden age of dirigibles was over.

Exercise

Without referring to the article, answer the following questions.

1. Why was the *Shenandoah* on a cross-country flight in 1924?

2. What two countries were leaders in the development of dirigibles in the 1930s?

3. How were the *Akron* and *Macon* different from the *Shenandoah*?

4. What happened to the *Hindenburg*?

5. What effect did the *Hindenburg* have on the development of dirigibles?

Name _____ Class _____ Date _____

Lesson 6
What Is Imagery?

Does it snow in your part of the country? In some areas of the United States, sudden, heavy snowstorms in cities make skiing down a snow-covered sidewalk or the street faster than walking. You may never have used skis on a city sidewalk or street, but imagine what it would be like.

1. What effects of the snowstorm would you see as you skied?
2. What sounds might you hear?
3. What might you taste?
4. What physical sensations would you feel as you moved?

Some details you may have imagined could include the heavy snowfall, the white-covered city, and the cars covered with snow. The crunching sound as the skis glide over the snow, possibly the taste of a few snowflakes, and the fumes from a car engine that is being warmed up might be other physical sensations in this situation. You might also have felt warm from exercise.

When you put yourself in a scene or react to the details in a photograph, you imagine the sights, sounds, smells, tastes, and feelings of that experience. When you read, physical sensations are described with words that the writer hopes will help you to create mental pictures called images or **imagery**.

Exercise A
As you read the selection below, try to imagine the physical sensations that are being described. Answer the questions that follow.

> Father started to trudge up the hill. I had to run to catch up with him. The road was muddy and our boots made wet, sucking noises. My jacket was not really thick enough to hold out the wind, and I pulled the collar tighter about my neck. It was a cold, sharp wind, but with a salt-sea smell. Father glanced at me, but still he said nothing. The setting sun behind us cast long shadows, which raced up and up ahead of us along the road.
>
> And then at the very top of the hill we turned off, walking to the very edge of it and looking down on the barn below us. Father crossed his arms, slipping his hands into his armpits to keep them warm.

1. Circle the letter that describes the location. They are
   a. in a city.
   b. in a rural area.
   c. on a beach.

2. What sounds are made by the two pairs of boots?

_____

3. Write one of the details that helps you to imagine the weather.

Grade Eight SkillBook, Reading

Name _____ Class _____ Date _____

4. What smell is described?
_____

5. What image helps you to imagine the effect of the setting sun?
_____

Exercise B
Write a descriptive paragraph on the lines provided below. Use imagery in your description.

_____
_____
_____
_____
_____
_____
_____
_____
_____
_____
_____
_____
_____
_____
_____
_____
_____
_____
_____
_____

Lesson 7
Recognizing Imagery

Exercise A.
Sensory descriptions can appeal to more than one sense at a time. After you read the words below, write the sense(s)—sight, sound, smell, taste, or feeling—to which each of the phrases appeals most strongly.

1. squealing tires making skid marks

2. damp socks

3. oval, cherry-flavored cough drop

4. rain hitting a windowpane

5. wind

Exercise B
Each pair of sentences below describes the same event. Put a check in front of the one in each pair that uses more vivid imagery.

1. _____ a. Silence hung over the courtroom as the attorney stared unblinkingly at the witness until he began to fidget in his chair and glance nervously around the room.

   _____ b. There was absolute silence in the courtroom while the attorney stared at the witness until he became more and more nervous.

2. _____ a. Dr. Mathis looked at the accident victim's face, saw that there were many injuries, and began to treat the patient.

   _____ b. Dr. Mathis gently turned the patient's face to the light and carefully treated the ragged cuts and bluish bruises with antiseptic-soaked cotton pads.

3. _____ a. Phil rode down the street on his bike, passing a runner with his dog and some small children riding on their tricycles.

   _____ b. As Phil bicycled down the shady, tree-lined streets, he passed a jogger in a tan warm-up suit with his German shepherd running beside him and some small children racing each other on their tricycles.

Grade Eight SkillBook, Reading

4. _____ a. For two days there was thunder and lightning as a heavy summer rain flooded the city streets with swirling, muddy water.

   _____ b. A two-day heavy rain filled the streets with water.

5. _____ a. The radio announcer reported that a leopard was missing from the zoo and that it could be hungry and dangerous.

   _____ b. The excited voice of the radio announcer warned everyone to stay off the streets as the escaped leopard might suddenly attack out of fear or hunger.

Exercise C
Read the following passage. Underline ten words or groups of words that create sharp, clear images.

The haunted house was half in the shadows of the clump of elms in which it stood. The elms were almost bare now, and the ground around the house was yellow with damp leaves. The late afternoon light had a greenish cast which the blank windows reflected in a sinister way. An unhinged shutter thumped. Something else creaked. Meg did not wonder that the house had a reputation for being haunted.

A board was nailed across the front door, but Charles Wallace led the way around to the back. The door there appeared to be nailed shut, too, but Charles Wallace knocked, and the door swung slowly outward, creaking on rusty hinges. Up in one of the elms an old black crow gave its raucous cry, and a woodpecker went into a wild ratatattat. A large gray rat scuttled around the corner of the house and Meg let out a stifled shriek.

Name _____ Class _____ Date _____

Lesson 8
Responding to Imagery

Exercise A
Imagine that you are a witness to the earthquake that is described below. Then answer the questions that follow.

> At Turnagain, on the edge of Anchorage, people first heard a deep rumble, like the sound of thunder. Next their houses began to shake. They rushed to their doors, looked out, and thought the world was coming to an end. The earth at their feet was churning and crumbling and sinking away. It was cracking into huge, tilted blocks. Neighbor helped neighbor to escape. Behind them trees fell. Houses were ripped in two or upended.

1. What sound first alerted the people?
   _____

2. Describe what the people felt inside their houses.
   _____

3. Why did the people think "the world was coming to an end"?
   _____
   _____

4. Write the image that describes the way the earth was cracking.
   _____
   _____

5. What images do you have of the trees and houses?
   _____
   _____

The experience of an actual earthquake may be unfamiliar to you, but the imagery in this description should help you to imagine what such an experience would be like.

Exercise B
Continue the earthquake story and then answer the questions that follow. Circle the correct letter for each one.

> Turnagain was built on high ground, on a bluff overlooking the water. The violent shaking triggered a landslide. The front of the bluff slid away, carrying houses and garages with it.
> In the city of Anchorage, big buildings creaked and groaned. Their

Grade Eight SkillBook, Reading

floors rose and fell in waves. Automobiles bounced like rubber balls. Great chunks of buildings crashed to the street. A movie theater dropped thirty feet into a hole that opened beneath it. A flower shop snapped in two.

    Anchorage was not alone in this nightmare. As it shook and cracked and jolted, so did much of Alaska. Buildings trembled and fell. Land tore open. Highways buckled. Railroad tracks were twisted into curls of steel. Snow-capped mountains shuddered, and ice and rock swept down their slopes.

    All along the coast, port towns suffered great damage. One reason was the kind of land on which they stood. Seward was both a port and the end of a rail line. The rail line brought in oil, which was stored in tanks before being shipped. When the earthquake hit, the tanks broke and the oil caught fire.

    Flames roared along the waterfront. Then a great landslide occurred. The entire waterfront slid into the bay.

1. Houses and garages in Turnagain slid into the water because of
    a. poor construction.
    b. heavy rain.
    c. shaking of the earth.

2. Which sound could be heard in downtown Anchorage?
    a. buildings collapsing
    b. automobiles crashing
    c. both *a* and *b*

3. Write a sentence containing a sight or sound image from the third paragraph.

    _____

4. To which sense or senses does the image "flames roared along the waterfront" appeal?
    a. sight
    b. sight and sound
    c. sight, sound, and touch

5. What image explains the severe damage in Seward?
    a. oil tanks on fire
    b. waterfront landslide
    c. both images

Lesson 9
Visualizing What Happens

  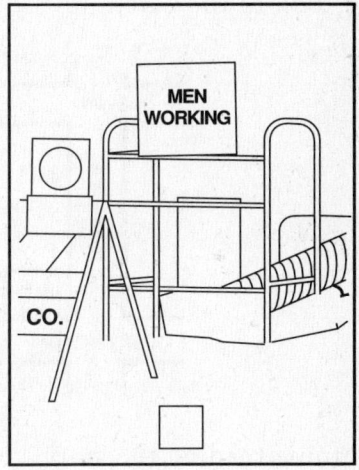

Which picture looks most like the scene that is described in the paragraph below?

    Because a broken sewer pipe was being repaired, the street in front of the bank on the corner had been torn up for several days. It was blocked off from all traffic. At 9:45 A.M. on Tuesday morning the sidewalks were deserted and few parked cars were on the streets. Everybody was already at work in the surrounding offices and factories.

How did you decide which picture to check? If you imagined what was being described, you knew that the picture should show a city street, an open sewer cover, traffic barriers, and warning signs—picture C. You realized that an unpaved country road and lines of traffic did not fit the description. One reason to form mental pictures or visualize as you read is to understand what is happening in a story or article. Find other details that help you visualize what is happening as you read more of this story.

    Two guards stepped out of the armored truck which had parked on the next street behind the bank. Actually the truck was only a very short block away from the bank. Each of the guards held a canvas bag of money in his left hand, and a gun in his right hand. As they turned the corner to go south, they walked out of the sight of a third guard who had remained inside the armored car. Then they began to walk the short block to the bank.

Grade Eight SkillBook, Reading

Exercise A

1. On the map below, draw a square to show where the armored truck was parked. Then draw a line with an arrow to show the route the guards took to the bank.

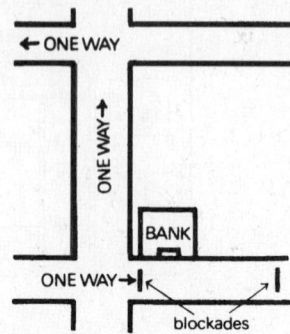 

Continue reading the story, keeping this scene in mind.

About halfway up the street, there was a man standing beside a battered old motorcycle with a sidecar that had been converted into a small hot dog stand. The motorcycle stood between two parked cars. The guards noticed the man as they walked toward where he stood on the sidewalk. Hot dog vendors were common in New York, and a motorcycle converted into a hot dog stand was a familiar sight in the neighborhood. However, the "hot dog man" usually drove up shortly before noon. He was early.

2. Put an "X" on the map to show where the motorcycle was.

3. Why did the guards not become more suspicious when they saw the hot dog man?

___

Go on with the story.

What the guards did not know was that the motorcycle had been stolen less than an hour before and the stocky little man wearing the dirty apron had never sold a hot dog in his life. He was a hoodlum who was about to commit a bold robbery.

4. How do you visualize the man beside the motorcycle? (Circle the letter of one or more.)
   a. tall and thin
   b. short and stout
   c. acting nervous
   d. looking untidy

5. How do you "see" the guards at this point in the story? (Circle one letter.)
   a. walking casually toward the hot dog stand
   b. stopping to speak to the man with the apron
   c. turning around and returning to the armored truck
   d. walking with drawn guns but without alarm as they get closer to the hot dog stand

Exercise B

Read about the actual robbery below. Then answer the questions.

   As the two guards passed the motorcycle, a tall man who was holding a bundle of old newspapers on his broad shoulder came walking down the street toward them. His battered hat hid the man's tough, hard face with its long, pointy nose and a scar above his right eye.

   With perfect timing, the tall man passed the first guard and quickly hurled his heavy bundle at him. The guard was knocked down. His head struck the pavement and he lay there, stunned. At the same time—before the other guard could protect himself—the hot dog man hit him from behind with a blackjack, a small weighted leather weapon that the man held by the handle. The second guard crumpled to the ground, unconscious.

   The hot dog man then jumped on the motorcycle's worn leather seat and started the engine. The taller man picked up the bags of money and put them into a chrome container on the sidecar which usually held supplies for hot dogs. Then the hot dog man started the motorcycle, made a U-turn, and quickly sped away. His hard-faced partner walked to the corner, actually passed the armored truck, and crossed the street to where his stolen getaway car was parked.

1. From what direction does the man with the newspapers approach the guards?

   _____

2. What does the man with the newspapers look like?

   _____

3. Which of the drawings below shows what a blackjack looks like?

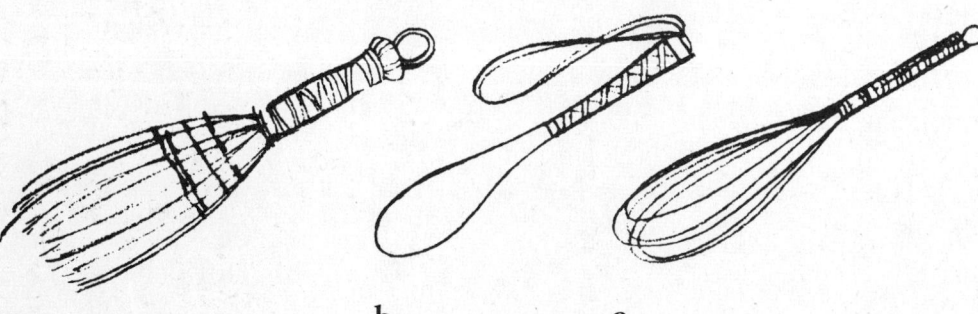

a.   b.   c.

Grade Eight SkillBook, Reading

Name _____ Class _____ Date _____

4. In what direction does the hot dog man escape?

   _____

5. What is the only possible clue that the two thieves have left at the scene of the crime (other than the information the two guards can give when they come to)?

   _____

Name _____ Class _____ Date _____

Lesson 10
Reviewing the Use of Imagery

As you read the following passage, try to imagine the sights, sounds, smells, tastes, and feelings that are being described. Use your own experience to help you respond to the images. Then answer the questions that follow.

from I WOULD RATHER BE A TURNIP
by Vera and Bill Cleaver

The library was old and gloomy and cool and smelled of old, moth-scented coverings and new, slick ones. Its hushed atmosphere was solitary. There was a vase of faded roses on the entrance desk and there was Miss Velda Dishman behind the desk.

Annie and Calvin stood in front of the desk and Miss Dishman looked up at them and Calvin's grin was ecstatic. "Want to look at your books," he whispered. "All of them." He had removed his hat and his white head glinted like tinsel in the strong light streaming in through the bare windows.

Miss Dishman smiled at Calvin and gave him permission to look at the books and he tiptoed away from the desk to the first aisle and knelt there. He clasped his hands over his stomach and gazed in rapture at the books and in a minute selected one, opened it, and was immediately lost.

Annie continued to stand at the desk, smelling the faded roses in the vase and looking at Miss Dishman who was leafing through a catalog and making notes on a separate sheet. The backs of her hands were peppered with little brown spots and her scalp, shining pinkly through the puffs of her silver hair, looked clean and smooth.

Annie reflected that Miss Dishman must be at least fifty years old—an incredible age.

Annie stood first on one foot and then another. Her feet hurt her; she could feel them growing. The atmosphere in this place was strange; it seemed so far removed from real, earthly things. After a minute she said, "You've sure got a lot of books in here. I never noticed before how many. . . ."

Annie locked her knees and fingered her hair. "Books've never interested me much although I'm writing one in my spare time."

"I know," said Miss Dishman. "Your father told me."

"It smells funny in here," said Annie.

Miss Dishman's fragile hands were taking the wilted roses from the vase; she was rolling them in a piece of newspaper and placing them in the wastebasket. "That's because you're not accustomed to the odor of books. Actually what you smell is not an odor; it's a scent."

"It just smells odd," murmured Annie. "That's all I meant to say."

Grade Eight SkillBook, Reading

Name _____ Class _____ Date _____

Exercise

1. Write one image from the first paragraph which appeals to one of these senses—sight, sound, smell, or feeling.

   _____

2. Describe the scene in which Calvin loses himself in a book.

   _____

   _____

3. Which of the following probably makes Annie think that Miss Dishman is old? (Circle one letter.)
   a. the smell of the roses
   b. the scratch of Dishman's pen as she writes
   c. Miss Dishman's scalp showing through her hair
   d. Miss Dishman's answers to her questions

4. What smells odd to Annie? How does Miss Dishman explain the smell?

   _____

   _____

5. Which images below could be added to those that are found in this selection? Write **Y** (yes) or **N** (no) on the space in front of each item.

   _____ a. old-fashioned tables and chairs

   _____ b. computerized card catalog system

   _____ c. lace curtains at the windows

   _____ d. Calvin's bored expression

   _____ e. shelves of books of various sizes and colors

   _____ f. rose petals that have fallen on the desk

Grade Eight SkillBook, Reading

Lesson 11
What Is Figurative Language?

What would you think if you heard a friend or classmate called a "clown"? Most likely, you would not think that person was really, literally, a clown. Rather, you would think the person tends to act funny or silly, somewhat like a real clown. The word is being used in a *figurative* sense to mean something different from the literal meaning.

Is the following sentence meant to be understood in a literal or a figurative way?

"Ernie, quit horsing around."

Ernie is not actually a horse. He is not eating hay or jumping fences. The phrase *horsing around* means "acting silly" or "fooling around." It can also mean "getting into mischief," the way a horse might if it were running around where it shouldn't be. *Horsing around* is **figurative language** because its meaning differs from the literal meaning of the individual words in the phrase.

The expression above is very common and probably is familiar to you. (If not, you would have been able to find its definition in most dictionaries.)

Other expressions will not be as familiar to you. Good writers and speakers create fresh, original figurative language. They express their ideas in a way that lets their readers see something in a new, often surprising way. In the following sentence, underline the words that describe the puppy in a figurative way.

After the puppy had finished eating, it was a soft, furry ball that just rolled around the floor.

Obviously, the puppy is not really, or literally, a ball. The writer could have written a literal description: "After the puppy had finished eating, it was so full and round that it couldn't walk without its belly touching the floor." But the figurative language gives a cleaner and more imaginative understanding of the fat, clumsy puppy.

In the paragraph below, underline the words and phrases that are meant to be understood figuratively, not literally.

On my cousin's eighth birthday, my family got together and bought her a new bicycle. When she saw it on the sidewalk all tied up in ribbons, she froze solid. My heart sank to my feet. "Oh," I thought, "she doesn't like it. It's not what she wanted after all." She looked back at us, then at the bicycle again, and her jaw dropped to the ground. She was off the front steps and down to the bike faster than an Olympic sprinter. Her eyes sparkled like stars, and I knew we had done the right thing.

The bicycle was, literally, tied up in ribbons. Have you ever heard the phrase *all tied up* used in a figurative way? Is the phrase used literally or figuratively in the following sentence?

I can't go to the movie with you tonight because I'm *all tied up* with homework.

Grade Eight SkillBook, Reading

The person is not literally tied up in any way. When used figuratively, the phrase *all tied up* means "busy and unable to get away." As this example shows, the same words and phrases can be used either literally or figuratively, depending on the context in which they appear. If a sentence doesn't make sense when you read each word literally, look for words or phrases that might be used figuratively.

Exercise A
One sentence in each pair below uses a figurative expression. Circle the letter of that sentence.

1. a. The eagle swooped down on the scared rabbit.
   b. Amy can run like a scared rabbit.

2. a. Phil's insult felt like a karate chop.
   b. Phil can break a board with a karate chop.

3. a. The boy paraded around the circus ring on top of a pair of stilts.
   b. With his long legs and awkward movements, Carl is a pair of walking stilts.

4. a. From somewhere in the west wing, footsteps sounded like the ticking of a clock.
   b. The car's engine was so quiet that he could hear the ticking of a clock on the dashboard.

5. a. Unable to land, the plane went around and around in circles overhead.
   b. Donald goes around and around in circles trying to make a decision.

Exercise B
Read each sentence below. Some sentences contain figurative language; others do not. Write **F** in the blank if the sentence has figurative language. Write **L** if the sentence is entirely literal.

_____ 1. When it comes to things that need special care, Hester's repair work is the best.

_____ 2. Our Loan Department provides a speedy detour around the financial traffic jams of life.

_____ 3. When the truck was driven onto the ice, it skidded and flipped over.

_____ 4. That little dog can be as brave as a lion.

_____ 5. The hail is coming down so fast it sounds like machine gun bullets.

_____ 6. Some people enjoy potatoes with eggs for breakfast.

_____ 7. The steeple towered two hundred feet above the surrounding village.

_____ 8. Hank has a loudspeaker for a mouth.

_____ 9. In spite of her problems, Doris seems to skate along smoothly through life.

_____ 10. The bulldozer quickly knocked down the remaining wall.

_____ 11. The cost of all this sports equipment is so high I'll have to borrow money from my father.

_____ 12. When the waiter accidentally tipped the pizza, the browned cheese slid onto the salad like a mudslide into a valley.

_____ 13. The rose garden is a beautiful quilt of reds, whites, and yellows.

_____ 14. The race car swung perfectly balanced on the edge of the curve—like a model plane flown on a string in a tight circle.

_____ 15. Someone had overturned the trash cans and littered the sidewalk.

Exercise C
Write your own examples of figurative language on the lines provided below. If possible, work in pairs or small groups to complete the assignment. Compare your work with your classmates.

_____
_____
_____
_____
_____
_____
_____
_____
_____
_____
_____
_____

Grade Eight SkillBook, Reading

Name _____ Class _____ Date _____

Exercise D
Write a brief composition using figurative language. You may get some ideas from your work on Exercise C.

Lesson 12
Making Sense of Figurative Language

Read the poem below and look for the figurative language.

DREAMS
by Langston Hughes

Hold fast to dreams
For if dreams die
Life is a broken-winged bird
That cannot fly.

Hold fast to dreams
For when dreams go
Life is a barren field
Frozen with snow.

    The poet says that if hope is given up ("if dreams die"), then life is "a broken-winged bird that cannot fly." Of course, life is not literally a bird. What does the poet mean by this figurative expression?
    A bird that can't fly would certainly be very unhappy. But more than that, the bird wouldn't be able to search for food or escape its enemies. A broken-winged bird would soon die. Without hopes and dreams, the poet tells us, life would not hold much for the future.

Exercise
Each sentence below contains figurative language. Circle the letter for the literal meaning that best explains the italicized figurative expression.

1. The hamburger buns at Barnie's Burgers taste *like cardboard*.
    a. The buns are dry, tough, and flavorless.
    b. The buns are very thin.
    c. The buns are made of paper.

2. Doris knows how to keep friends; she *sticks to them like tape*.
    a. She keeps her distance from her friends.
    b. She stays close to her friends.
    c. She gets her friends into sticky situations.

3. When the outfielders ran into each other, they bumped heads and *flopped to the ground like rag dolls*.
    a. They lay sprawled on the ground without moving.
    b. Their clothes were torn.
    c. They looked tiny.

4. After a two-hour workout, I felt as if I'd been *run through a cement mixer*.
    a. I felt I was in great shape.
    b. I was so tired I had an accident.
    c. I was sore and completely worn out.

Grade Eight SkillBook, Reading

5. The weather has left the country roads in terrible shape; they look *like chocolate pudding*.
   a. They're full of holes.
   b. They're dark brown and muddy.
   c. They are narrow and winding.

6. When school was over, the students streamed out of the building *like ants leaving an ant hill*.
   a. They marched slowly in a single line.
   b. They moved quickly in many directions.
   c. They crawled over the grass.

7. His advice was about *as useful as a newspaper left out in a hard rain*.
   a. His advice concerns the weather.
   b. His advice is very clear.
   c. His advice is of no use.

8. Her temper can be *as hot as chili peppers*.
   a. She is slow to become angry.
   b. She has a bad temper.
   c. Her temper makes her hungry.

9. We can always tell where Mr. Ruz is because his voice is *like ten kettle drums all being drummed at the same time*.
   a. His voice is very musical.
   b. His voice sets the beat for everyone else's.
   c. His voice is very loud and deep.

10. That carrot cake looked and smelled so good I ate *like a five-hundred-pound hog*.
    a. I ate without a fork.
    b. I felt I was too fat.
    c. I ate much, much more than I usually do.

Name _____ Class _____ Date _____

Lesson 13
Understanding Figurative Comparisons

Most figurative language involves comparisons. Figurative comparisons can help you understand familiar things in new ways. They can also help explain something unfamiliar by comparing it to something you already know. For example, if you have never been near an ocean, would the following comparison help you understand the sounds the sea makes?

The sounds of the sea were like the moans of a sorrowful dog.

Exercise A
Each sentence below has a figurative comparison. Circle the letter of the two things being compared.

1. For a half hour almost every night, Ben and his son play on the rug like two puppies.
   a. Ben—his son
   b. Ben and his son—two puppies
   c. puppies—rug

2. There's a woodpecker in these woods that sounds like a jackhammer.
   a. woodpecker—jackhammer
   b. woodpecker—sounds
   c. woods—jackhammer

3. After the explosion, people poured out of the building like water bursting from a dam.
   a. explosion—water
   b. people—water
   c. building—water

4. Larry is such a stock-car racing fan that you can almost hear gears shift as he walks.
   a. race car—fan
   b. Larry—gears
   c. Larry—race car

5. The wind turned the branches into whips that lashed against the side of the house.
   a. branches—whips
   b. branches—house
   c. wind—whips

Figurative comparisons compare things that may have one or two similarities. But the two things are mostly not alike. Figurative comparisons may be short, or they may continue through several sentences, paragraphs, or lines of a poem.

Grade Eight SkillBook, Reading

Exercise B
Read the following poem, and then answer the questions about the figurative comparisons.

MOTOR CARS
by Rowena Bennett

From a city window, 'way up high,
I like to watch the cars go by.
They look like burnished beetles, black,
That leave a little muddy track
5 Behind them as they slowly crawl.
Sometimes they do not move at all
But huddle close with hum and drone
As though they feared to be alone.
They grope their way through fog and night
10 With the golden feelers of their light.

1. How are the cars, as seen from a high window, like beetles?
   a. They seem as small as beetles.
   b. They are all black like beetles.
   c. They are shaped like beetles and even have feelers.

2. What does line 3 suggest about how the tops of the cars look? Does the word *burnished* (or "polished") suggest that they are dull black or shiny black?

_____

3. How are beetles and cars similar in what they leave behind them?

_____

4. What is actually happening in lines 6–8?
   a. The cars are moving down the street in a long line.
   b. The cars are parked at the curb very close to each other.
   c. The cars are bunched up at intersections waiting for the light to change.

5. What are the "golden feelers" in the last line?

_____

Exercise C
The preceding poem had one figurative comparison: Cars compared to beetles. The following poem uses several comparisons to describe gathering leaves in fall. Read the poem, and answer the questions.

GATHERING LEAVES
by Robert Frost

Spades take up leaves
No better than spoons,
And bags full of leaves
Are light as balloons.

5   I make a great noise
Of rustling all day
Like rabbit and deer
Running away.

But the mountains I raise
10 Elude my embrace,
Flowing over my arms
And into my face.

I may load and unload
Again and again
15 Till I fill the whole shed,
And what have I then?

Next to nothing for weight,
And since they grew duller
From contact with earth,
20 Next to nothing for color.

Next to nothing for use.
But a crop is a crop,
And who's to say where
The harvest shall stop?

1. The speaker compares picking up leaves with a spade (a flat shovel designed for turning earth) to gathering them with a spoon. What does this comparison suggest about the effectiveness of the spade?

2. Could the bags of leaves actually be as "light as balloons"? Why or why not?

3. How are the speaker and the rabbit and deer alike?

4. How does the speaker suggest the great size of the piles of leaves in the third stanza?

   _____

5. The speaker has compared gathering the leaves to harvesting a crop. How are these two activities *not* alike?

   _____

Exercise D
Write your own poem using a comparison.

Lesson 14
Reviewing Figurative Language

As you read the following passage from the novel *The Survivor*, notice the use of figurative language. Then, answer the questions.

from **THE SURVIVOR**
by James Forman

    An old man and a boy stood on the high dunes overlooking the sea, which was dark violet-blue and feathered white where the wind kissed it. No boat was out. Below, the beach lay golden yellow in the late afternoon light. A horseman trotting his mount splashed through the shallows. The hoofmarks were brief silver coins.

    There were other figures on the beach making the most of summer's end, and the old man smiled to see them there, his family. The boy beside him was his favorite grandchild. Moses Ullman was seventy years old. He had found much pleasure in growing old. The years had been good and full of adventure. They had turned him from a rather ugly, awkward youth with a diving nose, so fiercely hooked that it might have chopped wood, into an old gentleman with a splendid snowstorm of silver-white hair. Lines of ugliness had come to rest in lines of strength and peace. He still had his strength: strong bony wrists, hands twisted and knotted, the nails yellow and thick as sea shells. His digestion was perfect. He could eat anything.

Exercise

1. Which of the following does the figurative expression "feathered white" make you see?
   a. heavy waves rolling in to the beach
   b. tiny whitecaps on the surface of the sea
   c. gulls flying over the sea

2. What kind of wind "kissed" the sea?
   a. a soft, very light wind
   b. a strong, steady wind
   c. a cold, violent storm wind

3. Why are the hoofmarks called "brief silver coins" at the end of the first paragraph?
   a. The horseshoes left traces of metal in the sand that reflected the sunlight.
   b. The water that collected in the round hoofmarks reflected light, but the waves quickly washed the marks away.
   c. Sand blew into the hoofmarks and quickly filled them up so that they became hard to see.

Name _____ Class _____ Date _____

4. To what is Ullman's hair compared? How might these two things be alike?

   _____

5. To what are Ullman's fingernails compared? How are these things alike?

   _____

Now use your own figurative language to make some comparisons. Think of something that will describe the look or feel of the following items by comparison. Write the word or phrase in the blank next to each.

    Item   is like:

6. the classroom around me   _____

7. the weather today   _____

8. an old pair of shoes   _____

9. my favorite t-shirt   _____

10. the loudness of a crowd   _____

Grade Eight SkillBook, Reading

| Name | Class | Date |

Lesson 15
Making Inferences

When you use a clue to make a reasonable guess, you are making an **inference**.

Study these two sentences. Decide to whom the speaker is talking.

"I don't care who you are, fat man. Get your reindeer off my roof."

1. Who is the "fat man"?
2. Which words in the sentences can be used as clues.

When you look at pictures and when you read, you frequently use clues to make inferences. In the example above, you know that the fat man is Santa Claus. You can infer this because he is fat and has reindeer on someone's roof. The more clues you find, the more likely it is that your inferences will be correct.

Exercise
Read the following letters and answer the questions.

Dear Cousin Kay,   Jan. 12
   Heavens, I can't believe it's January 12 already and I still haven't thanked you for the delightful ceramic ~~doorsto cookie j cuspid~~ ceramic. The modern ceramic work is so interesting, I think, and the colors of this ~~thi~~ one are just beautiful. . . . . .

1. Which of the following sentences is the best inference about the situation? (Circle the letter of the best answer.)
   a. The writer doesn't want to say that the ceramic arrived broken.
   b. The writer can't figure out what the ceramic is supposed to be.
   c. The writer already owns a ceramic just like the one received.

2. Underline the words in the letter that you used as clues.

Jim-Dandy Youth Publications   Jan. 12
Box 4207 New York NY.

Dear Sirs,

   My aunt Miss Carrie Lundy gave me a suscription to The Growing Boy for Christmas I notice that you print other magazines too and so I would like to change it to Bill Blaze Space Demon and if there is any difference in price send it to
   Herbert Lundy Jr.
   13150 S.W. Fielding Rd.
   Oswego Oreg.

as I do not want to bother Aunt Carrie...

Name _____ Class _____ Date _____

3. Which of the following sentences is the best inference about what this second letter reveals? (Circle the letter.)
   a. The boy has never had a magazine subscription before.
   b. The boy doesn't want his aunt to know that he wants a different magazine.
   c. The boy wants subscriptions to two magazines.

4. Circle the words in the letter that you used as a clue.

5. Underline at least one part of the letter that allows you to infer that Herbert is not a careful writer.

Name _____ Class _____ Date _____

Lesson 16
Identifying Clues

Reading sometimes involves detective work. When you need to make inferences, you search for clues and put the clues together with what you already know. You then can make inferences about what is happening and what the characters believe or feel. Sometimes there are many clues, and it is easy to find them. Other times there are only a few clues, and they are hidden.

Exercise A

Read this mystery about the robbery of a police officer on vacation. Look for clues as you read.

Police Captain Tom Reilly had been driving in the mountains all day. It was midnight before he went winding down the steep mountain road in his Volkswagen.

On his way down, Reilly passed several mountain cabins tucked away in the woods. But he never saw anyone. That was why he was surprised when his car's headlights outlined a large automobile parked in the middle of the road.

Reilly hit the brakes, and his small car careened out of control. As he swerved up on the shoulder of the road, Reilly heard his tires blow.

Before he could get out of the VW, three masked men surrounded his car. One of the men demanded his wallet.

Reilly handed the man his wallet. The three leaped into their car and sped down the road.

After they left, Reilly examined his tires. He picked up a handful of tacks off the road. "That was planned pretty well," he muttered to himself.

Remembering a cabin about two miles back, Reilly started walking. After he had knocked on the door several times, a farmer appeared.

"I was just robbed down the road," Reilly said through the cabin's screened door. "I'd appreciate it if you'd call a garage to get me a new set of tires. And then call the sheriff."

Reilly could hear the man dial the number. "Hello, Okie's Garage? Sorry to get you up at this hour, Okie. Got a man stranded out here. Needs a set of VW tires. Right, see you in a while." Then the man called the sheriff.

A few hours later, Reilly told his story to the sheriff. Then Reilly turned toward the farmer.

"I'm thankful for this man's hospitality," Reilly said, "but I'm afraid you're going to have to arrest him for robbery."

Were you a good detective? Complete the exercise on the next page.

Grade Eight SkillBook, Reading   **67**

1. Why did Reilly hit his brakes as he was driving down the steep mountain road?

2. How were his tires damaged?

3. Underline what Reilly told the farmer.

4. When the farmer called Okie's Garage, what did he tell Okie?

5. Why did Captain Reilly suspect that the farmer was in on the robbery?

Exercise B
Read the selection below. Write as many clues as you can to support the inferences that follow the selection.

"Yes," said Baird. "Radio ahead that we have three serious cases of suspected food poisoning and that there seem to be others developing. You can say we're not sure but we suspect that the poisoning could have been caused by fish served on board. Better ask them to put a ban on all food originating from the same source as ours."

Baird stepped to the door. The lines in his face had deepened, but his eyes were steady.

"See that the passengers are not alarmed," he instructed Janet as they stepped out of the cockpit. "We'll be depending on you a great deal. Now, if you'll locate my bag, I'll be attending to Mrs. Childer."

Then he suddenly stopped as if something had occurred to him. "By the way, what did *you* eat for dinner?"

"I had meat," the young woman answered him.

"Thank heavens for that, then." Janet smiled and made to go on again, but he gripped her suddenly, very hard by the arm. "I suppose the pilot had meat, too?" He shot the question at her.

She looked up at him, as if at the same time trying both to remember and to grasp the meaning of what he had asked.

Then, suddenly, shock and realization flooded into her, and her eyes dilated with an immense and overpowering fear.

Name _____ Class _____ Date _____

1. The action is taking place aboard an airplane.

   _____

2. Baird is a doctor.

   _____

3. Janet is a stewardess.

   _____

   _____

4. The pilot ate fish.

   _____

   _____

5. Janet thinks that the pilot may not be able to finish the flight.

   _____

   _____

Grade Eight SkillBook, Reading

Lesson 17
Inferences About Time and Place

As you read stories, you need to know the place and time of the happenings. Sometimes the writer may tell you directly where and when the story is taking place. The writers of the next selections, however, do not directly tell you time and place. Instead, you must find clues. Read the selections and make inferences about the time and place.

Exercise
Read the following selections and answer the questions.

A. Bean season was almost over. School started in two weeks. The girls walked along the road, tired to the bone.
   The girls passed the Baxters' and were almost home when Sandy held out her hands, stopping Marie and June abruptly. Her sisters looked up questioningly and then followed her gaze. A black-and-white car sat in front of the house, the word *Sheriff* across its doors.
   "What'll we do?" whispered June, biting her lower lip.
   "We'll hide," said Sandy. "Come on!"
   She headed across the road and held up the fence while Marie and June scurried beneath it. Then she climbed through the barbed wires. As they ran, the three girls ducked low. They circled around, coming in behind the barn, where they stopped in a thick clump of tall, willowy weed and settled down to watch.

1. This story probably takes place
   a. in a large city
   b. at a trailer park
   c. on a farm
   d. on a small island

2. The time of year in this selection is probably
   a. early May
   b. late August
   c. late December
   d. late March or early April

B. The rain started about mid-afternoon. Thunder rumbled across the prairie and lightning split the sky. The clouds hung low and full. Joey dug out his slicker and put it on. The rain pelted against him fiercely.
   The trail that had once been deep with ruts and dust, now was slippery with mud. The mules strained forward, pulling hard to keep the wagons moving. Every little while, a wagon bogged down. Precious hours were lost getting it out and moving again.
   Darkness dropped early, the clouds still black and threatening as they pulled into their circle. Joey tried to build a fire under the wagon but the

wood was too wet. Finally his mother prepared a cold supper inside and they crowded together in the small space.

"What about the watch tonight?" Jenny whispered.

"I'll take it. We don't want to be caught off guard," Joey returned.

He finished eating and leaped down, his boots squooshing in the rain-soaked earth. He circled around until he was near George Logan's wagon. Everything seemed quiet. He climbed up in a lone tree that grew nearby. The livestock were grazing a short distance away, still a little restless from the storm.

3. What is the time of day at the end of this selection?

_____

4. This selection takes place on a
   a. wagon trail
   b. paved mountain road
   c. desert plain
   d. path through a forest

5. This selection occurs sometime shortly after the
   a. discovery of America
   b. opening up of the West
   c. first landing on the moon
   d. twentieth century

Grade Eight SkillBook, Reading

Name _____ Class _____ Date _____

Lesson 18
Inferences About Characters

When you read, you make inferences about characters—based on clues. The major clues you use to make inferences about characters come from their appearances, their actions, and the situations they are in. You can also learn about characters from what they say and how they say it.

Exercise A
Read the following selection and make some inferences about Claudia.

    Claudia knew that she could never pull off the old-fashioned kind of running away. That is, running away in the heat of anger with a knapsack on her back. She didn't like discomfort; even picnics were untidy and inconvenient: all those insects and the sun melting the icing on the cupcakes. Therefore, she decided that her leaving home would not be just running from somewhere but would be running to somewhere. To a large place, a comfortable place, an indoor place, and preferably a beautiful place. And that's why she decided upon the Metropolitan Museum of Art in New York City.
    She planned very carefully; she saved her allowance and she chose her companion. She chose Jamie, the second youngest of her three younger brothers. He could be counted on to be quiet, and now and then he was good for a laugh. Besides, he was rich; unlike most boys his age, he had never even begun collecting baseball cards. He saved almost every penny he got.
    But Claudia waited to tell Jamie that she had decided upon him. She couldn't count on him to be *that* quiet for *that* long. And she calculated needing *that* long to save her weekly allowances. It seemed senseless to run away without money.
    She had to save enough for train fare and a few expenses before she could tell Jamie or make final plans. In the meantime she almost forgot why she was running away. But not entirely. Claudia knew that it had to do with injustice. She was the oldest child and the only girl and was subject to a lot of injustice. Perhaps it was because she had to both empty the dishwasher and set the table on the same night while her brothers got out of everything. And, perhaps, there was another reason. A reason that had to do with the sameness of each and every week. She was bored with simply being straight-A's Claudia Kincaid.

Read each statement. If the statement is a correct inference, write **T** for true on the line. If the statement is incorrect, write **F** for false on the line. If there is no evidence in the story, write **CT** for can't tell. Be ready to tell what clues you used.

_____ 1. Claudia would enjoy a camping trip in the wilderness.

_____ 2. Claudia wants to be an artist someday.

Name _____ Class _____ Date _____

_____ 3. Claudia wants Jamie to run away with her because she knows he feels the same way she does.

_____ 4. Claudia believes she does more than her share of the chores at home.

_____ 5. Claudia likes Jamie better than she likes her other two brothers.

Exercise B

In this selection you learn about the characters through their conversations. The night before this selection begins, Nick, in a hurry to leave town, dived into an open boxcar in a moving train; inside he found the boxcar already occupied by a man called Idaho. After a night of traveling, the train is about to pull into the railroad yard in the town of North Forks. . . .

from **RUN FAR, RUN FAST**
by Walt Morey

"Now then," Idaho said in a businesslike voice, "the first thing you've got to learn is how and when to get into and out of a boxcar. Never dive in head first. You could smash your head on some cargo or be sucked out, as you almost were."

"I'll do whatever you say," Nick said.

The train's speed dropped off fast. Idaho stood up. "Come on. We're due to leave this private luxury coach in a few minutes."

They stood in the open door while the freight crawled into the yard and stopped. Nick started to jump to the ground but Idaho held him back. "Never jump without lookin' first. Okay! All clear. Go ahead."

Fine snow covered the ground. A biting wind picked it up and swirled it across the freight yard. Cold knifed through Nick's thin suit.

Idaho said, "First thing is to get you some clothes. Come on. I know a place."

"How'll I get clothes without money?"

"I'll show you. We're going to a place called The Lighthouse."

Nick fell in beside him. "We going to steal 'em?"

"I never steal."

They hiked six frigid blocks and turned into an old store building whose dusty windows were packed with an assortment of used clothing. Inside row on row of clothing hung on racks. Halfway down an aisle a tall, lean old man with a full beard bore down on them. "Idaho! Idaho!" he boomed. "As I live and breathe! I'd about give up on you this year."

Idaho was pawing through a pile of caps and hats. "Nick," he said, "this's Cap Small. Don't ask what he was captain of, a rowboat most likely if anything."

Cap Small's knowing blue eyes kept studying Idaho. He nodded his head wisely.

"I'll take this cap," Idaho said. "Nick's travelin' with me. He needs to trade in these fancy duds for some decent clothes. You know. Wool pants, shirt, jacket, heavy shoes."

Grade Eight SkillBook, Reading

"Trade!" Cap Small almost shouted. "I'm in th' business of sellin'. Can't you get that through your bald head?"

"You trade me."

"You're always broke—so you say. Anyway, you're a special case."

"So's Nick. He's my partner."

"They're always your partner."

They both sounded angry. But Nick could see they had trouble not smiling. This was their greeting.

"Well, all right. Just this once more." Cap Small headed for the back of the store grumbling.

Read each statement. If the statement is a correct inference, write **T** for true on the line. If the statement is incorrect, write **F** for false on the line. If there is no evidence in the story, write **CT** for can't tell. Be ready to tell what clues you used.

_____ 1. Idaho has been in this part of the country before.

_____ 2. Idaho is probably older than Nick.

_____ 3. Idaho wishes that Nick would leave him alone.

_____ 4. Nick does not have much experience in getting on and off boxcars.

_____ 5. Idaho stops in at The Lighthouse at least once a year.

_____ 6. Idaho probably used to work for Cap Small.

_____ 7. Idaho and Cap Small are good friends.

_____ 8. Idaho has always been alone before when he has seen Cap Small.

_____ 9. Idaho is probably dishonest.

_____ 10. Cap Small probably doesn't mean it when he says, "Just this once more."

Exercise C

Read the following selection and look for clues about a teenager named Frances and her mother who is a nurse for a rural community health service. Fran is alone in the house, doing her homework.

The next call came at ten to eight. She knew at once that it was the old man again.

"Will you give me your name?" she asked.

"Is that the nurse?" the voice demanded.

"What is your name?"

"This is Mr. Treloar. . . . I didn't want to trouble you, but . . ." He seemed unable to continue.

Frances wished her mother had been there to take the call. She would have known exactly what to do.

"You see . . . my wife has fallen down . . ." he continued.
"You must phone the doctor," she said almost coldly.
"I don't like to disturb him."
"That's what he's there for."
"And the nurses are always so good. . . . I thought if she could have a look . . ."
"Phone the doctor."
"Is the nurse there?"
"No, you must phone the doctor."

She put the receiver down. The last time she had taken a message of despair, and written it all down, her mother had come home and said, "Oh not him again! Why didn't he ring one of his daughters? There are two living on the same estate. And he's got neighbors, hasn't he? I wish I'd answered the phone. I'd have given him a good telling off!"

But if the old man's wife had fallen down, then she needed help. At least Fran had covered herself by telling him to call the doctor.

People were always speaking to her on the phone as though she was her mother. She was always being given personal details.

What did you learn about Fran and her mother? Put "T" for true or "F" for false before each statement.

_____ 1. Fran is uneasy about having this responsibility of answering her mother's phone calls.

_____ 2. Fran feels very sorry for the old man.

_____ 3. Fran's mother is probably too sympathetic toward her patients.

_____ 4. Fran's mother would probably approve of the way Fran handled Mr. Treloar.

You probably decided that Fran is uncomfortable in emotional situations and would rather avoid them if possible. And, as a nurse, Fran's mother seems strangely to have little patience with people. Based on the clues in actions and speech, you were able to make inferences about Fran and her mother.

Lesson 19
Inferences About Fantasy

Stories can have impossible or highly improbable situations, events, and characters. Such stories are called **fantasies**. Dickens's *A Christmas Carol*, Stevenson's *Strange Case of Dr. Jekyll and Mr. Hyde*, and the tale of Cinderella are fantasies.

You use your inference skills to identify a fantasy. Then you make inferences about the characters, the events, and the time and place of the story, just as you do for other stories. In fact, you may find that a fantasy is making a point about the real world.

Exercise
Read this selection and answer the questions.

THE CHOICE
by W. Hilton-Young

Before Williams went into the future she bought a camera and a tape recording machine and learned shorthand. That night, when all was ready, we made coffee and put out brandy and glasses against her return.

"Good-bye," I said. "Don't stay too long."

"I won't," she answered.

I watched her carefully, and she hardly flickered. She must have made a perfect landing on the very second she had taken off from. She seemed not a day older; we had expected she might spend several years away.

"Well?"

"Well," said she, "let's have some coffee."

I poured it out, hardly able to contain my impatience. As I gave it to her, I said again, "Well?"

"Well, the thing is, I can't remember."

"Can't remember? Not a thing?"

She thought for a moment and answered sadly, "Not a thing."

"But your notes? The camera? The recording machine?"

The notebook was empty, the indicator of the camera rested at "1" where we had set it, the tape was not even loaded into the recording machine.

"But good heavens," I protested, "why? How did it happen? Can you remember nothing at all?"

"I can remember only one thing."

"What was that?"

"I was shown everything, and I was given the choice whether I should remember it or not after I got back."

"And you chose not to? But what an extraordinary thing to—"

"Isn't it? she said. "One can't help wondering why."

Name _____ Class _____ Date _____

1. What is meant by "she hardly flickered"?
   _____
   _____

2. What one thing can Williams remember about where she went?
   _____
   _____

3. What choice did Williams make?
   _____
   _____

4. Give at least one possible reason why she might have made the choice she did.
   _____
   _____

5. Underline three clues that tell you this is a fantasy.

Grade Eight SkillBook, Reading

Lesson 20
Reviewing Inferences

Exercise
Read the following selection about Geir and Peter. Then answer the questions.

from LEAP INTO DANGER
by Leif Hamre

The days passed.

The weather remained unchanged as did life in the camp. Geir kept the fire going always, and the stone wall at the back of the hut became so warm that the temperature inside the hut remained even and comfortable. Their beds, with the cushions from the plane as mattresses, were warmer and softer.

Food supplies had increased so that they were now able to have two or three satisfactory meals a day. They had more fish than they could eat.

Geir had not so much to do any longer. He spent one day making an enormous SOS of branches, which he laid out on the ice, but when that was finished, he had only the daily routine work to do. He collected wood, cooked food, and examined the fishing lines and the snares morning and evening.

He sat for hours brooding over the fact that they had not yet been found and wondering why this was. He had now no doubt in his mind that they had given a wrong position; otherwise, the helicopter or the patrol would surely have found them.

One bitter cold night Geir woke because he was shivering. The fire had nearly burned itself out, and he leaned forward toward the door and threw on a few branches.

Suddenly he heard a noise from the darkness. He could not say what it was, but it was at any rate something different from the soft sighing of the wind and the crackling of the fire. He listened for a moment, every nerve stretched, but the sound was not repeated.

"It must have been something—I'm absolutely sure of that," he thought. "It sounded almost like a shout."

There! There it was again, far away—a shout. It must be a shout.

"Peter!" he yelled. "Peter!"

He unrolled himself quickly from his parachute and pushed his feet into his boots.

"They're coming! We're saved!" he cried, deeply moved.

Peter sat bolt upright, his face a mixture of sleepy confusion and wide-awake expectation.

"Is it true?" he burst out. He looked through the door opening. "Now? In the middle of the night?"

"Sure," said Geir. "They shouted. I heard it clearly—far away."

He wriggled out of the door and stood up beside the fire.

"Ahoy!" he shouted out into the darkness. "A-hoy! A-hoy!"

They listened eagerly for a minute or two. Then Geir shouted again, cupping his mouth with his hands and shouting in all directions.

But the night remained quite silent.

"You must have dreamed it," said Peter, disappointed.

Geir shouted again, but still all was quiet. "The shouts may have come with the wind," he said. "And *mine* don't carry against it. I must stand against it. I must stand against the wind and shout until I get an answer."

He fetched his snowshoes and bent down to put them on. Then they both heard it again—a long drawn-out howl that rose and sank as if it were carried on an uneven wind.

Geir arose. "Did you hear it?" he whispered.

"Stand still!" cried Peter sharply. "Don't shout!"

Something in Peter's voice made Geir pause and listen. A minute passed. Then they heard it again as if it were nearer.

The boys did not move for a long time. There was no longer any doubt. That was not a human voice.

"Wolves," said Peter firmly.

Geir did not answer. Disappointment and horror were written all over his face.

1. Does this story take place on a frozen sea near the North Pole, in a wooded wilderness, or somewhere in the Florida Everglades?

   _____

2. What has happened to Geir and Peter?

   _____
   _____

3. When does this story probably take place—in the distant past, the present, or the far-off future?

   _____

4. What evidence suggests that Geir is an experienced outdoorsman?

   _____
   _____

5. Is this story a fantasy? Why or why not?

   _____
   _____

Grade Eight SkillBook, Reading

Name _____ Class _____ Date _____

Lesson 21
Finding the Direct Statement of Main Idea

The **topic** identifies the general subject of a selection, but the **main idea** states *what is said about the topic.*

As you read, you have to put together the details and decide what one main idea they all emphasize. But sometimes, as in this passage, the author includes a sentence that actually states the main idea. This is called a **direct statement of the main idea**.

A direct statement of the main idea will often, but not necessarily, be at the very beginning or at the end of a passage. At times the writer takes a sentence or two to introduce the topic and doesn't state the main idea until the middle of the paragraph.

Exercise
Read each paragraph and then answer the questions.

A. Glenn D. Prestwich, a chemist at the university in Stony Brook, New York, has a rather unusual interest. He studies the chemical defenses of bazooka termites and snapping termites, corking termites and pincer termites, and even termites that explosively self-destruct. Each of these groups has a special way of holding off enemies and competitors. There seems to be a wide range of defensive weapons among the termites Prestwich studies.

1. Which is the topic of paragraph A?
   a. insect pests
   b. Glenn D. Prestwich
   c. termite defenses

2. Which of the following statements is the most important thing said about the topic?
   a. Some termites self-destruct.
   b. Termites cause a great deal of damage.
   c. Prestwich is interested in a broad range of termite defenses.
   d. There are many different kinds of termites.

3. Is there a direct statement of the main idea in paragraph A? Circle your answer.
   Yes
   No

B. Prestwich has found that most of these termite weapons owe more to chemistry than to muscle power. Bazooka termites, for example, shoot a glue out of their long foreheads. This glue is a chemical that is slightly water-repellent. It sticks easily to the body of an ant, a major termite enemy. Unable to scrape the glue off, the ant usually dies. The soldierless termite goes to even greater extremes to punish any attackers. This unarmed worker bursts apart when pinched. But as it explodes, it spurts digestive juices that eat into its enemies like acid.

4. Which of the following is the topic of paragraph B?
   a. bazooka termites
   b. soldierless termites
   c. termite defenses

5. The main idea of paragraph B is
   a. Bazooka termites shoot a water-repellent glue from their foreheads.
   b. Termites are more complex creatures than we usually think.
   c. Ants and termites, though enemies, are closely related.
   d. Termite defenses depend chiefly on chemical weapons.

6. Underline the direct statement of the main idea in paragraph B.

C. While most termites are slow-moving, soldier Rhinotermes (named after their long, noselike upper lip) dash about painting the faces of attacking insects with insecticide dispensed through the upper lip. This paintbrush defense system is another very effective and complex form of chemical warfare. Prestwich has found that the poison used by one branch of the paintbrush termites will kill members of another family. But he still hasn't been able to figure out what prevents each clan of termites from poisoning themselves.

7. What type of termites is the topic of paragraph C?

8. Underline the sentence that directly states the main idea that is being made about this group's defense system.

D. None of Prestwich's termites are of the crop-eating, house-chomping varieties that have given termites their bad name. In fact, in the temperate regions of the United States only the snapping mandible termites are pests. These other termites, it seems, are different. Prestwich's termites are more interested in keeping their enemies at bay than doing battle with homeowners and farmers.

9. The main idea of paragraph D is
   a. Termites keep their enemies at bay.
   b. Prestwich's termites concentrate on doing battle with termite enemies.
   c. Snapping mandible termites are pests and will eat houses.
   d. All termites deserve their bad name.

10. Underline the direct statement of the main idea in paragraph D.

Grade Eight SkillBook, Reading

Name _____ Class _____ Date _____

Lesson 22
Identifying the Implied Main Idea

Written selections very often will not contain a sentence that directly states the main idea. In such cases, the main idea is only **implied**, or suggested. You must put together everything that is said to arrive at the main idea of the selection.

Exercise A
As you read the next paragraph, notice the arrangement and emphasis of details.

> Who is responsible for our country's pollution problem, and who can do something about it? Newspaper headlines point the finger at industry for wastes in our rivers, smog in the air, and poisonous chemicals buried underground. Citizens' groups discuss governmental control and self-policing by industry. But what about the crumpled gum and candy wrappers blowing down the sidewalk? How about the broken glass, metal cans, and plastic cups left scattered after a family picnic? Or the way people prefer riding two blocks to the store instead of walking? Is it really fair to blame big business for the abandoned cars, rusty bikes, and useless appliances that can be found in back alleys and ditches all over the country?

1. Circle the letter of the phrase that best suggests the topic of this paragraph.
   a. industrial pollution
   b. family picnics
   c. problems in our cities
   d. our country's pollution problems

2. Now circle the letter of the statement that best summarizes the main idea of the paragraph—that is, what is said about the topic.
   a. Pollution is our country's number one problem.
   b. Responsibility for our country's pollution problem lies with individuals as well as with big business.
   c. Citizens' groups are responsible for pollution and must assume responsibility for cleaning it up.
   d. Abandoned cars and appliances add to pollution.

The writer expects you to understand the point being made about the pollution problem from the questions asked and the examples given. A good statement of main idea summarizes the understanding you get from the whole selection.

Main Idea in Literature
Stories and poems also contain details that build up a main idea or impression. Usually the writer wants readers to come to understand the point

on their own. You will find that the main idea of a poem or story is very often implied rather than directly stated.

You will find, too, that all the details in a poem count toward developing the main idea. It can take almost as many words to say what a poem is about as are in the poem itself. In a good poem every word is important.

Exercise B

As you read this poem by Carl Sandburg, notice how the poet builds up the understanding he wants you to have.

SOUP

I saw a famous man eating soup.
I say he was lifting a fat broth
Into his mouth with a spoon.
His name was in the newspapers that day
5 Spelled out in tall black headlines
And thousands of people were talking about him.

When I saw him,
He sat bending his head over a plate
Putting soup in his mouth with a spoon.

1. What is the topic of this poem? (Circle one.)
    a. a famous man eating soup
    b. eating soup with a spoon
    c. newspaper headlines

2. Which of the following statements best states the main idea suggested by the poem?
    a. If you are alert, you can sometimes spot famous people eating in a restaurant.
    b. Even famous people do ordinary things, like eating soup, in ordinary ways.
    c. Famous people have their names in newspaper headlines.
    d. It is unusual for a famous person to eat soup.

Lesson 23
Evaluating Details

As you read, you will find that writers often include details that add interest or give a fuller sense of the subject, but these could be changed or left out without changing the main idea of the selection.

Exercise
Read each paragraph and answer the questions by circling the letter of the correct answer.

    A. One thousand students, mostly boys, from twenty elementary schools in New York City and its suburbs, are busy practicing ballet leaps for a huge dance festival in the Felt Forum of Madison Square Garden. These dancers, all between the ages of eight and thirteen, are the most talented of the seven thousand students that have been selected and trained by the great American dancer, Jacques d'Amboise (zhäk däN bwaz´).

1. What is the main idea of paragraph A?
    a. Jacques d'Amboise is organizing a huge dance performance by one thousand students.
    b. The dancers in the program at Madison Square Garden will be between eight and thirteen years old.
    c. Ballet is enjoyed by many students in the New York area.
    d. It takes a lot of hard work to teach dance to students.

2. Which details are important to understanding the main idea?
    a. Students came from twenty schools in the New York City area.
    b. There will be a big performance in Madison Square Garden featuring eight- to thirteen-year-old dancers.
    c. The young dancers are practicing ballet leaps now.
    d. Jacques d'Amboise selected and trained the dancers for the program.

    B. D'Amboise was only fifteen himself when he became a member of the newly formed New York City Ballet more than thirty years ago. He rose very swiftly to become the world-famous dance troupe's principal male dancer. It wasn't easy in those days for an American boy to choose ballet as a career—particularly one who grew up among the gangs of Washington Heights as d'Amboise did. He took a real chance of being called a sissy. D'Amboise hasn't forgotten. The National Dance Institute (NDI) was started in 1966 by d'Amboise so that his sons, then ten and seven, could discover the joys of dancing without being forced to go to formal ballet classes. The brothers asked a few of their schoolmates to join in. They wore ordinary street clothes; d'Amboise had them pile their coats on the floor. Then they were invited to jump over the coats while a pianist played "jumping music." Thus did eight little boys learn the basics of the *grand jeté* (gRäN zhə tā´), an important movement in ballet.

84   Grade Eight SkillBook, Reading

3. What is the main idea of paragraph B?
   a. Boys have to learn at an early age to put up with a certain amount of teasing.
   b. D'Amboise was the principal male dancer in the New York City Ballet.
   c. D'Amboise started the National Dance Institute so his sons could learn to enjoy dance without the problems he had.
   d. Boys can become successful ballet dancers.

4. Which details are important for understanding the main idea in paragraph B?
   a. D'Amboise became a member of the New York City Ballet more than thirty years ago.
   b. D'Amboise remembers how hard it can be for a boy to study ballet.
   c. D'Amboise grew up among boys who were likely to laugh at him.
   d. There were eight boys in the first group that d'Amboise worked with.
   e. D'Amboise made the classes for his sons and their friends fun and informal.

C. Today, d'Amboise and an assisting faculty of professional dancers bring ballet, modern dance, jazz, and other forms to thousands of kids in public, private, and parochial schools in New York City, Long Island, Westchester County, and parts of New Jersey through the National Dance Institute. The goal, simply stated, is "to establish dance as an everyday part of the cultural life of America." But d'Amboise continues to feel a special interest in encouraging boys to see dance as an enjoyable and challenging activity. As he begins his programs each fall in the schools the NDI serves, he permits only boys to sign up. He feels that otherwise social pressure would bring in all girls. Around Christmas, when the boys are having too much fun to want to drop out, girls are allowed to fill out the groups.

5. What is the main idea of paragraph C?
   a. Boys start in the fall; girls can join NDI classes only around Christmas.
   b. The NDI arranges classes in schools around New York City to help kids, and especially boys, to see dance as a part of their everyday lives.
   c. There are thousands of elementary school students in New York City and the surrounding communities who do not benefit from cultural programs.
   d. Dance is an important part of American life.

Name _____ Class _____ Date _____

Lesson 24
Reviewing Main Idea

Exercise
Read through the following article and answer the questions.

KIDS IN THE KITCHEN

(A) The first thing Nicholas and Sebastian Yeager do when they get home from school is check the refrigerator. It may be that they grab an apple or a piece of cold chicken for a snack. But the boys' main interest is in making sure that all the necessary ingredients for that night's meal are on hand. The Yeager brothers are experienced family cooks and they like it that way.
(B) Nicholas, 12, and Sebastian, 14, are each responsible for preparing dinner for themselves and their mother two nights a week. The boys are expected to plan the meal and do any necessary last minute shopping, as well as the cooking. They try to have everything ready to eat by the time their mother gets home from work at 6:15.
(C) The two Yeagers are old hands in the kitchen. As preschoolers, they helped their mother scrape carrots and cut up fruit salad. She let them pour tomato sauce when she made spaghetti and turn the mixer on and off for cookies. As they got a little older, Mrs. Yeager guided her sons through the directions in simple cookbooks. In time, they were comfortable doing it all on their own.
(D) Then, too, shopping has always been a family affair in the Yeager household. By the time they were eight or so, the boys knew how to compare prices and to check ingredients as well as how to look for giveaways on the backs of cereal boxes.
(E) There are days when Nicholas and Sebastian would much rather play ball than peel potatoes. But they realize that it is a real help to their mother to come home to a prepared meal after a hard day. Both boys are also pleased that they won't be limited to TV dinners or cheap restaurants once they move out on their own. But there are immediate rewards to being the family cooks too. As Nicholas says, "When you are the cook, you cook what *you* like." Sebastian, whose specialty is cheesecake, adds that when there are leftovers, "The cook eats!"

1. What topic is introduced in paragraph A? (Underline one.)
   The Yeager brothers are always looking for something to eat.
   The boys love to make a snack from chicken and apples.
   The boys want to make certain all the ingredients for dinner are on hand.
   The boys hope to someday become famous chefs.

2. Write what you feel is the main idea of paragraph B.

_____

_____

86 Grade Eight SkillBook, Reading

Name _____ Class _____ Date _____

3. What is the direct statement of the main idea of paragraph C?

   _____

   _____

4. List two details that are important for developing the main idea in paragraph C.

   _____

   _____

5. Write what you feel is the main idea of paragraph D.

   _____

   _____

6. What topic is introduced in paragraph E? (Underline one.)
   The boys like to play ball.
   Mrs. Yeager works hard.
   The boys know they are helping out.
   Sebastian's specialty is cheesecake.

7. List a detail in paragraph E that is important for developing the main idea.

   _____

8. Write an original sentence that states the main idea of the whole article.

   _____

   _____

Grade Eight SkillBook, Reading

Lesson 25
What Are Judgments?

Good judgments are well-supported opinions. They are based on dependable evidence, and they agree with certain standards and with good sense.

Your own judgments about clothing probably depend on the standards set by the people around you. For example, if most of the players on your softball team wear gym shoes to practice, you probably do too, even though you may wear cleats in a game. Of course, your judgment also agrees with common sense. It would not be good sense to wear your brand-new dress shoes to softball practice! You probably also considered some evidence in making your judgment to wear gym shoes. You might have thought that it is hot at the practice field, that you will be running, and that you want to practice sliding into bases. Such evidence would discourage you from wearing heavy hiking boots or loafers!

Exercise
Below are statements by people who have made judgments about how to spend their money. Decide if each has made a good judgment or a bad judgment. Circle the correct answer. Then, on the blank, list evidence, if any, that they considered.

1. Kendra: "I want to buy ice skates for figure-skating contests. I need the proper equipment; I can't get ordinary skates. The skates must fit perfectly. I'll be competing in five contests this winter, so quality is very important to me."
   good judgment / bad judgment

   Evidence: _____

2. Ted: "I bought a jacket to wear to parties and dances. I chose gray because that color goes with my favorite pants. I didn't have too much money to spend; I had to shop around for the best price."
   good judgment / bad judgment

   Evidence: _____

3. Gail: "I think we ought to go to the Sea and Range for dinner. Dad likes steak, and Mom likes seafood. And there are some dinners that have both, which I would like."
   good judgment / bad judgment

   Evidence: _____

4. Karen: "I bought a ticket to a concert. The ticket is expensive, even though the seat is way back. It's worth it. The group's albums sell millions of copies."
good judgment / bad judgment

Evidence: _____

5. Sam: "I want to buy the biggest speakers for my stereo. We live in a small apartment, and I can't play the stereo very loud. But my friend Rob has speakers that big."
good judgment / bad judgment

Evidence: _____

6. Mary: "The fish in my saltwater aquarium require special care and food. They are ocean fish. The local pet shop didn't carry special saltwater fish food. They only had food for freshwater fish that live in lakes and ponds. I bought that instead because it was cheaper and the fish probably won't care. Fish are fish."
good judgment / bad judgment

Evidence: _____

7. Juan: "I've wanted a new computer for a long time. It's a big investment. I found an excellent deal on one in the local paper. The owner said it worked great. He said he was selling it because the manufacturer had discontinued that model and it was getting more difficult to find repair service for it. I'm so happy to have found this computer!"
good judgment / bad judgment

Evidence: _____

8. Kim: "I'm so excited about going on my trip to visit my cousin. I've worked all summer to save enough money. I wanted to fly out in the afternoon so I'd have time to pack in the morning, but I saved $100 by getting up early and taking the 7:00 a.m. flight instead."
good judgment / bad judgment

Evidence: _____

Grade Eight SkillBook, Reading

Lesson 26
Fact and Opinion

Would you accept any of the following statements as facts?

A **fact** can be proved to be either true or false. An **opinion**, on the other hand, cannot be proved to be true or false. Opinions are expressions of personal feelings, beliefs, or evaluations. All of the statements above are opinions.

Just because someone *says* or strongly *suggests* that something is a fact doesn't make it a fact. Take another look at what is being called "a fact," and "the truth." When you are making judgments, you need to think carefully about such statements.

In the first two statements, there is no way that anyone can *prove* that dancing is the *best* means of self-expression or that adults are "hard to get along with."

As for the third statement, it predicts a future event. Something must already have happened before it can be proved true or false. Therefore, all statements that deal with the future are opinions.

Which of the following is a fact?

1. *Swan Lake* is a ballet.
2. Social workers spend half of their time on problems parents have with their children.
3. On November 7, 1995, the mayor was re-elected for a second term.

Each of these sentences is a statement of fact. We could prove each to be true or false.

For sentence 1, we could check books about ballet or music and find that *Swan Lake* is indeed a ballet. For sentence 2, we could interview social workers or read reports about what they do and how much time they spend on their different duties. We might find that the statement is false. But since we can prove it to be either true or false, it is still a statement of fact. For the third statement, we could check newspapers, election records, or almanacs that list city officials.

90   Grade Eight SkillBook, Reading

Name _____ Class _____ Date _____

Exercise
Make a decision about each of the statements below. On the blank, write **F** if the sentence is a fact, which can be proved true or false. Write **O** if the sentence is an opinion, which cannot be proved true or false.

_____ 1. In last night's basketball game, Mary Ortega scored twenty points.

_____ 2. Sailboats will become more popular as gasoline becomes more expensive.

_____ 3. In 1925, Amy Lowell won the Pulitzer Prize for poetry.

_____ 4. There is no way a pro football team will ever win the Super Bowl five times in a row.

_____ 5. India has more people than any other country.

_____ 6. Many people moved to California during the Gold Rush of 1849.

_____ 7. Soccer is the best sport for children to play.

_____ 8. Canada, the United States, and Mexico trade goods back and forth.

_____ 9. The President gave a speech in March about the importance of reading.

_____ 10. Next year Julia will win a medal at the Olympics.

Lesson 27
Mixed Statements

The greatest achievement for amateur athletes is to be in the Olympic Games, where athletes from all over the world come to compete.

The first part of the sentence expresses a personal opinion about how people feel about participating in the Olympics. Does the rest of the sentence present facts or opinions?

It is common to find sentences that present both fact and opinion. Such statements are called **mixed statements**. When you read such statements, you need to be able to sort out the facts from the opinions.

In the following mixed statement, which part expresses a fact?

Over two thousand athletes competed in the Junior Olympics in 1980, and more and more young people will compete in future Junior Olympics.

Only "Over two thousand athletes competed in the Junior Olympics in 1980" is a fact that can be proved true or false. The rest of the sentence is an opinion.

Exercise

Read each item below and decide which kind of statement it is. On the blank, write **F** if the item is a fact or **O** if it is an opinion. If the item is a mixed statement, write **M** on the blank.

Then, for the mixed statements, underline the part of the statement that is a fact.

_____ 1. An example of a devoted athlete is Mandeva Jackson, who runs six miles every day for practice.

_____ 2. You will find Mandeva on the track every day at 5 a.m.

_____ 3. Alice Hagan practices gymnastics for three to four hours every day, six days a week, eight months a year.

_____ 4. Alice has been practicing for eight years, but the daily routine of exercise is still not easy.

_____ 5. These and other young athletes prepare for such sports as track, gymnastics, swimming, and judo.

_____ 6. As part of their preparation, they attend several weekend competitions throughout the year.

_____ 7. The athletes also participate in activities to raise money for travel expenses.

_____ 8. One hard-working swim club used imaginative ways to raise money; they sold doughnuts, held paper drives, and had a swim marathon.

Name _____ Class _____ Date _____

_____ 9. These young athletes work harder than other teenagers to meet their goals.

_____ 10. As the best reward possible for all their hard work, athletes aged eight to eighteen compete in the Junior Olympics.

_____ 11. They enjoy competing, even if they don't win, and they enjoy meeting the other athletes, who come from all parts of the country.

_____ 12. Competitions are held for several weeks, giving athletes a chance to meet exciting new friends.

_____ 13. Gold, silver, and bronze medals are awarded in each event.

_____ 14. Sometimes only a fraction of a second or a point marks the difference between first place and second place.

_____ 15. Only a small fraction of the population will ever compete in the Olympics—those athletes are very special people.

Lesson 28
Valid and Objective Opinions

When we need to make judgments, it is easy to see that statements of fact can help us. But what about opinions? Can they be helpful? Under certain conditions, opinions can be valuable.

Do you think any of the following statements has value?

Parent: "Billy will be sick in bed by tomorrow. His forehead feels hot, and he says he aches all over."

Teacher: "I bet Billy will pretend to be sick tomorrow. Everybody cuts school at least once in spring."

Classmate: "Billy's probably sick all right—with spring fever."

Which person supports the opinion with facts? Which person's opinion can you accept?

You should be willing to accept only the parent's opinion. The other two opinions are not worth much, because there are no facts to support them. On the other hand, the parent's opinion is supported by two facts: 1) Billy's forehead feels hot, and 2) he says he aches all over. The parent uses these two facts to make the judgment that Billy will soon be sick in bed and expresses a valid opinion that should be taken seriously. Would you accept the following opinion about Billy, even though there are no facts given to support the opinion? If so, check it.

Dr. Valdez: "Billy won't be going to school tomorrow. He'll have a fully developed case of flu by then."

You probably accepted Dr. Valdez's opinion. A doctor is an authority, or expert, on illness because of training and experience. Therefore, his opinion is probably valid, even without fact.

Here are four of Dr. Valdez's other opinions. Would you accept any as valid?

1. "The Buick is the best car made today."
2. "The Tigers will win the pennant this year."
3. "The new vaccine should control the disease."
4. "Joseph Greenburg should be elected mayor."

Dr. Valdez is an authority on medicine. This does not mean that he is necessarily an authority on other subjects. Sometimes, advertisers will try to make us believe that an authority in one area is also an authority in another area. For example, a baseball player may do an ad for toothpaste because the advertiser thinks people will accept his opinion without looking for facts. Don't be fooled into accepting such opinions as necessarily valid. The baseball player may be influenced by personal feelings, beliefs, or evaluations that may make his opinions invalid.

94   Grade Eight SkillBook, Reading

Exercise

Check each opinion below that you can accept as valid because the speaker is an authority and/or there are facts to support the opinion.

_____ 1. Nursery school teacher: "Young children before the age of five are constantly learning things. They probably absorb more during these early years than at any other time."

_____ 2. Actor: "Comic roles are often more difficult to play than serious, dramatic roles."

_____ 3. Student: "I like working with my hands, and I got all A's in my shop classes. I would probably make a good carpenter."

_____ 4. Tennis star: "Pop-O Treats are delicious and nourishing. They are a real pick-me-up that are also good for you."

_____ 5. Plumber: "Building a new freeway is unnecessary and would be a waste of the taxpayers' money."

Grade Eight SkillBook, Reading

Lesson 29
Words with Emotional Effect

When you read, you should beware of words intended to distract your thinking by making you react emotionally. Sometimes these emotionally loaded words are used to cover up a lack of facts to support a writer's opinions.

Writers can also cover up true situations by using words intended to prevent you from reacting emotionally. Usually the situations they are trying to hide would make you react negatively. The words writers use in these cases are intended to avoid or lessen a negative emotional reaction you probably would have.

Which italicized word or phrase in each sentence below is intended to be more pleasant, or less offensive?

"I don't *gossip*; I'm just curious about people and I like to *talk about* them."

"I wouldn't say my little sister *tells lies*; she just has a lot of *imaginative stories*."

The phrase *talk about* sounds less offensive than the word *gossip*, and *imaginative stories* is less offensive than *tells lies*.

Exercise A
Check the sentence in each pair that avoids or softens the negative effect of the situation.

1. _____ a. No contact has been made yet with the astronauts.
   _____ b. The astronauts are feared lost.

2. _____ a. The President is closely watching the international disagreement.
   _____ b. The President is worried about the threat of another foreign war.

3. _____ a. Thousands of children die yearly from hunger.
   _____ b. Some parts of the world face food shortages.

4. _____ a. The community theater group puts on a consistent show.
   _____ b. Everything about the community theater group's show was just awful.

5. _____ a. Vandalism at this school nearly doubles from year to year.
   _____ b. Damage to our school property continues to grow.

When you hear someone make a speech, you should be alert for words intended to appeal to your emotions. Speakers often try to persuade an audience to agree with them. They may want to convince people to vote a certain way, to take action on some issue, or to believe in a particular cause.

Name _____ Class _____ Date _____

Exercise B
Read the statements below. Underline two words or phrases that contribute to the emotional effect of each. (Note: a hint is given in parentheses that tells you what the emotional effect is.)

1. We can no longer allow other countries to fish in our waters. These greedy foreigners are stealing our food. Giving them fishing rights is a surrender of our own rights. (negative attitude toward foreign fishing boats)

2. Cats are terrible pets. They cry and cry when they are hungry. We feed them and what do we get? They give us unfriendly stares and scratched furniture. (negative attitude toward cats)

3. Calculators and electronic games are wonderful aids for studying mathematics. They make math fun and exciting. Students can easily learn to master complex problems with them. (positive attitude toward calculators and electronic games)

4. A strict curfew is needed to protect us from unruly teenagers. They roar up and down our streets at night, and they deafen us with their music. They hang out at the shopping center, looking for trouble. (negative attitude toward teenagers)

5. The planned urban renewal project is a must. Our downtown area will come alive again. Think of gleaming office buildings, dazzling cultural events, and appealing shops along a mall with no cars. (positive attitude toward the renewal project)

Grade Eight SkillBook, Reading

Lesson 30
Appeal in Advertising

Exercise A

1. What is the price for the Phantom listed on the sign in the showroom window?

   _____

2. Would you regard the items mentioned in the "deluxe option package" as optional or extra? What will the car cost with these features?

   _____

You've seen advertising claims in all sorts of places—newspapers, magazines, billboards, and television. The main purpose of advertising is to sell a product or service. To sell a product or service, the advertiser must make it sound as appealing as possible. The advertiser uses words that make you react in a positive way, often in an emotional way. You will find very few ads that mention anything negative about a product or service!

Because ads are usually one-sided to create a positive impression, they often fail to provide certain facts. They may omit important details buyers need to know in order to make up their own minds. The kinds of words used in ads often try to create an extraordinary picture of something quite ordinary.

Exercise B

The advertisements below use many words intended to make you react in a positive way toward the product. For each item, underline four words or phrases that contribute to the positive appeal of the ad. Then, on the blank,

Name _____ Class _____ Date _____

write one fact, if any are given, about the product being advertised. If no facts are given, write "none."

1. Sunstreak, the new breakfast cereal, starts your day the natural way. Try a hearty, wholesome bowlful in the morning and you'll feel better all day!

   Fact: _____

2. Don't leave those great stereo sounds at home! Enjoy the galaxy of sounds of your favorite tapes as you drive. For the low, low price of only $89.95 (plus a small installation charge), you can have the Outward Car Stereo Speaker System today! Take the beauty of music with you, wherever you go!

   Fact: _____

3. Are you bored with ordinary pizza? Try new On-the-Roll Pizza, a totally different taste treat. Zesty sauce, lots of cheese, and spicy toppings are baked on a chewy Italian bread. The world has changed; it's time pizza changed too.

   Fact: _____

4. Capture your special events for all time with the Eventor camera. You will treasure the vivid color photographs of your family and friends at school activities, parties, and sports events.

   Fact: _____

5. Be on top of your studies with the OnTop Organizer. This is no everyday notebook. The OnTop has tabs, divider sheets, and pockets to help you organize all your notes and other school materials. An organized student will be a successful student!

   Fact: _____

Grade Eight SkillBook, Reading

Name _____ Class _____ Date _____

Lesson 1
Main Idea in a Paragraph

A paragraph is a group of sentences about one main idea. All the details and sentences in a paragraph should develop the main idea.

A paragraph is a group of sentences that tells about one **main idea**. All the sentences should help develop this idea. Before you write a paragraph, find a main idea on which to focus. Then list details about this idea. Imagine, for example, that one morning you saw a spider catch a grasshopper. List details about the event.

    grasshopper wound in thread   web shimmered
    yellow and black spider   web stretched between branches

    Now think of the main idea that you want to express about these details. You might want to suggest that the web was both beautiful and deadly. Throughout your paragraph, use details that help develop this main idea. Make sure all your sentences stick to this main idea. Your paragraph might read something like this:

> One morning I saw a spider capture a victim in her beautiful deathtrap. The yellow and black spider was sleeping in her web, which stretched like a silvery veil. Suddenly, the whole web shivered and shimmered. A grasshopper had landed on it. The spider awakened and raced to her prey. Soon the spider had encased her victim in white thread. I backed away from the doomed victim and its lovely tomb. I still wonder how an incident so deadly could be so beautiful.

    Some paragraphs, especially narrative paragraphs, do not state the main idea in a single sentence. If the main idea is not directly stated, you must draw a conclusion about it. Use details from the paragraph and information you have learned about drawing conclusions.

Exercise A
Answer these questions about the paragraph you have just read with your class.

1. Which details express beauty?

   _____

2. Which show something deadly?

   _____

Exercise B
Imagine that you were writing a paragraph about each of the following main ideas. Then write three details that could be used to support each main idea.

100   Grade Eight SkillBook, Writing

1. Losing your sense of direction can be embarrassing.

2. Our new pet causes family debate.

3. Not all prizes are worth winning.

Exercise C
Decide which sentences do not support the main idea in the paragraph below. Then write the paragraph as it should be on a separate sheet of paper.

    Chaos struck our house one morning. As I tried to brush my teeth, the faucet just groaned; no water came out. I couldn't wash my hair, so Dad used my hair dryer to heat the pipes. I had just bought the dryer at Kimbol's on sale. We couldn't have our usual breakfast of poached eggs, so we had cornflakes instead. My brother finished his homework upstairs. Finally, the pipes gurgled and water came out of the faucet. We gave Dad a cheer for restoring order to the house.

Exercise D
Each set of details could be used to support a main idea. For each numbered item, write a sentence suggesting, but not stating, your main idea. Use wording that makes your reader draw a conclusion.

    Example: engine sputters; smoke billows from hood; dashboard panel lights up
    Answer: Trouble always occurs at the worst possible time.

1. face grows hot; palms are moist; skin feels prickly

2. racquet smacks ball; opponent lunges forward; crowd applauds

3. police sirens scream; red lights flash; car screeches around corner

4. my turn in checkout line; load groceries on conveyor belt; discover I forgot my money

Grade Eight SkillBook, Writing

Lesson 2
Topic Sentences

A sentence that states the main idea is called a topic sentence.

The topic of a paragraph is the specific subject of that paragraph. A sentence that states the main idea is called a **topic sentence**. The other sentences are called **detail sentences**. They give details that support or tell about the main idea.

A topic sentence often, but not always, appears at the beginning of a paragraph that explains something. Topic sentences should be placed in a paragraph where they will be most effective. For example, a topic sentence may appear at the end of a paragraph in order to sum up the details in the sentences. Or, a topic sentence might be preceded by one or more sentences that provide information and also introduce the topic.

Read the following paragraph. Find the topic sentence.

> Lonely and homesick people were not unknown to me by any means. Living just across the bay from San Francisco where ships from the Orient deposited their store of lonely students and travelers, our family was a ready source of solace. My parents were graduates of a well-known university in Japan, and it seemed that every alumnus arriving in California came directly to our home as though reporting in to an alumni office. They came in growing numbers over the years, to do graduate work at the university or at the Divinity School, and whenever they longed to unburden themselves in their native tongue or sip a bowl of steaming bean-curd soup, they found both a willing ear and a generous table at our home.
>
> —*from* **OH BROOM, GET TO WORK** by Yoshiko Uchida

Exercise A
Answer these questions about the paragraph above.

1. What is the main idea of the paragraph?

   _____

2. Is the topic sentence:
   a. the first sentence?
   b. the last sentence?
   c. in the middle of the paragraph?

Exercise B
The topic sentence has been omitted from each of the following paragraphs. Read the paragraphs and the topic sentences that follow them, choosing the best topic sentence for each paragraph. Then tell where each topic sentence should appear in each paragraph. Remember that the topic sentence is not always the first sentence in a paragraph.

If you are looking for a companion that is easy to get along with and doesn't talk back, look no further. Cats don't need to be taken out for walks and they don't talk back. They also tend to mind their own business as long as you stay out of it. Aside from their curiosity about small moving objects and a tendency to chew plants, cats don't look for trouble either.

1. a. Cats and dogs are the best pets.
   b. A cat is an ideal pet, since it can keep you company and is generally content with food, water, and a warm spot for sleeping.
   c. Although cats are good pets, be careful if you have a bird.

_____

_____

Almost every night, somewhere in the South, slaves slipped away from the quarter. They hid in swamps. They walked incredible distances. Some of them reached the North and freedom. Others were caught and brought back in chains. There were few plantations that would boast that they had never had a slave run away.
—*from* **HARRIET TUBMAN: CONDUCTOR ON THE UNDERGROUND RAILROAD** by Ann Petry

2. a. Long before our forefathers realized its consequences, slavery had taken its toll.
   b. Harriet Tubman was a wonderful humanitarian who spent her life dedicated to the abolition of slavery.
   c. Early in the nineteenth century, the dream of freedom had begun spreading through the slave cabins on all the plantations.

_____

_____

Grade Eight SkillBook, Writing

Lesson 3
Writing a Narrative Paragraph

A narrative paragraph tells a story. The events in a narrative paragraph are usually arranged in chronological order.

A **narrative** is a story in which the events are usually told in the order in which they occur. Note the sequence and transition words in the narrative paragraph below.

> . . . We had heard the creak of a step in the passage.
> Very stealthily we heard it pass along until it died away in the distance. Then the baronet gently opened his door and we set out in pursuit. Already our man had gone round the gallery, and the corridor was all in darkness. Softly we stole along until we had come into the other wing. We were just in time to catch a glimpse of the tall, black-bearded figure, his shoulders rounded, as he tiptoed down the passage.
> —*from* **THE HOUND OF THE BASKERVILLES**
> by Arthur Conan Doyle

You have also learned that narrative writing does not always include all the details or facts of a certain event. In such cases, the reader draws conclusions based on what is given.

The following list shows some possible details that might be included in a narrative paragraph.

Jane's family is away on vacation.
Jane is alone in the house.
She hears a noise in her bedroom.
There is an open window in the bedroom.
An intruder has been in the room.
A pearl ring and money are still on the dresser.
Grandmother's portrait is gone.
The portrait contains a family secret.
The portrait means something to someone other than the family.

Some of these details would not contribute to a narrative paragraph. If Jane's family is on vacation, then she would probably be alone in the house. We can also infer that an intruder has been in the room if the portrait is missing, and that the portrait means something to the intruder if he or she has gone to the trouble to steal it.

Exercise A
Rewrite the paragraph below on a separate sheet of paper. Make it clearer and more interesting by adding transition words and vivid details.

> A group of people traveled by car through a dense jungle area. A large overturned truck blocked both sides of the road. What were they to do? Jungles were on both sides of them. Their destination was too far away to

walk to. They had no camping gear. The driver saw a car stop on the other side of the truck and quickly thought of a solution. The drivers could exchange people and luggage. Each would go back the way he had come with the other's passengers.

Exercise B

Based on the main idea given below, number the list of details in the correct order, crossing out any that are not necessary.

Main Idea: A lone sailor on a lake is caught in a storm.

Details:
_____ Boat drifts toward rocks

_____ Helicopter is on its way

_____ High winds blow up

_____ Pilot acts quickly

_____ Helicopter arrives in nick of time

_____ Sailor radios for help

_____ Sailor lowers sails

_____ Sailor is relieved

_____ Boat drifts away from rocks

_____ Sailor is safe

_____ Helicopter blades create wind

Grade Eight SkillBook, Writing

Name _____ Class _____ Date _____

Lesson 4
Plot

Plot creates action in a story by raising a conflict that must be resolved.

At the end of this unit, you will write a short story. Before you write, you will review the essential elements of a well-written story. The first of these is plot. **Plot** is the series of related events or actions that move a story along. It is the plot that keeps you interested and wondering, "What will happen next?"

A diagram of a plot might look like this.

Early in the story, a **conflict** arises that must be resolved. Much of a story may be devoted to a character's struggle with the conflict.

Meanwhile, as the saying goes, "the plot thickens" and events grow more complicated. The tension or suspense build to a **climax**, or high point of the story. When the climax occurs, a new light may be shed on the problem, or a dramatic event may occur.

From then on, the story moves swiftly to its **resolution**, or end. If the conflict is resolved in a convincing way, the resolution is satisfying.

Below is a plot summary of Hemingway's story "A Day's Wait." Think about how the plot summary follows the diagram discussed above.

> The boy's father realizes that his son is running a fever. A doctor is called, and he confirms that the boy has a temperature of one hundred and two degrees Fahrenheit. Overhearing the doctor, the boy thinks he means Celsius. The boy assumes he is dying. He becomes tense and withdrawn. He refuses to nap and tells his father not to stay with him. The father goes out hunting for a while. When he returns, he finds his son still acting strange. Finally, the boy asks his father when he is going to die. He mentions he had heard at his French school that people can't live with a fever above forty-four degrees. At last, the father realizes what has been upsetting his son. He explains the difference between Fahrenheit and Celsius. Finally, the boy relaxes. The next day he cries over little things.

Exercise A
Answer these questions about the plot summary.

1. What conflict or problem is raised early in the story?

   _____

2. How does the plot grow more complicated?

   _____

Name _____ Class _____ Date _____

3. What do you consider to be the climax of the story?

_____

_____

4. How is the conflict resolved at the end of the story?

_____

_____

5. Do you find this resolution satisfying? Explain why the death of the boy would have been a good or bad ending.

_____

_____

_____

Exercise B

Choose one of the following and write a plot summary on a separate sheet of paper. Label and identify (**1**) the conflict; (**2**) the climax; and (**3**) the resolution.

1. a movie, play, or drama on television that you enjoyed
2. a short story you read and would recommend to others

Name _____ Class _____ Date _____

Lesson 5
Character and Dialogue

Use description and dialogue to bring your characters to life.

Writers can make their **characters** come to life by describing their appearance and feelings. At the beginning of "A Day's Wait," Hemingway describes the main character as "a very sick and miserable boy of nine years."

Writers can also make their characters appear realistic by describing their thoughts and actions. Read the description below from "The Drummer Boy of Shiloh." Notice how Ray Bradbury brings Joby to life by describing his thoughts.

> If he stayed still, when the dawn came up and the soldiers put on their bravery with their caps, perhaps they might go away, the war with them, and not notice him living small here, no more than a toy himself.

Writers also make their characters believable through **dialogue**, or speech. Notice how the relationship between the young soldier, Joby, and the general is revealed through their dialogue.

> "What's your name, boy?" he asked.
> "Joby, sir," whispered the boy, starting to sit up.
> "All right, Joby, don't stir." A hand pressed his chest gently, and the boy relaxed. "How long you been with us, Joby?"
> "Three weeks, sir."
> "Run off from home or join legitimate, boy?"
> Silence.
> "Fool question," said the general. "Do you shave yet, boy? Even more of a fool. There's your cheek, fell right off the tree overhead. And the others here, not much older. Raw, raw, the lot of you. You ready for tomorrow or the next day, Joby?"
> "I think so, sir."
> "You want to cry some more, go on ahead. I did the same last night."

You will want to bring your own characters to life through dialogue. Try to make the dialogue sound natural and appropriate to the speaker. You can develop an ear for dialogue by noting conversations you overhear in a store, cafeteria, or playground.

Guidelines for Writing and Punctuating Dialogue
1. Begin a new paragraph each time the speaker changes.
2. Enclose a speaker's exact words in quotation marks.
3. Begin a direct quotation with a capital letter.
4. Set off a direct quotation with a comma when it is preceded or followed by a phrase such as *he said* or *she muttered*.
5. Establish the name of each speaker the first time that person speaks in the dialogue. You do not need to repeat the speaker's name throughout the dialogue or to say *he said, she said,* or *he answered* again and again.
6. Avoid overusing the word *said* when writing dialogue. Consider verbs from the Word Bank at the right, or think of other words.

Word Bank
replied
mocked
boasted
taunted
murmured
whispered
shouted
mumbled
scolded

Name _____ Class _____ Date _____

Exercise A

Answer these questions about the dialogue on the previous page.

1. What can you conclude about the relationship between Joby and the general?

   _____

   _____

2. What does the dialogue reveal about Joby?

   _____

   _____

Exercise B

Read the partial plot summary below. Then list details that will help develop the characters of Martha and David. Describe their appearance, actions, thoughts, and feelings.

   Martha's father is laid off from his job, and suddenly there is no money for Martha to go to college. David, Martha's boyfriend, offers to lend her the money she needs, but Martha is too proud to accept. She prefers to apply for a student loan and work part-time as a waitress. David's feelings are hurt and he stops calling Martha. Martha is upset, but too proud to call David. Then things take a turn for the better. Martha's father finds a better job that pays more. . . .

_____

_____

_____

_____

_____

Grade Eight SkillBook, Writing

Lesson 6
Classifying

You can classify information by arranging it into similar groups.

Classifying is organizing information by arranging it into similar groups. Classifying information is a useful prewriting skill to help organize your material.

Suppose you decide to build some Word Banks of descriptive words. In one Word Bank you put all the words that describe sound. In another, you put all the words that describe taste. You make three other Word Banks to describe the sensations of smell, touch, and sight. By organizing the words this way, you have classified them according to the senses they describe. Here is how your Word Bank might look.

Sound	Taste	Smell	Touch	Sight
thunderous	sour	pungent	soft	radiant
harmonious	bitter	acrid	rough	colorful
scratchy	tart	rank	prickly	lustrous
shrill	oily	smoky	sticky	violet
squeaky	spicy	musty	furry	craggy

Before you write, think of ways to classify your information. You might make a Word Bank like the one above. You might use a dictionary to help classify words according to their meanings. Or you might classify specific details about a person you want to describe under headings such as these: *Physical Features*, *Actions*, *Speech*. Whenever you want to classify information, think of category headings that will help you organize your material.

Exercise A

The words below are grouped according to something they have in common. Cross out the word that does *not* fit the classification. You may need to use a dictionary.

Example: polished, sleek, uneven, smooth
Answer: uneven

1. powerful, mighty, frail, strong
2. vacant, jammed, empty, deserted
3. silly, grave, serious, earnest
4. image, stone, likeness, copy
5. odd, peculiar, weird, normal

6. fear, dread, alarm, joy
7. stand, nod, bow, droop
8. aid, neglect, assist, help
9. mature, ripen, develop, die
10. crimson, blue, ruby, red

Name _____ Class _____ Date _____

Exercise B
Each of the following groups has one or more common characteristics. Write the common characteristic that makes each group a class. Some groups may have more than one common characteristic.

Example: meter, centimeter, decimeter
Answer: metric measure, all contain the word *meter*

1. groan, scream, sigh _____
2. purple, violet, lavender _____
3. lock, rock, dock _____
4. sociology, psychology, anthropology _____
5. America, Japan, Russia _____
6. farmer, fiddler, furrier _____
7. ballet, waltz, samba _____
8. dirty, foul, filthy _____
9. daisy, daffodil, day lily _____
10. Hawaii, Kansas, Alabama _____
11. wool, cotton, silk _____
12. water, milk, vinegar _____
13. lamp, flashlight, match _____
14. smile, smirk, sneer _____
15. ocean, sea, pond _____
16. string, rope, twine _____
17. pitcher, cup, bottle _____
18. piano, guitar, flute _____
19. nail, hammer, saw _____
20. lettuce, cucumber, celery _____

Grade Eight SkillBook, Writing

Name _____ Class _____ Date _____

Lesson 7
Arranging Details in Spatial Order

You can use spatial order to help organize supporting details clearly.

One effective way to organize supporting details is to use **spatial order**. Spatial order describes a scene from the viewpoint of an observer and arranges details according to their location. For example, you may describe the room you are sitting in from top to bottom or from left to right. Be sure to follow whatever spatial order you establish so your reader's mental image moves smoothly along with your words. The words at the right can help you express spatial relationships. You can also use phrases such as *across the street* or *near the edge* to give your reader an accurate sense of direction and distance.

Read the following paragraph carefully. Note the words and phrases the author uses to indicate the spatial order of his father's hut in their West African village.

Spatial Order
above
away
back
down
up
toward
far
in
under
ahead
near
over
right
left
beyond
through
bottom
distance
closer
farther

> My father's hut was near the workshop, and I would often play there beneath the veranda that ran round the outside. It was my father's private hut. It was built like all our huts, of mud that had been pounded and molded into bricks with water; it was round, and proudly helmeted with thatch. It was entered by a rectangular doorway. Inside, a tiny window let in a thin shaft of daylight. On the right there was the bed, made of beaten earth like the bricks, spread with a simple wicker-work mat on which was a pillow stuffed with kapok leaves. At the rear of the hut, right under the window where the light was strongest, were the toolboxes. On the left were the *boubous* [loose cotton garments draping the whole figure] and the prayer rugs. Finally, at the head of the bed, hanging over the pillow and watching over my father's slumber, there was a series of pots that contained extracts from plants and the barks of trees.
>
> —*from* **THE DARK CHILD** by Camara Laye

Exercise A
Answer the following questions about the paragraph above.

1. Where was the author standing as he described the hut?

   _____

2. What type of spatial order—near to far, top to bottom, or right to left—is apparent in the passage?

   _____

112 Grade Eight SkillBook, Writing

Name _____ Class _____ Date _____

Exercise B
Read the following paragraph and write answers to the questions that follow it.

    The *Half Moon* glided easily over the calm waters. Henry Hudson directed his men to steer a straight course upriver, remaining dead center between the banks. He grinned as he spotted the New World riches he'd been searching for: large sturgeon swimming alongside the ship; harvest-ready rows of maize near the shore; and packs of deer running silently through forests of oak. The mountainsides glistened in the distance, promising precious metals and ores.

1. Are details presented mostly from near to far, left to right, or top to bottom?

   _____

2. Write the words and phrases from the paragraph above that show the main spatial order used.

   _____

3. Where was Henry Hudson as he spotted the New World riches?

   _____

Grade Eight SkillBook, Writing

Lesson 8
Writing a Descriptive Paragraph

A descriptive paragraph is used to create a vivid image of a person, place, or thing.

A well-written descriptive paragraph can appeal to all the senses of a reader. In addition, a writer can describe a subject using spatial order, as you studied in the previous lesson. The writer can also show differing aspects of the same subject—a person as both happy and sad, an object from the front and the back, or a place at night and in the daytime.

A writer can show the internal as well as the external aspects of a subject. You can learn about the feelings of people or the inner workings of nonhuman subjects, such as volcanoes and watches.

Notice the way Willa Cather makes her subject come alive in the following description.

> She was a spare, tall woman, a little stooped, and she was apt to carry her head thrust forward in an attitude of attention, as if she were looking at something, or listening to something, far away. As I grew older, I came to believe that it was only because she was so often thinking of things that were far away. She was quick-footed and energetic in all her movements. Her voice was high and rather shrill, and she often spoke with an anxious inflection, for she was exceedingly desirous that everything should go with due order and decorum. Her laugh, too, was high, and perhaps a little strident, but there was a lively intelligence in it. She was then fifty-five years old, a strong woman, of unusual endurance.
>
> —*from* **MY ÁNTONIA** by Willa Cather

Exercise A
On a separate sheet of paper, list the most important details about a person and then classify them according to such headings as appearance, personality, manner of speaking and dressing and so forth. Make your details as specific as possible.

Exercise B
Read the following paragraph that describes a special place for Gaucho, a young boy growing up in New York City. Answer the questions that follow.

> That's why he loved his room—if you could call it that—because he could be alone yet not too alone. It wasn't even a real room. It used to be the kitchen pantry—a long, deep, dark closet that you walked into, which had a lot of shelves along the wall to store canned food. He and Mama had removed the shelves, except for the ones high up, near the ceiling, where he now kept his personal belongings. With the wooden shelves gone, there was just enough space to stick in a comfortable cot against the wall and a bureau and mirror at the rear of the tiny box-like space. Since there wasn't

Name _____ Class _____ Date _____

any electric outlet in the former closet, Mama and Gaucho had removed the heavy door, which led to the kitchen, and replaced it with a thin, almost transparent floral drapery that allowed the kitchen light to filter in and make the room glow softly. The curtain also assured Gaucho of privacy. He and Mama had a silent understanding that when the curtain was drawn across the doorway, she would knock on the nearby wall or call out to him before entering.

—*from* **GAUCHO** by Gloria Gonzalez

1. What details help you visualize the room?
   _____
   _____

2. What words and phrases are used to show spatial order?
   _____
   _____

Grade Eight SkillBook, Writing 115

Name _____ Class _____ Date _____

Lesson 9
Comparing and Contrasting

To compare means to identify likenesses among things. To contrast means to identify differences.

One way to learn more about something is by finding out how it is like something else you know. When you see how persons or things are alike, you are **comparing** them. When you see how they are different, you are **contrasting** them. The words and phrases in the list at the right will help you express the comparisons and contrasts you make. Study them before you read the following paragraph. As you read the description in this paragraph, note the words and phrases the author uses to compare and contrast.

For Comparisons
both
like
just as
similarly
the same as

For Contrasts
yet
however
on the contrary
different from
but

> Both Canada and the United States share a common heritage and the same continent but are very different culturally. The major portions of the countries were settled primarily by French and English explorers. However, the French did not maintain as strong a hold anywhere in the United States as they did in Canada. You can see the result of this difference when you compare some Canadian and American cities. In Montreal and Quebec City, for example, you can walk amid French-speaking street vendors selling fruit-filled crepes (pancakes) and golden brown pommes frites (fried potatoes). Billboards advertise their goods in English and French, the official languages of Canada. In the United States, on the contrary, there are few places of such French character. Part of cities may reflect the French influence in place names—the Vieux Carré, or French Quarter, of New Orleans, for example—yet you will hear little French being spoken, as most Americans speak English.

Exercise A
Write your answers to each of these questions.

1. In what ways are Canada and the United States alike?
   _____
   _____

2. In what ways are Canada and the United States different?
   _____
   _____

3. Which words and phrases in this paragraph signal comparisons?
   _____
   _____

Exercise B

When you describe similarities and differences between things, you may find it helpful to create a chart of the information you plan to compare and contrast. Place the items you are comparing and contrasting in the left column, and write the points to compare and contrast at the top. Fill in the missing information in this chart.

	Shape	Color of skin	Color of fruit	Taste	Texture of skin
honeydew melon	round	pale green			smooth
cantaloupe	round	light brown			rough

Exercise C

For each pair of items below, write a descriptive sentence that compares the items and a sentence that contrasts them. Use words and phrases that signal comparisons and contrasts.

    Example: appearance of honeydew melon, appearance of cantaloupe
    Answer: Both honeydew melon and cantaloupe are round, but their colors and textures vary. Honeydew melon is green and smooth, yet cantaloupe is light brown and rough.

1. car, horse

_____

_____

2. house, tent

_____

_____

3. eye, camera

_____

_____

4. brain, computer

_____

_____

Grade Eight SkillBook, Writing

Name _____ Class _____ Date _____

Lesson 10
Writing a Compare/Contrast Description

In a composition describing places, each paragraph can describe different details.

In previous lessons, you learned how to arrange details in spatial order in a descriptive paragraph and how to focus on certain details to describe a particular subject, such as a person or place. You are now ready to compare and contrast places in a **descriptive composition** of more than one paragraph. Read the following description.

A HOUSE WITH TWO MOODS

The purple house has always delighted and frightened its young inhabitants. The attic of the house is a favorite room. The narrow stairs leading up are covered with a carpet woven with images of odd birds and animals. A huge, cuddly stuffed bear is propped up on a brightly decorated wooden chest that rests under a lovely stained-glass window. A large skylight in the center of the ceiling brightens the square room during the day. The back of the attic is crowded with trunks full of interesting clothes, games, and other relics of the past. There is a musty but comforting smell. The attic is friendly and fun, and it is visited often.

The basement of this house, like the attic, is a hidden, quiet place. The basement must also be reached by a narrow stairway. However, bare wood steps lead to a place that, unlike the attic, has frightened the children of the house. It is an oddly-shaped, dark room with spooky shadows cast by objects such as old hat trees and forgotten crates. Cobwebs hang from the low ceiling; insects dart along the slimy floor. Most young visitors explore the basement only once.

Exercise A
On a separate sheet of paper, create a comparison chart like the one on page 117 of Lesson 9 and base it on the composition above. In the first column, list the things being compared and contrasted: the attic and the basement. Fill in the chart to see similarities and differences—for example, *light: attic/bright, basement/dark*.

Exercise B
Think of two places that you could compare and contrast. For example, you could write about your home during Halloween and during Thanksgiving. You could also write about the school cafeteria and your kitchen at home. After choosing two places, complete the exercises on the next page. Use the checklist below to help you.

Comparison/Contrast Description Revision Checklist
√ Have I included words and phrases that indicate comparison and contrast, such as *just as*, *similarly*, *on the contrary*, *however*, *but*, and *although*?

Name _____ Class _____ Date _____

√ Have I included appropriate sensory details so that my readers can visualize these places clearly?
√ Are my details arranged in a logical spatial order? Have I included words and phrases that make this spatial order clear?

1. List details about the places you are going to describe. Think of ways to classify these details.

2. Arrange the details you thought of in number 1 in a logical spatial order. Use words that show spatial order such as *left*, *right*, *up*, and *down*.

Grade Eight SkillBook, Writing   119

Name _____ Class _____ Date _____

Lesson 11
Writing an Explanatory Paragraph

An explanatory paragraph uses facts and ideas to explain something.

An **explanatory paragraph** explains something by using facts. In this type of paragraph, you can explain what causes dew on grass, why there are tides at sea, or how to develop a photograph.

One kind of explanatory paragraph explains an idea by giving reasons or examples. Transition words and phrases can serve to signal examples or help make the logical order of ideas clear. Notice how words and phrases from the box at the right help clarify information in the following paragraph.

Reasons/Examples
as a result
because
consequently
due to
for example
for instance
furthermore
however
in addition
in other words
nevertheless
therefore
to illustrate

Mountain climbing, especially that done on rocks, is a challenging sport. Rock climbers pull themselves up steep rock faces; therefore, they use special shoes, rope, and steel spikes. Ice climbers, however, face additional difficulties. To climb over ice and snow, they use ice axes and boot spikes, called crampons, to gain footing. In addition, they build rest spots at several points during their ascent. Mountain climbing—on rock or ice—is a sport that requires both skill and daring. Nevertheless, it attracts many enthusiasts.

Another kind of explanatory paragraph explains a process, such as assembling a kite or building a birdhouse. Transition words are especially important in explaining the specific sequence of steps in a process. Notice how some of the words in the box at the left are used to indicate time order in the following paragraph about how a special bread is made by the Blackfoot tribe.

Time Order
after
as
before
finally
first
last
next
now
then
until
when
while

While the water was beginning to boil, SoodaWa made tea. She always made the tea first. Then while the water boiled rapidly, she prepared the flour for making bannock bread. She kneaded a batch of dough, and then she greased her big frying pan with fat and spread the dough upon it very evenly. She placed the pan on a red-glowing bed of coals that she had scraped away from the fire, and she held it there until a wonderful aroma rose from the bread as it slowly browned.
—*from* **LEGEND DAYS** by Jamake Highwater

Exercise A
Answer these questions about the preceding paragraphs.

1. Underline the topic sentence in the paragraph about mountain climbing.

2. What transition words are used to signal examples and reasons in the first paragraph?

_____

_____

Name _____ Class _____ Date _____

3. What transition words are used to signal time order in the second paragraph?

_____

_____

Exercise B
The following paragraph tells how to move a plant to a new pot. Read it and then answer the questions.

> You can repot a plant in the following way. First put pebbles in the bottom of a new flowerpot for drainage. Then put an inch of fresh potting soil on top of the pebbles. Now use a knife to loosen the soil around the plant in the old pot. Carefully empty the old pot upside down into your hand. Stand the plant in the new pot. Place the top of the roots at least one inch below the rim of the pot. Finally, press more potting soil around the roots and water the plant.

1. Is the paragraph developed by presenting reasons and examples or by presenting steps in a process?

_____

2. What transition words make the time order clear?

_____

Exercise C
Choose a topic from the following list, or come up with one of your own. Then write a topic sentence and three detail sentences. Arrange the sentences in a logical order. Use the checklist below to evaluate and improve your sentences.

Explanatory Paragraph Revision Checklist
√ Does my topic sentence appear where it is most effective?
√ Have I arranged my detail sentences in a clear order?
√ Do transition words signal a step-by-step or logical order?

- how to make a sub sandwich
- how to roller-skate safely
- why some animals have hooves
- stamp collecting as a hobby
- what causes tornadoes
- the craft of woodworking

_____

_____

_____

_____

Grade Eight SkillBook, Writing

Name _____ Class _____ Date _____

Lesson 12
Cause and Effect

Recognizing cause-and-effect relationships improves your reading comprehension and your writing.

A **cause** is what makes something happen. An **effect** is what happens due to a cause. Read the following sentence:

Because it rained Saturday, Theresa could not play softball.

The rain is what makes Theresa unable to play; it is the cause. Theresa's inability to play is what happened because of the rain; it is the effect.

You often encounter causes and effects in explanatory writing. Sometimes one cause can have several effects, or one effect can have several causes.

A sequence of events—things that happen one after another—does not necessarily involve a cause-and-effect relationship. For example, Juanita may put the cake into the oven, and then the doorbell rings; however, the first event does not cause the second.

Exercise A
Identify the cause and effect in each sentence.

1. Julio memorized all the assigned spelling words; therefore, he won the spelling bee.

   _____

2. I am taking my dog to the vet because she needs her shots.

   _____

3. Keiko sang the part better than anyone else, and thus she won the lead in the school musical.

   _____

4. Ice covered the road, so traffic moved slowly.

   _____

Exercise B
Read the following paragraph. Then answer the questions that follow it.

(1) As we look back on it, we can realize that Jay's Treaty was a good thing for the young nation. (2) It gave the United States full control in law, and, in fact over the Northwest Territory. (3) It prevented a war that could have brought disaster to the country. (4) It started what amounted to ten years of friendly relations with Great Britain. (5) It had one other effect too. (6) When the members of the Spanish royal court heard of Jay's Treaty, they were terror-stricken. (7) Did Jay's Treaty really mean England

and America were secretly in alliance? (**8**) If that were the case, then America's frontiersmen could turn against the Southwest and take it from Spain. (**9**) Worried about the longer-range meanings of the treaty, the Spanish court courteously received Thomas Pinckney, a special envoy from the United States. (**10**) The Spaniards now agreed to allow Americans to navigate the Mississippi River freely and to place goods on deposit in Spanish New Orleans—two things the Americans had hitherto been unable to do. (**11**) Spain also recognized the Mississippi River as the western boundary of the United States and the 31st parallel as the southern boundary. (**12**) As a result, a long struggle by the Americans to use the Mississippi River and to obtain living room west of the mountains came to a triumphant climax.
—*from* **THE FOUNDING OF THE REPUBLIC** by Richard B. Morris

1. Underline the cause in the above paragraph.

2. What were the first three effects of this cause?

3. Which of the following summarizes the effect described in sentences 6–9?
    a. The Spanish began fearing the Americans.
    b. American pioneers and Spain went to war.
    c. Thomas Pinckney was trained to become a spy.

4. What other effects are mentioned in the paragraph?

5. What sentence is an effect of sentence 1 but also the cause of sentence 2?

Name _____ Class _____ Date _____

Lesson 13
Writing a Cause-and-Effect Paragraph

A cause-effect paragraph clearly states how one person, thing, idea, or action influences another.

A **cause-effect paragraph** is a type of explanatory paragraph that shows how one action causes another, or proves that a certain belief or action will lead to a certain behavior. Paragraphs of cause and effect often use transitions to clarify the logic of the argument or position being put forth. The words in the list at the right can be used to express the relationships between causes and effects. Sometimes you may want to explain how one event, action, or idea caused more than one thing to happen. For example, in *The Founding of the Republic* you learned how one event—the signing of Jay's Treaty—changed the course of U.S. history in many ways. Read the following paragraph, which explains how one idea triggered innumerable effects. Note the words and phrases used to signal the cause-and-effect relationships.

Cause and Effect
if . . . then
because
since
for
consequently
cause
therefore
thus
hence
as a result

> The storm was over in several minutes, but the damage it created was extensive. Trees had been uprooted and were lying across the highway. Swollen rivers overflowed their banks. Barn roofs were partially blown off. The town found itself without electricity for several hours and all flights to and from the local airports were canceled. Since the storm was so brief, people were unprepared and were caught in drenching rain. Some vehicles stalled, and several motorists abandoned their cars along the highway. As a result of all this, many people decided to make preparations in case of another bad storm.

Exercise A
Answer these questions about the paragraph above.

1. What sentence states the cause?

   _____

2. What sentences contain the effects?

   _____

3. What words and phrases signaling cause and effect are used?

   _____

Exercise B
Fill in the blanks to complete each cause-and-effect relationship.

1. If I finish my homework on time, then _____

2. Hyon-Joo is allergic to tomatoes; therefore _____

3. Fatima watered the plant weekly, consequently _____

124 Grade Eight SkillBook, Writing

4. Since I enjoyed that book so much, _____

5. We worked quickly and thus _____

Exercise C
Read the following paragraph about how an airplane flies. List the cause-and-effect relationships you find.

> Have you ever marveled at how an airplane stays aloft? The secret lies in the shape of its wings and the fact that air moves constantly. Both wings are curved on the top side, but straight on the bottom. When the plane begins to move, it causes the wings to cut through the air. Because the air meets with the resistance of the wings, it breaks up. The air that breaks over the wing pushes down on it. The air that breaks under the wing pushes up. Since the air traveling over the wings has to travel farther than the air under the wings, it flows faster than and pushes less on the wing than does the air flowing under the wing. Therefore the air flowing over the bottom wing portion pushes the wings up. As a result, the plane leaves the ground. Consequently, as long as the plane keeps moving, the wings act to lift the plane and keep it airborne.

_____

_____

_____

Grade Eight SkillBook, Writing   **125**

Name _____ Class _____ Date _____

Lesson 14
Writing a Persuasive Paragraph

In a persuasive paragraph the writer tries to convince the audience to accept an opinion by giving strong reasons to support it.

When you write a **persuasive paragraph**, you are trying to convince your audience to agree with your opinion or to follow your advice. Make sure you clearly state your opinion or identify the action you are urging. To persuade others, you may proceed in one or more of the following ways:

1. Express your opinion clearly in a topic sentence.
2. Give relevant, accurate reasons or facts as evidence.
3. Give specific examples from your personal observations or experience.
4. Quote statements of authority, such as the comments of experts or the results of public-opinion polls.
5. Use words and phrases to signal your supporting evidence. These include *first, next, finally, because, since, more important, furthermore,* and *therefore*.

Your paragraph should have a conclusion. This may be a strong summary statement. It may also state what you will do or expect others to do as a result of your advice or opinion. Notice the conclusion in the following persuasive paragraph.

> We, the children of America, should become aware of how many hours of our lives we are killing with television. I discovered this when I looked at my own life. I found that I spent six hours one Saturday watching television. That was one-fourth of my entire day. Furthermore, when I subtracted the eight hours I slept, I was left with almost half my waking hours in front of the set. More important, I learned that I was not alone. *Media America* magazine reports that the average American my age spends seven hours each day watching television. Isn't it time for us to become more active and productive citizens?

Exercise A
Answer the following questions about the preceding persuasive paragraph.

1. What is the topic sentence?

   _____

2. What reasons does the writer give to back up the opinion expressed?

   _____

3. Which of these reasons is based on personal experience? Which is based on a valid outside authority?

   _____

Name _____ Class _____ Date _____

Exercise B
Choose five of the ten general topics below. For each one, write a sentence that states an opinion, explains a problem to be considered, or urges some action concerning the topic.

1. your school motto

   _____

2. television reruns

   _____

3. local bus service

   _____

4. comic books

   _____

5. behavior of fans at games

   _____

6. billboard advertising

   _____

7. children's birthday parties

   _____

8. youth sports competition

   _____

9. baby-sitting

   _____

10. littering penalties

    _____

Grade Eight SkillBook, Writing

Lesson 15
Writing a Summary Paragraph

A good summary paragraph keeps to main ideas and omits unimportant details.

A **summary** is a brief statement of the main ideas of an article or the major events in a story. Read these two paragraphs. Which one seems to do a better job of summarizing the novel excerpt?

1. In *Banner in the Sky*, by James Ramsey Ullman, Frau Matt's young son, Rudi, wants to climb a mountain in the Swiss Alps with Captain Winter. The captain believes that Rudi will be safe and that he has earned the right to make the climb, but Frau Matt objects. She wants Rudi to continue his training as a hotel worker. Rudi convinces her that he will not lose his job if he makes the climb. Reluctantly, Frau Matt gives in, and Rudi is overjoyed.

2. Frau Matt looks at her hands. Sure, she's proud of her son, but he could get hurt. Suppose he loses his job as a mountain guide? Rudi says old Teo will let him go. Besides, there's Toni Hassler. Rudi spoke to him last week. Toni could substitute for him. Frau Matt agrees.

Summary 1 is better because it follows the guidelines below. Study these guidelines. Then do the exercise that follows.

Guidelines for Summarizing Fiction
1. Mention the title and author, the setting and main characters, the conflict, and the major events in the story.
2. Note only important events. Leave out unimportant details.
3. Be brief. Instead of listing a series of actions or ideas, try to sum them all up in a single phrase or sentence.
4. Check over your summary to make sure your facts are accurate.

Exercise A
Discuss these questions about the summaries.

1. What important information does Summary 2 leave out?

   _____

   _____

2. What unimportant information does it include?

   _____

   _____

Name _____ Class _____ Date _____

3. Which sentence in Summary 1 sums up sentences 3–6 in Summary 2?

   _____
   _____

4. Which fact given in Summary 2 is not accurate?

   _____
   _____

Exercise B
Read the summary paragraphs below. Tell which is better and why. Use the guidelines above to direct you.

1. "A Day's Wait," by Ernest Hemingway, takes place on an icy winter morning in the country. Schatz, a nine-year-old boy, is sick in bed. His father tries to comfort him, but Schatz remains tense and silent. The doctor examines him, says he has the flu, and leaves medicine for him. Schatz's father reads to him. Later, he learns that Schatz is confused about his high temperature and thinks he's going to die. The boy relaxes when the father explains that he has confused the Celsius scale with the Fahrenheit scale and will be all right.

2. The doctor says the boy has pneumonia and leaves medicine to help the fever, a purgative, and a third medicine to deal with acid. His father reads to him from Howard Pyle's *Book of Pirates*. There is ice on the ground. The dog falls on it. The father kills two quail and misses five others. The boy mixes up miles with kilometers. The father explains the difference to him again and that makes him feel better. The boy doesn't die, but the next day he is very sad and cries.

_____
_____
_____
_____
_____
_____
_____
_____

Grade Eight SkillBook, Writing

Name _____ Class _____ Date _____

Lesson 16
Research: Choosing a Topic

The first step in planning a research report is choosing your topic and the type of report you will write.

At least once during the year you will probably write a **research report**, a composition based on information gathered through research. In this lesson you will begin planning your report.

First you would list people, places, events, and things that interest you. You may find ideas in your journal. A good topic is narrow enough to handle in six to eight paragraphs. The Revolutionary War is too broad, but a single event connected with it, such as the Boston Tea Party, should work. Narrow any topics that seem too broad.

Next, you would choose the type of report most suitable to your topic. Here are some examples.

- A **cause/effect report** might focus on the causes of a historical event or what happened as a result of it. It might also focus on a science topic such as The Birth of a Hurricane.
- A **narrative report** might recount someone's life from birth to death or tell what happens during a typical day in a factory.
- A **comparison/contrast report** deals with two subjects that have marked similarities and differences. The Telephone and the Telegraph would work well; Caves and Rainbows would not.
- An **explanatory report** explains important aspects of a topic, such as how a branch of government works or what it was like to live in another century, by focusing on one aspect at a time.

Finally, you would write a list of five to ten questions you will want your report to answer. This will further narrow your topic. Here is a list of questions for the topic Pioneer Children.

1. What did they eat?
2. What were their houses like?
3. What were their schools like?
4. What were their communities like?
5. What kinds of chores did they do?
6. What did they do in their free time?

Exercise A
Write *Cause/Effect, Comparison/Contrast, Explanatory,* or *Narrative* to tell which type of report you would write for each topic on the next page. Then briefly explain why.

Example: How a Candle Is Made
Answer: Narrative—I would tell about the process from start to finish, one step at a time.

Name _____ Class _____ Date _____

1. Butterflies and Moths
   _____

2. How a Comet Comes to Be
   _____

3. Superhighways Have Changed the American Landscape
   _____

4. The Building of the Panama Canal
   _____

5. The Voyages of Christopher Columbus
   _____

6. The Computer and the Human Brain
   _____

7. Flood Damage Along the Mississippi
   _____

8. Early Methods of Flight
   _____

9. Automobiles and Air Pollution
   _____

10. The Achievements of Albert Einstein
    _____

Exercise B
On a separate sheet of paper, make a list of topics that interest you. Narrow any that seem too broad. Choose a topic and the type of report you will write. You might choose one of the types discussed in this lesson. Then write six to ten questions you will want your report to answer. Save your work for the next lesson.

Grade Eight SkillBook, Writing

Lesson 17
Research: Using Reference Sources

Use reference sources to research your topic.

Your next step is to find information on your topic. **Reference sources** contain specific information that is classified so that you can locate it easily. They usually are kept together in a separate section of the library. Here are some examples.

Encyclopedia   An encyclopedia is a book or a set of books with articles covering many topics. There are also specialized encyclopedias on one subject, such as *The Baseball Encyclopedia*.

Almanac   An almanac contains up-to-date information on many subjects, such as sports and weather. Published yearly, almanacs arrange facts and figures into tables and charts.

Atlas   This is a book of maps and geographical information. It contains maps that show cities, oceans, and other land features.

Biographical Reference Books   These are works like *Who's Who in America* and *Biographical Dictionary of English Literature*. These books give short biographies of well-known people in politics, business, sports, and the arts.

Specialized Subject Dictionaries   Specialized dictionaries, such as *Compton's Dictionary of the Natural Sciences* and *The Harvard Dictionary of Music*, define terms in a particular area.

Nonprint Media   These include collections of films, filmstrips, records, tape cassettes, microfilm, and microfiche.

Readers' Guide to Periodical Literature   This is an index that helps you find articles published in magazines. The *Readers' Guide* lists articles by subject and author. Study the sample entry.

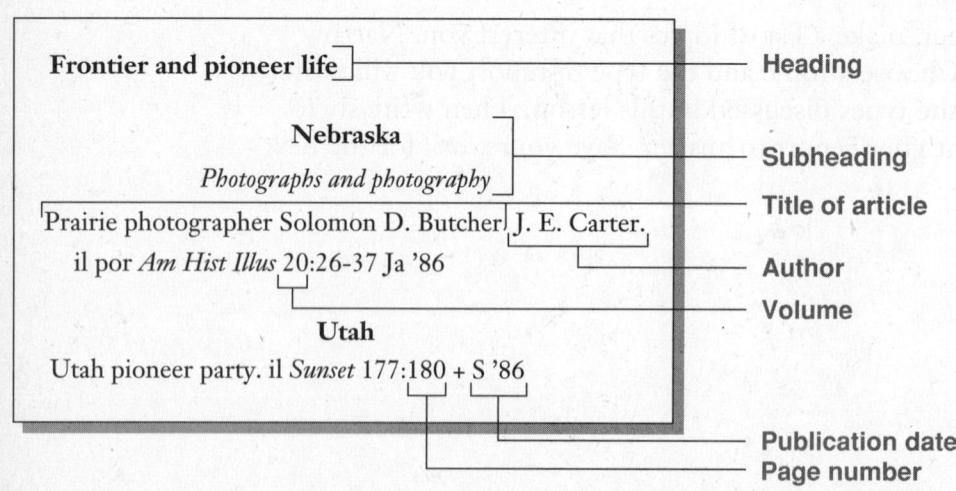

Name _____ Class _____ Date _____

Exercise A

Circle the reference source in parentheses that would contain the following information.

Example: a list of sunrise times for 1987 (atlas, almanac)
Answer: almanac

1. a map of Alberta, Canada (atlas, specialized subject dictionary)
2. information about the history of motion pictures (encyclopedia, biographical reference book)
3. a 1959 magazine article on Hawaii becoming a state (atlas, *Readers' Guide*)
4. a detailed description of a violin (specialized subject dictionary, almanac)
5. a film of the first walk on the moon (encyclopedia, nonprint media)
6. some recent magazine articles about trends in music (encyclopedia, *Readers' Guide*)
7. lists of botanical and zoological terms (almanac, specialized subject dictionary)
8. the final standings of the East Division American League in 1986 (specialized subject dictionary, almanac)
9. some facts about the early life of poet Gwendolyn Brooks (biographical reference book, specialized subject dictionary)
10. slides showing the Rocky Mountains (*Readers' Guide*, nonprint media)

Exercise B

Take out the questions you wrote in Lesson 17. For each one, jot down the reference source or sources you would use to find information on each question.

Grade Eight SkillBook, Writing

133

Lesson 18
Research: Taking Notes

As you research your topic, take notes on information that will help answer the questions you have written.

You have chosen your topic, type of report, and questions. Now you will find information in the library and elsewhere. As you use reference sources, take notes on important facts and details.

Read this passage from a magazine article. Then notice how the information has been recorded on the note card that follows.

> Between the moments of excitement fell inevitable hours of boredom. Parents packed small libraries and organized school lessons to fill these hours; the children made up games. Many of their games would be instantly recognizable to both earlier and later generations—London Bridge, run-sheep-run, leapfrog, button-button. Girls and younger boys made wreaths and necklaces from wildflowers, a favorite pastime before the present century, and chanted handed-down rhymes and rounds.

6
West, Elliot. "The Youngest Pioneers."
<u>American Heritage</u>, Vol. 37 (Dec., 1985). p. 93

To combat boredom on wagon trail, kids:
1. Read books and did school lessons
2. Played games: London Bridge, leapfrog
3. Made flower necklaces
4. Chanted rhymes

The number at the top of the card corresponds to the question that the information helps answer. Number each of your note cards or pages in this way. Below the number, note the source of the information. Underline book or magazine titles. Put quotation marks around article titles. Include the author's name and the page reference. Then write the note itself.

You have seen a card with information from a magazine. Notice how two other kinds of sources are identified on these cards.

Nonfiction Book

> 1
> Carpenter, Allen. <u>Kansas.</u> Chicago: Children's Press, 1979. p. 35
>
> Food often scarce:
> 1. Fires burned crops
> 2. Grasshopper hordes ate green plants

Encyclopedia Article

> 1
> "Pioneer Life in America," <u>World Book Encyclopedia,</u> 1986. Vol. 15, p. 439
>
> Got supplies from Indian people:
> 1. Vegetables
> 2. Buffalo meat

Each card contains a main idea and numbered details supporting it. In your notes, highlight facts in this way. Begin most note cards or pages with a main idea and then add details. Others may contain only a single fact or a definition of a term. Whatever kind of note you make, always head the card or group of notes with your question number and the information source.

While doing research, you may decide to change the focus of your report by adding or changing questions. Take care that your report doesn't become too broad in the process.

Exercise A

Read the passage below. On a separate sheet of paper, write the number of the question on page 130 of Lesson 16 that it helps answer. Next, write a note identifying the source. Then summarize the information that helps answer the question.

1. From page 118 of the article "Frontier Life," in volume 12 of *The Encyclopedia Americana*, published in 1986:

    Frontier homes were of many designs and were constructed of various materials. Perhaps the most characteristic of the first houses built on the frontier were the pole, or log, cabins. These structures could be raised quickly by relatively untrained laborers using materials immediately at

Grade Eight SkillBook, Writing

hand. They were square pens without windows, but usually with large doorways on both sides and stone fireplaces with mud and stick chimneys. Roofs were made of riven boards, and cracks were sealed with mud daubing. Floors were of either tamped clay or split-log puncheons. . . .

The log cabin came nearest to being the universal pioneer dwelling across the wooded frontier. On the prairies, where timber was not readily available, settlers generally erected sod houses, made of earth blocks, as their first dwellings.

2. From page 160 of the book *Pioneer Women* by Joanna L. Stratton, published in New York by Simon and Schuster in 1981:

Generally, the classroom structure was informal, even if the discipline was strict. The school terms were usually short, lasting only a few months at a time. Although most students were interested in their studies, they attended only as their farm chores and the weather permitted. The clanging of a sturdy iron bell that hung outside the schoolhouse door called the youngsters to class each morning. Arriving by foot or horseback, students of assorted ages and various grades took their seats together in one room. The curriculum, usually ungraded, was left largely to the discretion of the teacher herself.

Exercise B
Research your questions from Exercise B at the end of Lesson 16. Find at least two reference sources and read information about your topic. Take notes according to the procedures discussed in this lesson.

Name _____ Class _____ Date _____

Lesson 19
Research: Organizing Information

Organize your information according to the type of report you plan to write.

Once you have taken notes based on your research, review each note card or page. Is the information really important and interesting enough to include in the report? Set aside any cards or notes that don't measure up.

Sort your notes into piles, one for each question. Now decide on the sequence in which you will deal with your questions. For a narrative report, use **time order** to recount the life, event, or process from start to finish.

For a cause/effect report, you might deal with the causes first, then the effects. Present multiple causes and multiple effects in **order of importance**, from least to most important or from most to least important, whichever you think works better. Use order of importance for comparison/contrast and explanatory reports too. Here is how the questions on page 130 were sequenced. Notice that the writer also revised the wording of the questions slightly.

1. What were pioneer communities like?
2. What kind of houses did they have?
3. What were their schools like?
4. What kind of food did children eat?
5. What work did pioneer children do?
6. What recreation did children enjoy?

Communities, houses, and schools are first because they are the places in which pioneer children spent most of their time. Diet is next because the growing and raising of food was a vital part of every pioneer child's life. The last two questions are paired because they present a good contrast. This is not the only sequence in which these questions could be presented. Order of importance sometimes is a matter of opinion. Just be sure that you have good reasons for whatever sequence you choose.

Exercise A
Read each set of questions. Renumber each set in the sequence you think might work best in a research report. Then, briefly, explain why you would use each sequence.

1. This set is for a report on Air Pollution in Big Cities:

    _____ How does air pollution make people uncomfortable?

    _____ How do factories contribute to air pollution?

    _____ How do airplanes contribute to air pollution?

    _____ How does air pollution affect trees and flowers?

    _____ How does air pollution endanger people's health?

Grade Eight SkillBook, Writing

| | How do automobiles contribute to air pollution?
| | How do buses contribute to air pollution?
| | How does air pollution affect the surfaces of buildings?

_____

2. This set is for a report on Old Time Baseball and Modern Baseball:

| | How is the equipment alike and different?
| | How do the numbers of professional teams compare?
| | How do players' salaries compare or contrast?
| | How have the rules changed?
| | How do playing fields and stadiums compare?
| | How do the skills of the players compare?
| | How do the numbers of spectators compare?
| | How does the media coverage compare?

_____

Exercise B

Review your note cards or note pages. Decide which ones you will use in your report. Sort them into piles according to the questions they help answer. Then decide on the sequence in which you will deal with the questions.

Lesson 20
Research: Outlining

Use your classifying and sequencing skills when making an outline.

An **outline** is a general plan for your report. The first step in making an outline is to group your note cards according to the questions they answer. Then arrange these groups in the sequence you worked out in the last lesson. Now use the information in each group to work out the main topics, subtopics, and details that will make up your outline. Before you begin, study the outline below. Notice that it uses the sequence of questions from page 137.

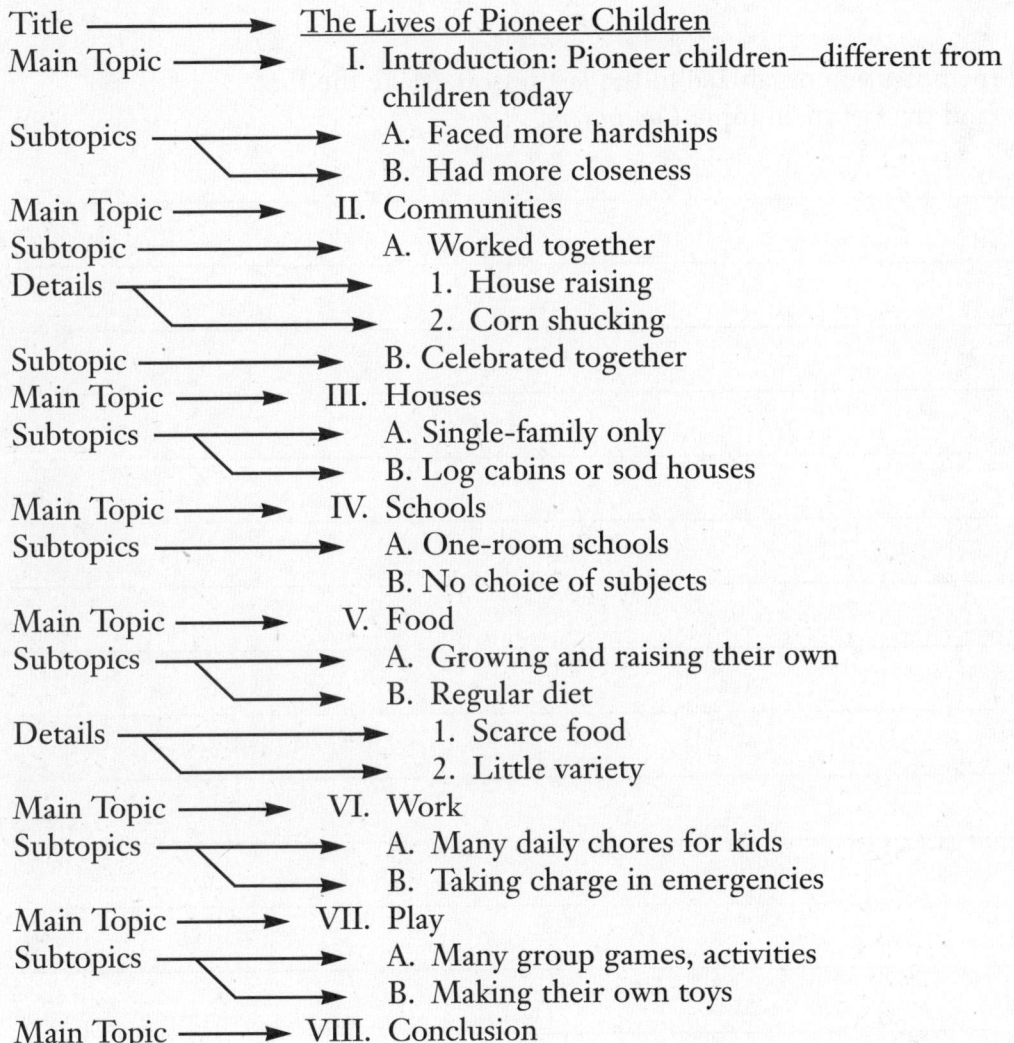

Title ⟶	The Lives of Pioneer Children
Main Topic ⟶	I. Introduction: Pioneer children—different from children today
Subtopics ⟶	A. Faced more hardships
	B. Had more closeness
Main Topic ⟶	II. Communities
Subtopic ⟶	A. Worked together
Details ⟶	1. House raising
	2. Corn shucking
Subtopic ⟶	B. Celebrated together
Main Topic ⟶	III. Houses
Subtopics ⟶	A. Single-family only
	B. Log cabins or sod houses
Main Topic ⟶	IV. Schools
Subtopics ⟶	A. One-room schools
	B. No choice of subjects
Main Topic ⟶	V. Food
Subtopics ⟶	A. Growing and raising their own
	B. Regular diet
Details ⟶	1. Scarce food
	2. Little variety
Main Topic ⟶	VI. Work
Subtopics ⟶	A. Many daily chores for kids
	B. Taking charge in emergencies
Main Topic ⟶	VII. Play
Subtopics ⟶	A. Many group games, activities
	B. Making their own toys
Main Topic ⟶	VIII. Conclusion

When you make your outline, follow the format used in the sample outline shown in this lesson. Remember to capitalize the first word of each line. Indent subtopics and details. Make sure subtopics support main topics and that details support subtopics. What precedes each main topic? each subtopic? each detail?

Grade Eight SkillBook, Writing

Exercise A

Create an outline on a separate sheet of paper for a research report based on the information below. Arrange the information in what you think is the best order.

- Title: The Telephone
- Main Topics: Early History, Telephone Services, Modern Developments
- Subtopics: Car phones, Local service, Invented by Bell in 1875, Long distance service, AT&T formed in 1885, Overseas service, Touch-Tone buttons, Picturephones
- Details: Came to U.S. in 1871, Reaches 190 countries, Teacher for the deaf, Uses undersea cable

Exercise B

Make an outline from the notes you organized in the last lesson. Make the first main topic *Introduction* and the last main topic *Conclusion*.

Name _____ Class _____ Date _____

Lesson 1
Kinds of Sentences

There are four kinds of sentences: declarative, interrogative, imperative, and exclamatory.

A **sentence** begins with a capital letter, expresses a complete thought, and ends with a punctuation mark. Read the following examples of sentence types.

Declarative: The president brought the meeting to order.
Interrogative: Is every member of the club present?
Imperative: Give me your attention, please. Stop talking out there!
Exclamatory: You are out of order! What a commotion you're making!

A **declarative sentence** makes a statement. It gives information and ends with a period.

An **interrogative sentence** asks a question. It ends with a question mark.

An **imperative sentence** gives a command or makes a request. It ends with a period or an exclamation mark. The subject is nearly always *you*, understood and not stated.

An **exclamatory sentence** is a statement or command made with strong feeling. It ends with an exclamation mark.

Exercise A
Read each sentence below and answer the questions.

Who will take the minutes
Please raise your hands for the vote
How quickly this vote came
Clearly, the ayes have it

1. Write the sentence that is interrogative and should end with a question mark.

   _____

2. Write the sentence that is an exclamation and should end with an exclamation mark.

   _____

3. Write the two sentences that should end with periods.

   _____

   _____

Grade Eight SkillBook, Grammar, Usage, and Mechanics

Name _____ Class _____ Date _____

Exercise B

Read each sentence and write what kind it is in the blank.

1. This is Uncle Ted, who works at a center for training guide dogs. _____
2. Give us a chance to ask you a few questions. _____
3. How did you happen to get into this kind of work? _____
4. Have you ever wondered who trains army dogs for sentry duty? _____
5. I was a member of the K-9 Corps in the army. _____
6. After the army, I visited a training center where blind students were working with dogs on an obstacle course. _____
7. What a great idea it was! _____
8. Tell us more about how you train dogs. _____
9. Dogs are trained on leashes and harnesses first for six months. _____
10. What should owners teach their dogs? _____

Exercise C

For each item, write a sentence using the group of words. Make your sentence the kind shown.

Example: Declarative sentence: many creaky floors
Answer: There were too many creaky floors to count.

1. Interrogative sentence: the haunted house

   _____

2. Imperative sentence: hold my hand

   _____

3. Declarative sentence: in the front door

   _____

4. Exclamatory sentence: something cold

   _____

5. Interrogative sentence: your flashlight

   _____

Name _____ Class _____ Date _____

Lesson 2
Subjects and Predicates

A sentence has a simple and complete subject and predicate.

A simple sentence has two parts: the complete subject and the complete predicate. The **complete subject** tells whom or what the sentence is about. The **complete predicate** tells what the subject does or is. Both the complete subject and the complete predicate can consist of one word or several words.

> The wide **river** | *meanders* slowly across the plain.
> Small **beaches** | *have appeared* here and there along its banks.
> **We** | *are* happy on our graceful boat with its billowing sails.
> An **otter** on a rocky perch | suddenly *dives*.

The main word in the complete subject is the **simple subject**. The simple subject is the noun or pronoun that the sentence is about. In the sentences above, the simple subjects are in dark type. They may be modified by adjectives or prepositional phrases.

The main word in the complete predicate is the **simple predicate**, usually called the **verb**. The verb may be a one-word verb or a verb phrase. The complete predicate may also contain adverbs and prepositional phrases that modify the verb or other words that complete its meaning. In the sentences above, the verbs are shown in italics.

A simple sentence has only one complete subject and one complete predicate, but each of these may be compound. A **compound subject** consists of two or more subjects, usually joined by the conjunction *and* or *or*. A **compound predicate** consists of two or more predicates joined by *and*, *but*, or *or*.

> An **otter** or that **seagull** | **took** my bait and **swam** away with it.

Exercise A
Draw a vertical line between the complete subject and the complete predicate. Underline the simple subject once and the verb twice.

> **Example:** Lazy turtles sleep soundly on the wet rocks.
> **Answer:** Lazy <u>turtles</u> | <u>sleep</u> soundly on the wet rocks.

1. Tiny fish in schools dart back and forth in the shadows.

2. Bullfrogs and crickets fill the air with their commotion.

Exercise B
Draw a vertical line between the complete subject and the complete predicate.

1. People from many countries gather for the helium-inflated balloon's liftoff.

2. The lone balloonist prepares her craft for the flight.

Grade Eight SkillBook, Grammar, Usage, and Mechanics

3. She will navigate her balloon across the Atlantic.
4. The happy balloonist jumps into the gondola.
5. The crew on the ground releases the moorings.
6. The large and colorful monster floats upward into the wind.
7. The strong, gusty wind propels it over the water.
8. A noisy crowd of well-wishers cheers at the impressive sight.
9. The balloon will rise during the day and dip in the evening.
10. Favorable winds and good weather should carry the craft more than two thousand miles.

Exercise C
Draw a vertical line between the complete subject and the complete predicate. Then underline the simple subject once and the verb twice. Some sentences may have compound subjects or predicates.

Example: The horse of modern times evolved from an animal no larger than a wolf.
Answer: The horse of modern times | evolved from an animal no larger than a wolf.

11. This small creature was called the dawn horse, or eohippus.
12. The four-toed eohippus could run on tiptoe.
13. Its toes changed and developed over thousands of years.
14. The result of the changes was the modern horse's hoof.
15. Ponies of today resemble another early animal, equus.
16. The primitive equus lived and thrived in North America.
17. Glaciers and colder temperatures made life difficult.
18. The animals abandoned North America and migrated to other parts of the world.
19. Modern horses were brought back to North America in 1537.
20. They quickly multiplied and roamed the West in wild bands.

Name _____ Class _____ Date _____

Lesson 3
Simple and Compound Sentences

A simple sentence has a complete subject and a complete predicate. A compound sentence consists of two or more simple sentences.

A **simple sentence** has one complete subject and one complete predicate. Either the subject or the predicate, or both, may be compound. Study these sentences.

            S   V
The royal yacht | attracted a huge crowd.
       S   S   V   V
The king and queen in their finery | nodded and smiled at the people.

You cannot break either simple sentence into two sentences without changing the word order.

There is a kind of sentence, however, that can be divided. A **compound sentence** is made by joining two or more simple sentences that are closely related. A conjunction such as *and*, *but*, or *or* is used to join them. A comma precedes the conjunction unless the two sentences are very short. Two closely related sentences can also be joined by a semicolon (;).

Notice the simple sentences underlined in these compound sentences.

<u>The king | looks quite bored today</u>, but <u>the queen | seems fairly happy.</u>
<u>The queen | talks to a subject</u>; <u>the king | rudely yawns.</u>

Exercise A
Tell what is compound in this sentence.

    Helen and Tomi sat on the porch and talked until midnight.

Exercise B
Place an *S* above each subject and a *V* above each verb. Some sentences have compound subjects or compound predicates.

    Example: Holland grows and exports tulips.
                        S   V   V
    Answer: Holland grows and exports tulips. —compound predicate

1. Tulip growers around the world import these handsome flowers.

2. The tulip originated in Turkey and means *turban* in Turkish.

3. Horticulturists and amateur gardeners plant tulips in the fall and enjoy them the following spring.

4. A variety of shapes attract tulip buyers.

5. Actually, the modern tulip is a member of the lily family.

6. Unusual colors and patterns in hybrid flowers require years of research.

7. Either bulbs or seeds may produce new plants.
8. Individual bulbs divide into several bulbs and yield flowers sooner than seeds.
9. Producers remove diseased plants and develop hardier hybrids.
10. Tulips are attractive flowers and remain very popular.

Exercise C
Write *simple* or *compound* for each sentence.

Example: Many gardeners and farmers grow flowers and vegetables.
Answer: simple

11. Healthy plants require sunshine and water; they also need protection from disease. _____
12. Successful gardeners weed and hoe their plants often. _____
13. Tomatoes should not be planted too early; they may become stunted by the cold. _____
14. Many other kinds of produce are less temperamental and require less care. _____
15. There is nothing like fresh vegetables from one's own garden! _____
16. Many gardeners can their produce, and others freeze it. _____
17. Farmers grow acres of corn or peas for commercial canneries. _____
18. Some people have outdoor gardens, but more have indoor gardens. _____
19. Indoor gardens usually consist of potted plants or herbs. _____
20. In almost every state, orchards of some kind produce fruit. _____

Lesson 4
Sentence Fragments and Run-ons

A sentence fragment may look and sound like a sentence, but it isn't a complete sentence. Sentence fragments are missing either a subject or a verb, or they don't express a complete thought.

A run-on is two or more sentences without proper punctuation between them.

A group of words punctuated like a sentence but not expressing a complete thought is called a **sentence fragment**. A fragment may contain a verb form or even a subject and a verb. However, a fragment does not make sense by itself.

You can correct fragments in two ways. Add words to the fragment to create a complete sentence, or if the fragment is a part broken off from a complete sentence, attach it to the sentence it belongs with. Appositive fragments should be set off with commas.

Fragment: Left for the picnic.
Corrected: We left for the picnic.

Sentence and fragment: We left for the picnic. Even though it was raining.
Corrected: We left for the picnic even though it was raining.

Sentences that run together with no punctuation or only a comma between them are called **run-on sentences**.

Al is doing the assignment he can't work the third problem.
The first test was difficult, the second one was easy.

Run-ons can be corrected in one of three ways.

- Use a period to separate the two complete sentences.
- If the sentences are closely related, use a comma and a conjunction like *and*, *but*, or *or* to connect them.
- Join two closely related sentences with a semicolon.

Al is doing the assignment. He can't work the third problem.
Al is doing the assignment, but he can't work the third problem.
Al is doing the assignment; he can't work the third problem.

Exercise A
Correct each fragment on the next page by joining it to the sentence from which it was separated. Add punctuation as needed.

Example: Many American women have succeeded as writers. And gained popularity during their lifetimes.
Answer: Many American women have succeeded as writers and gained popularity during their lifetimes.

Grade Eight SkillBook, Grammar, Usage, and Mechanics

1. Born in 1862, Edith Wharton was reluctant to become a writer. Because it was not considered proper for a woman.

2. Her most famous novel is *Ethan Frome*. A tale of love turned bitter.

3. Sarah Orne Jewett wrote about the difficult lives of people in rural America. Particularly her native Maine.

4. Jewett's characters were vividly drawn. And very realistic.

5. An example is "The Flight of Betsey Lane." A popular story.

6. Another famous writer, Willa Cather, grew up on a ranch in Nebraska. And used her memories of it in her novels too.

7. She won early fame with *O Pioneers!* But is better known for *Death Comes for the Archbishop*.

8. Katherine Anne Porter won national awards. For short stories.

9. She spent twenty-two years on her only novel. *Ship of Fools*.

10. These writers portrayed women. Who endured hard lives.

Name _____ Class _____ Date _____

Lesson 5
Combining Subjects, Predicates, and Sentences

Combine subjects, predicates, and sentences to show how ideas are related.

Short, choppy sentences can be monotonous if they are used too often. In the first example below, both sentences have the same predicate. Notice how much smoother the sentences sound when combined into one sentence with a compound subject.

Two sentences: Several old baby bonnets were ruined in the flood. A book of rare maps was ruined in the flood.
Combined: Several old baby bonnets and a book of rare maps were ruined in the flood.

The verb with this kind of compound subject should be plural.

A compound predicate can be formed by joining related sentences with the same subject.

Two sentences: Antique experts were called to the museum. Antique experts restored the damaged goods.
Combined: Antique experts were called to the museum to restore the damaged goods.

More than two subjects or predicates can also be combined. Then commas must be used. Notice how commas are used in punctuating such sentences.

Three sentences: The bird hit the kite. The bird tore the kite. It destroyed the kite.
Combined: The bird hit, tore, and destroyed the kite.

Related sentences can be joined into compound sentences. Use the conjunction *and* to show addition of ideas, *but* to show contrast, and *or* to show a choice.

Columbus discovered America. Other explorers soon followed.
Columbus discovered America, **and** other explorers soon followed.
Columbus landed first. He did not name America.
Columbus landed first, **but** he did not name America.
Was he an explorer? Was he just looking for adventure?
Was he an explorer, **or** was he just looking for adventure?

Exercise
Rewrite the sentences on the next page by combining subjects, predicates, or whole sentences. Change the verb number if needed.

Example: Doctors cure diseases. Good nutrition prevents illness.
Answer: Doctors cure diseases, but good nutrition prevents illness.

Grade Eight SkillBook, Grammar, Usage, and Mechanics

Name _____ Class _____ Date _____

1. Some proteins build muscles. Some proteins replace dead tissue.
   _____
   _____

2. Other proteins are less valuable to the body. Other proteins should be avoided.
   _____
   _____

3. Protein can be found in meat. Iron can be found in meat. Vitamins can be found in meat.
   _____
   _____

4. Do you have to eat meat? Can you be healthy without it?
   _____
   _____

5. Vegetarians eat fish. They don't eat meat.
   _____
   _____

6. Many fruits and vegetables contain important vitamins. Whole grains contain important vitamins too.
   _____
   _____

7. Food experts recommend eating whole grains. Doctors agree.
   _____
   _____

8. Many people have changed their eating habits. They are healthier as a result.
   _____
   _____

Grade Eight SkillBook, Grammar, Usage, and Mechanics

Lesson 6
Varying Sentence Structure

You can make your writing more interesting and effective by varying the length and kinds of sentences you use.

Sentences can be of various kinds and lengths. Parts of sentences can be combined to make new sentences. Read the paragraph and think of ways to improve it.

    (1) The city's transit workers were on strike. (2) They were on strike for more pay. (3) The buses and subways did not run during the strike. (4) The strike lasted ten days. (5) People found different ways to get to work. (6) Some people formed car pools and drove to work. (7) Some people rode bicycles. (8) Other people just walked. (9) The strike was inconvenient for everyone. (10) Many people sympathized with the striking workers.

Here are some ways this paragraph can be improved. Notice how they were carried out in the revised paragraph that follows.

- Sentences with very similar meaning such as **1** and **2** can be combined with a prepositional phrase.
- Vary sentence beginnings. The information in sentence **4** can be summarized in a phrase and put at the start of sentence **3.**
- Vary sentence type. Instead of using all declarative sentences, a sentence like **5** can be rephrased into a question.
- Sentences **6, 7,** and **8** can be combined.
- Sentences **9** and **10** can be combined with the conjunction *but*.

    The city's transit workers were on strike for more pay. For ten days no buses or subways ran. How did people manage to get to work? Some formed car pools and drove, some rode bicycles, and others just walked. The strike was inconvenient for everyone, but many people sympathized with the striking workers.

Exercise
Rewrite the following items, making the sentences more varied and interesting. Use the guidelines in this lesson.

    Example: The first subways were above ground. This was in London.
    Answer: The first subways in London were above ground.

1. Deep recesses were cut into the streets. The recesses were for the train tracks.

Name _____ Class _____ Date _____

2. They called it a subway. The train didn't run in a tunnel yet.
   _____
   _____

3. Real underground trains opened in 1860. It happened in London.
   _____
   _____

4. The tunnels resembled tubes. Londoners still call them that.
   _____
   _____

5. Boston built the first American trolley line. It was in 1897.
   _____
   _____

6. New York soon had a larger system. Boston had theirs earlier.
   _____
   _____

7. New York's subways travel underneath five counties. They are thousands of miles long.
   _____
   _____

8. Paris's subways have rubber wheels for a quieter ride. Montreal's subways have rubber wheels for the same reason.
   _____
   _____

9. Does Tokyo have crowded subways? Are Mexico City's worse?
   _____
   _____

10. Mexico City's subways cut through ancient Aztec pyramids. They look like a museum.
    _____
    _____

Grade Eight SkillBook, Grammar, Usage, and Mechanics

Name _____ Class _____ Date _____

Lesson 7
Direct Objects and Subject Complements

A direct object is a noun or pronoun that follows an action verb. A subject complement is a noun, pronoun, or adjective that follows a linking verb and refers to the subject.

A **direct object** is a noun or pronoun that follows an action verb and tells what or who receives the action of the verb. A direct object may be compound. Look at these examples.

> Jan defeated her **opponents** in the relay.
> One of her opponents congratulated **her** and her **coach**.

In the first sentence the noun *opponents* is the direct object. It tells who was defeated. Find the direct object in the second sentence. What does it tell?

An action verb with a direct object is a transitive verb.

A **subject complement** follows a linking verb and identifies or describes the subject. Study these examples.

> Jan was the **winner** of the relay.
> The winners last year were **she** and **Tony**.
> Jan was **happy** and **triumphant**.

In the first sentence the noun *winner* is the subject complement. It identifies the subject *Jan* as the winner. A noun used as a subject complement is called a **predicate noun**. The subject complement in the second sentence is a compound: *she* and *Tony*. In that sentence it consists of a **predicate pronoun** and a **predicate noun**. The third sentence contains a **compound predicate adjective**: *happy* and *triumphant*. An adjective used as a subject complement is called a **predicate adjective**.

A linking verb does not have an object. It is an intransitive verb.

Exercise A
Underline the direct object or subject complement in each sentence. Then tell if it is a direct object or whether the complements are predicate nouns, predicate pronouns, or predicate adjectives.

> **Example:** Jan ran the marathon.
> **Answer:** Jan ran the <u>marathon</u>.—direct object

1. The prize was hers. _____
2. Jan won the blue ribbon. _____
3. She played the game well. _____
4. Jan was the best athlete. _____

Grade Eight SkillBook, Grammar, Usage, and Mechanics

Name _____ Class _____ Date _____

Exercise B
Underline the direct object or subject complement in each sentence. Tell whether the verb is transitive or intransitive.

   Example: I enjoy track meets.
   Answer: I enjoy track <u>meets</u>.—transitive

1. Today we will hold a relay race at our school. _____
2. The captain of our team is Gerry. _____
3. Serita and Jeffrey are team members too. _____
4. Jeffrey runs the first leg of the race. _____
5. He relays the baton to Serita. _____
6. Serita hands the baton to Gerry. _____
7. Gerry is a faster runner than I. _____
8. The other teams are not local. _____
9. Our coach cheers us on eagerly. _____
10. I am still nervous during a race. _____
11. The race was a huge success. _____
12. Our coach congratulated us and the other team. _____

Exercise C
Write **DO** over direct objects. Write **SC** over subject complements. Tell whether each complement is a predicate noun, predicate pronoun, or predicate adjective.

   Example: Numismatics is the study of coins and medals.
                                    SC
   Answer: Numismatics is the study of coins and medals.—predicate noun

13. A numismatist is an expert in numismatics. _____
14. Mr. Gonzales sponsors our coin-collector's club. _____
15. Beryl Jacobs will be the president next year. _____
16. The two most dedicated club members are she and Tom Vaar. _____
17. Beryl and I joined the club last year. _____
18. We became collectors because of Mr. Gonzalez. _____
19. Coin collectors crowd his shop on weekends. _____
20. People of all ages can join our club. _____
21. Numismatics has been popular for many years. _____
22. I am a collector of Indian-head pennies myself. _____

Name _____ Class _____ Date _____

Lesson 8
Indirect Objects

An indirect object is a noun or pronoun that tells to whom or for whom the action of the verb is done.

A sentence that contains a direct object may also contain a noun or pronoun that serves as an indirect object. An **indirect object** tells *to whom* or *for whom* the action of the verb is done. Study the following examples.

    Mother gave the **girls** permission.
    Michael wrote **me** a letter.

In the first example above, *permission* is the direct object of the verb *gave*. The indirect object is *girls*. It tells *to whom* Mother gave permission. Find the direct object and the indirect object in the second sentence above.

Although a preposition (*to* or *for*) is implied when an indirect object is used, an indirect object is never part of a prepositional phrase. A noun or pronoun is an indirect object only if it precedes the direct object and is used without a preposition. If a noun or pronoun follows a preposition, it is the object of the preposition, not an indirect object. Compare these sentence pairs.

    Object of preposition: Leah gave her trophy to the school.
                                      Ralph bought a ticket for Sonya.
    Indirect object: Leah gave the school her trophy.
                                        Ralph bought Sonya a ticket.

Exercise A
Write *indirect object* or *object of a preposition* for each underlined word.

1. Lester sent <u>Jane</u> flowers on her birthday. _____
2. Her brother Stan baked <u>her</u> a cake. _____
3. Dad bought ice cream for <u>her</u>. _____
4. The whole family sang "Happy Birthday" to <u>her</u>. _____
5. She gave <u>Mother</u> a big hug. _____
6. Jane sent a thank-you note to <u>Lester</u>. _____
7. She offered <u>Stan</u> two baseball tickets. _____

Exercise B
Complete each sentence on the next page with an indirect object.

    Example: Uncle Denis sent _____ a collie puppy named Bouncer.
    Answer: Uncle Denis sent <u>Lincoln</u> a collie puppy named Bouncer.

Grade Eight SkillBook, Grammar, Usage, and Mechanics

1. The playful animal gave _____ a bouncy greeting.
2. Lincoln offered _____ a big bone.
3. Lincoln's mother fed his _____ some beef scraps.
4. Lincoln built _____ a doghouse.
5. The frisky puppy brought _____ a stick.
6. Cousin Francis sent _____ a collar for Bouncer.
7. Lincoln's sister bought _____ some bones.
8. Lincoln's little brother gave _____ a hug.
9. Bouncer gave _____ a friendly lick.
10. Lincoln sent _____ a thank-you letter.

Exercise C
Replace the prepositional phrases with indirect objects.

   Example: The children made some gifts for their friends.
   Answer: The children made their friends some gifts.

11. Bill painted a picture for his mother.

   _____

   _____

12. He built a pipe rack for his father.

   _____

   _____

13. Myron gave a gift certificate to his sister.

   _____

   _____

14. Tanya wove a scarf for her cousin.

   _____

   _____

15. Tanya's cousin sent some earrings to her.

   _____

   _____

Grade Eight SkillBook, Grammar, Usage, and Mechanics

Lesson 9
Independent and Dependent Clauses

A part of a sentence that has a subject and a verb and makes sense by itself is called an independent clause. A dependent clause has a subject and a verb but does not make sense by itself.

A **clause** is a group of words that contains a subject and a verb and is used as part of a sentence. An **independent clause** is a part of a sentence that is grammatically independent. It can stand alone and make sense by itself. Look at these examples:

> **Seth laughed heartily**, but **Martha just smiled**.
> Seth laughed heartily. Martha just smiled.

The first example is a compound sentence made up of two independent clauses joined by the conjunction *but*. In the second example, the two independent clauses are separated into two simple sentences.

Not all clauses, however, make sense or express a complete thought by themselves. Notice these clauses:

> that she brought to the picnic
> because he was late

A group of words that has a subject and verb but cannot stand alone is called a **dependent clause**. A dependent clause needs to be attached to an independent clause in order to make sense.

> Betty baked the bread **that she brought to the picnic**.
> **Because he was late**, Ken didn't stop to talk.

Dependent clauses begin with words like *who, which, that, because, when, if, until, before,* and *after*.

Exercise A
Underline the independent clauses once, and the dependent clauses twice.

> **Example:** A man who read the newspaper ad bought Mom's car.
> **Answer:**   <u>A man</u> <u><u>who read the newspaper ad</u></u> <u>bought Mom's car</u>.

1. I didn't meet the man who bought Mom's car.
2. When I got home, he had already left.
3. The car was old, but Mom got a good price for it.
4. She wants a new car that will seat more than two.
5. We will enjoy the new car, but we will miss the old one.

Grade Eight SkillBook, Grammar, Usage, and Mechanics

Exercise B
Underline the dependent clause in each sentence.

    Example: I lost the election that was held last Tuesday.
    Answer: I lost the election <u>that was held last Tuesday</u>.

6. There were three candidates in the election <u>that I lost</u>.
7. Bobbette DeBow was the one <u>who got the most votes</u>.
8. <u>After the votes were counted</u>, I congratulated her.
9. This is the second time <u>that I have run for class president</u>.
10. I might run in the science-club election, <u>which will be held next month</u>.
11. I am interested in going into politics <u>when I finish college</u>.
12. <u>If I do</u>, my parents will probably be disappointed.
13. They point to my uncle, <u>who has run for mayor three times and lost each time</u>.
14. <u>Before I decide on a political career</u>, I'll talk it over with my parents.
15. I might change my mind, <u>though I doubt it</u>.

Name _____ Class _____ Date _____

Lesson 10
Complex Sentences

A sentence that has one independent clause and one or more dependent clauses is called a complex sentence.

Though a dependent clause has a subject and a verb, it cannot stand alone. It has to be joined with an independent clause to make a sentence. A sentence with one independent clause and one or more dependent clauses is called a **complex sentence**.

> The championship game **that we attended** was played on Friday.
> **Before we went**, we called Sam, **who is an avid football fan**.

Notice in both complex sentences above that the dependent clauses appear in different places. A dependent clause may come before, after, or within the independent clause in a complex sentence. Find the independent and dependent clauses in these sentences.

> **After the game was over**, we ordered a pizza.
> We ate the pizza **while we discussed the game**.
> **Because it was delicious**, the pizza, **which we shared**, was soon gone.

Exercise A
Underline the independent clauses once, and the dependent clauses twice.

1. Until the rain started, we had been planning a picnic.
2. One boy that we knew waited an hour before he left the park.

Exercise B
Rewrite each sentence by adding a dependent clause to form a complex sentence. Use the word in parentheses to introduce the dependent clause.

Example: We were late for school. (because)
Answer: Because we missed the bus, we were late for school.

1. The magician made the elephant disappear. (after)

   _____
   _____

2. The chorus played dance music. (before)

   _____
   _____

3. School closings were announced on TV and radio. (because)

   _____
   _____

Grade Eight SkillBook, Grammar, Usage, and Mechanics

4. I saw an excellent play. (which)

_____

_____

5. Do your homework first. (if)

_____

_____

6. He couldn't remember the tune. (although)

_____

_____

Exercise C
Read each sentence below. If the sentence is complex, underline the dependent clause. Do not underline the other sentences.

    Example: Early astronomers, who were called "star arrangers," mapped about one-third of the star groups.
    Answer: Early astronomers, <u>who were called "star arrangers,"</u> mapped about one-third of the star groups.

7. The Egyptian astronomer Ptolemy, who learned a great deal about star groups, is known for his maps of the night sky.

8. His studies, which were conducted in the second century A.D., described the motion of the planets.

9. Ancient Greeks described stars, but they had no telescopes.

10. Hans Lippershey, who invented the telescope in 1608, contributed to the study of astronomy.

11. The scientist who made the first really effective telescope was Galileo.

12. The stars appear motionless, but they are all moving.

13. Centuries ago, the North Star that you see guided sailors who did not have today's modern equipment.

14. This star, which is also called Polaris, is seen in the Northern Hemisphere.

15. When you see the Big Dipper, you are looking at the most easily identifiable group of stars.

16. The Little Dipper is called Ursa Minor, and this star group is made up of seven bright stars.

17. Most people who study the skies have observed these star groups, which often can be seen without a telescope.

Lesson 11
Compound-Complex Sentences

A sentence that contains two or more independent clauses and one or more dependent clauses is a compound-complex sentence.

A compound sentence contains two independent clauses joined by a coordinating conjunction. A complex sentence contains one independent clause and one or more dependent clauses. A **compound-complex sentence** consists of two or more independent clauses and one or more dependent clauses. Study these compound-complex sentences.

David raked the leaves **before he mowed the lawn**, and Kiyo helped him. **After the lawn was mowed**, Marla trimmed the hedge, but Kiyo quit for the day **because it was late**.

In the first sentence, the independent clauses are *David raked the leaves* and *Kiyo helped him*. The dependent clause is *before he mowed the lawn*. In the second sentence, there are also two independent clauses. They are *Marla trimmed the hedge* and *Kiyo quit for the day*. In this sentence there are also two dependent clauses. They are *After the lawn was mowed* and *because it was late*.

Now look at the following two sentences. Find the complex sentence and the compound-complex sentence.

Whenever David mows a lawn, he also edges it and trims around the trees and shrubs.
After the three did such a good job on the yard, they deserved praise, and Mr. and Mrs. Tatara told them so.

Exercise A
Read each sentence and decide what kind of sentence it is. Underline your answer.

1. Since they started their DKM Lawn Service, the three have been busy five days of the week. (complex, compound-complex)

2. David suggested the service, and Kiyo and Marla were all for it when they heard his idea. (complex, compound-complex)

Exercise B
Read each sentence and decide what kind of sentence it is. Write *complex* or *compound-complex*.

1. In 1792 Whitney, who had just graduated from Yale, went to Georgia. _____

2. Whitney, who was mechanically minded since boyhood, was in Georgia only five days when he invented the cotton gin. _____

Grade Eight SkillBook, Grammar, Usage, and Mechanics

3. Because separating short-staple cotton from the seeds was difficult, a device that would make separation easier was needed. _____

4. Whitney put sawtooth disks on rollers that separated long-staple cotton, and this made the separation of short-staple cotton easier. _____

5. After the cotton gin became widely available, short-staple cotton became a profitable crop. _____

6. Whitney went back to Connecticut, where he opened a cotton-gin factory, but it was not a financial success. _____

7. The gin had a simple design, and after someone else saw it, Whitney expected competition. _____

8. Whitney sued his competitors, but when he finally won his case, he was deeply in debt. _____

Exercise C

Add one or more dependent clauses to each compound sentence to form a compound-complex sentence.

  Example: The rain poured down, and we had to huddle in a doorway.
  Answer: Just as we started for home, the rain poured down, and we had to huddle in a doorway.

9. The book was long and dull, but I read it.
_____

10. Dan played the song for Tina, and she liked it.
_____

11. Juanita did all the work, but she couldn't please them.
_____

12. The dancers were excellent, and the audience applauded loudly.
_____

13. Grandpa will shop for food, or maybe Aunt Ilona will do so.
_____

14. My favorite football team will play in the Rose Bowl, and I want success for them.
_____

Grade Eight SkillBook, Grammar, Usage, and Mechanics

Lesson 12
Adjective and Adverb Clauses

An adjective clause is a dependent clause that modifies a noun or pronoun. An adverb clause is a dependent clause that modifies a verb, adjective or another adverb.

A dependent clause that does the work of an adjective by modifying a noun or a pronoun is an **adjective clause**. Adjective clauses usually begin with words like *that*, *which*, *who*, *whom*, or *whose*, called **relative pronouns**. Study the sentences below.

>We hiked through the valley **that had been cultivated**.
>The fields, **which were a vivid green**, contained many crops.
>It was I **who suggested the hike**.

In the first sentence, the adjective clause *that had been cultivated* modifies the noun *valley*. In the second sentence, the adjective clause *which were a vivid green* modifies the noun *fields*. In the third sentence, the adjective clause *who suggested the hike* modifies the pronoun *I*.

Notice that no comma is used to set off the clause *that had been cultivated* in the first sentence. The clause is needed to tell which valley. In the second sentence, the clause *which were a vivid green* is set off by commas. It is not necessary to the basic meaning of the sentence, which is *The fields contained many crops*. In the third sentence, no comma is used because *who suggested the hike* is necessary information.

A dependent clause that modifies a verb is an **adverb clause**. Adverb clauses tell *how*, *when*, *where*, or *why* an action happened.

>Dana awakened [**before the winter sun rose**].
>She skated [**where her coach had told her**].
>She practiced daily [**because she wanted to become a champion**].

The adverb clause in each sentence tells about the action. Adverb clauses begin with **subordinating conjunctions**. Some of these are listed in the box at the side.

An adverb clause that begins a sentence is followed by a comma. Notice the punctuation in these sentences.

>Dana's coach watches her closely when she practices.
>When she practices, Dana's coach watches her closely.

Subordinating Conjunctions

after
although
as
because
before
if
since
though
unless
until
when
whenever
where
wherever
whether
while

Exercise A
Underline the adjective or adverb clause in each sentence.

1. Before he left, Tom closed and locked the window.

2. Leonard, who was with him, helped with the upstairs windows.

Grade Eight SkillBook, Grammar, Usage, and Mechanics

Exercise B

Underline the adjective or adverb clause in each sentence. Tell what kind of clause it is.

Example: When the clock struck six, Kenji started out.
Answer: <u>When the clock struck six</u>, Kenji started out.—adverb

1. Kenji hurried <u>because he was late</u>. _____
2. <u>As he approached the cemetery</u>, someone called his name. _____
3. He could think of no one <u>who might also be out this early</u>. _____
4. He peered into the shadows <u>that were cast by the tall trees</u>. _____
5. <u>Since he could see no one</u>, he continued on his way. _____
6. Suddenly a person <u>whom he recognized</u> came into view. _____
7. Kenji felt relieved <u>when he saw Martin</u>. _____
8. The two, <u>who were good friends</u>, walked along together. _____
9. They were going to band practice, <u>which was early today</u>. _____
10. <u>Before practice began</u>, the director handed out some new music. _____

Exercise C

Turn each simple sentence into a complex sentence by adding an adjective or adverb clause. Begin each clause with the relative pronoun or subordinating conjunction in parentheses.

Example: Sy joined the band. (when)
Answer: Sy joined the band when he transferred to our school.

11. The music contest was won by that girl. (who)

_____

_____

12. The restaurant used to be a bakery. (that)

_____

_____

13. We go to dinner there. (whenever)

_____

_____

14. A troupe of acrobats will entertain the picnickers. (after)

_____

_____

Lesson 13
Combining Sentences with Clauses

Use adjective and adverb clauses to combine sentences.

A string of simple sentences, especially short ones, can make your writing sound choppy. You can sometimes combine two such sentences by turning one of them into a clause. Read the following pairs of simple sentences.

> Lu read the manual. It told how to assemble the bike.
> Lu assembled the bike by herself. She is usually all thumbs.

These pairs of short sentences can be combined by making the second sentence in each an adjective clause introduced by a relative pronoun.

> Lu read the manual, **which told how to assemble the bike**.
> Lu, **who is usually all thumbs**, assembled the bike by herself.

In the first sentence, the relative pronoun *which* replaces the pronoun *It* from the second sentence in the first pair. The resulting adjective clause has been combined with the first sentence to form a complex sentence. Find the relative pronoun that replaces the pronoun *She* from the second sentence in the second pair.

Simple sentences can also be combined by making one sentence an adverb clause introduced by a subordinating conjunction. Study these examples.

> Lu read the directions.   **Before Lu assembled the bike**, she
> She assembled the bike.   read the directions.
>
> The assembly went fast.   The assembly went fast **because Lu**
> Lu followed the directions.   **followed the directions**.

In the first combined sentence, the subordinating conjunction *Before* is used to turn the second sentence into an adverb clause. Find the subordinating conjunction used to combine the second pair of simple sentences into a complex sentence.

Exercise A
Combine each sentence pair, using an adjective clause. Begin the clause with the relative pronoun *that*, *which*, *who*, or *whose*. Change wording as needed.

> **Example:** The book describes a utopia. I borrowed the book.
> **Answer:**   The book that I borrowed describes a utopia.

1. The word *utopia* comes from Greek words meaning "no place." It now means "ideal place."

_____

2. An ancient Greek book may have been the first tale of a utopia. Its author was Plato.

_____

Grade Eight SkillBook, Grammar, Usage, and Mechanics

3. Not all the people appreciated Plato's book. He wrote it for their improvement.

4. He wanted a land ruled by a king. The king was a philosopher.

5. Other books were written by Sir Thomas More and Voltaire. These books described utopias.

Exercise B

Combine each pair of sentences. Use the subordinating conjunction in parentheses to form an adverb clause. Set off any clause you place at the beginning of a sentence with a comma.

Example: We decided to take a vacation trip. The members of my family held a meeting. (when)

Answer: When we decided to take a vacation trip, the members of my family held a meeting.

6. We all wanted to go. We couldn't agree on where. (though)

7. Tony wanted to go to California. He wanted to try surfing. (because)

8. Allie was against the idea. She doesn't like water. (since)

9. No one else was very enthusiastic about a historic tour. Mom was all for it. (although)

10. We argued and argued. Dad got annoyed. (until)

Name _____ Class _____ Date _____

Lesson 14
Improving Sentences

Make your sentences clear and concise.

1. Place modifiers close to the words or phrases they modify. In each pair of sentences below, the first sentence contains a **misplaced modifier**; in the second sentence it has been placed next to the correct word.

> A farmer sold us a collie **who had gone to school with me**.
> A farmer **who had gone to school with me** sold us a collie.

> Dad decided that we should move **while watching the game**.
> **While watching the game**, Dad decided that we should move.

2. Make sure that items of equal importance in your sentences are balanced. This balance is called **parallel structure**. The second sentence in each pair has parallel structure.

> The speaker was **clear, calm,** and **gave an interesting talk**.
> The speaker was **clear, calm,** and **interesting**. (three adjectives)

> The ballet dancer moved **quickly** and **with grace**.
> The ballet dancer moved **quickly** and **gracefully**. (two adverbs)

3. Check your writing for **wordiness**—unnecessary repetition of words or ideas. The words in dark type make the sentence below wordy. These words should be deleted in the first two sentences. In the third, the words in dark type can be replaced with *because*.

> The **baby** puppies were brown **in color**.
> Marie was speechless **and couldn't say a word**.
> I am late **due to the fact that** I overslept.

Exercise A
Improve the sentences by making them parallel, by eliminating wordiness, or by repositioning the modifier.

> **Example:** Last summer in July we were invited to go to the Jaycee picnic.
> **Answer:** Last July we were invited to the Jaycee picnic.

1. There was food at the picnic that was frozen.

_____

2. The food and drinks were free and didn't cost anything.

_____

3. The day was sunny, hot, and it was humid.

_____

Grade Eight SkillBook, Grammar, Usage, and Mechanics

4. Some people sat in the shade and chatted and talked with each other.

5. The children and adults planned to play football while eating dessert.

6. A four-piece band played loudly and with energy.

7. I found a sheet of music that had been written by John Lennon under a tree.

8. The clowns were nimble, silly, and amused us.

9. People attended the picnic that came from all over.

10. The picnic is an annual event that is held every year.

Exercise B
On your paper rewrite the following paragraph, correcting misplaced modifiers, making words parallel, or deleting wordiness.

    The actor was tall, red-haired, and a homely person. His speaking voice was deep and low in pitch. He wore a brightly colored costume. While reciting soliloquies, several props were used by him. His character had an important effect on the audience who had a French accent. The character was boring, sarcastic, and a grouch. He bossed other characters around and told them what to say and do. Most of them spoke softly, hesitatingly, and with fear. When the play ended, the audience applauded loudly, rose to its feet, and gave the cast of actors a standing ovation.

Lesson 15
Expanding Sentences

Your sentences can become more interesting and exact when they are expanded with adjectives, adverbs, prepositional phrases, participial phrases, and appositives.

Read the first sentence below and the three expanded sentences that follow. Notice how each addition makes the original sentence more interesting and informative.

> Our team won.
> Our **energetic** team won.
> Our team won **easily**.
> Our **superior** team won **handily**.

Find the word that was added in the first expanded sentence. The adjective *energetic* modifies the noun *team*. Find the word that was added in the second expanded sentence. It modifies the verb *won*. Find the words that were added in the third expanded sentence. They modify the noun *team* and the verb *won*.

Prepositional phrases, participial phrases, and appositives can also be used to expand sentences. Read the expanded sentences below. Determine what kind of phrase is being used to expand each sentence.

> Our team won **in a remarkable finish**.
> Our team, **the current champions**, won.
> Our team, **outsmarting their opponents**, won.

Exercise A
Expand each sentence below by adding an adjective and an adverb.

> **Example:** A coach watched.
> **Answer:** A nervous coach watched anxiously.

1. The spectators cheered.

2. A player protested.

3. The guard hesitated.

4. Some cheerleaders shouted.

5. The whistle blew.

Grade Eight SkillBook, Grammar, Usage, and Mechanics

Name _____ Class _____ Date _____

Exercise B
Rewrite each sentence below, adding the kind of phrase in parentheses after the sentence. Underline the phrase.

Example: The game ended. (appositive)
Answer: The game, a furious battle, ended.

1. Many points were scored. (prepositional phrase)

2. Somebody slipped. (participial phrase)

3. The coach yelled. (appositive)

4. A cup spilled. (prepositional phrase)

5. The player shot. (participial phrase)

6. A guard dribbled. (participial phrase)

7. The center jumped. (prepositional phrase)

8. The buzzer sounded. (participial phrase)

Lesson 16
Appositives

An appositive is a noun or phrase that follows a noun and identifies or explains it. Appositives can be used to combine sentences.

A word or phrase that follows a noun to identify or explain it is an **appositive**. An appositive and its modifiers form an **appositive phrase**. Read these sentences.

> The world's busiest airport, **O'Hare**, is in Chicago.
> The Concorde, **a supersonic airliner**, flies from New York to Paris in three and a half hours.
> At the airport you will be met by Marty Baker, **your host**.

In the first sentence the noun *O'Hare* is an appositive that identifies the world's busiest airport. In the second sentence the phrase *a supersonic airliner* explains something about the Concorde. Find the appositive in the third sentence and the noun it explains.

Notice that when an appositive or an appositive phrase is in the middle of a sentence, it is set off by commas. An appositive at the end of a sentence takes only one comma.

You can use appositives to combine short, choppy sentences into longer, smoother sentences. Study these sentences.

> My dog has won prizes in dog shows all over the country. It is a terrier.
> My dog, **a terrier**, has won prizes in dog shows all over the country.

When an appositive is one word that is closely related to the preceding noun, it need not be set off by commas.

> My friend **Brian** has never flown in an airplane.

Exercise A
Underline the appositive phrase in each sentence once. Draw two lines under the noun that the appositive explains or identifies.

> **Example:** Our drama class wrote a play, *A Visit from Rion*.
> **Answer:** Our drama class wrote a play, *A Visit from Rion*.

1. The play is about the future, the year 2222.
2. It has two leading characters, Melody and Charley.
3. My brother David is playing a leading role.
4. Two other characters, Zelly and Rabo, are robots.
5. Zelly and Rabo live on the planet Rion.
6. The robots live in an underground city, their home on Rion.
7. They visit Charley and Melody in Omaha, a city in Nebraska.

Grade Eight SkillBook, Grammar, Usage, and Mechanics

Name _____ Class _____ Date _____

8. They arrive in a spaceship, a moon-powered craft.

9. The robots marvel at two pets, Sundae and Whiskers.

10. Charley's dog, a brown and white spaniel, is named Sundae.

Exercise B

Combine each pair of sentences into a single sentence with an appositive. Set off the appositive with a comma or commas.

Example: Lobsters live on ocean floors. They are hard-shelled animals.
Answer: Lobsters, hard-shelled animals, live on ocean floors.

11. Coastlines are homes of a strange animal. This strange animal is the spiny lobster.

12. A favorite food is cracked open by the lobster's claw. This favorite food is clams.

13. The lobster migration occurs in the fall. It is a curious sight.

14. The lobsters travel in a parade. It is an odd procession.

15. Scientists have organized SLURP. SLURP is the Spiny Lobsters Undersea Research Project.

Lesson 17
Identifying Nouns

A noun is a word that names a person, place, thing, or idea.

   engineer   Chicago   basketball   charity

The following clues will help you identify nouns.

- Many nouns are preceded by the articles *a*, *an*, and *the*. When you see an article in a sentence, you know a noun will soon follow. Study the example below.

The young artist painted **an** apple on **a** round table.

Nouns can be singular or plural. Study the examples.

Singular	**Plural**	
pig	pigs	Notice that some nouns change
glass	glasses	from singular to plural by adding
country	countries	*-s* or *-es*. Other nouns change their
fox	foxes	spellings when made plural. You
wolf	wolves	can use a dictionary to check the
child	children	spellings of plural nouns.

	Root Word	**+ Suffix**	**= Noun**
- Nouns may	attend	-ance	attendance
end with a	govern	-ment	government
noun-making	neighbor	-hood	neighborhood
suffix.	farm	-er	farmer
	act	-or	actor
	good	-ness	goodness

Exercise A
Underline the nouns in each sentence.

   Example: The rain stopped, and the sun broke through the clouds.
   Answer: The <u>rain</u> stopped, and the <u>sun</u> broke through the <u>clouds</u>.

1. We searched the sky and found a rainbow.
2. Its appearance gave the children great pleasure.
3. My little sister thinks that elves painted the rainbow.

Exercise B
Underline the nouns in each sentence.

1. I keep a scrapbook of photographs from my travels.
2. Each year my family travels to a different state.

Grade Eight SkillBook, Grammar, Usage, and Mechanics

3. We do months of research before we find a place.
4. Usually, Dad comes up with three or four suggestions.
5. By the end of spring, the family finds a place and makes reservations.
6. Then Mom writes to the bureau of tourism for information.
7. Places like Arizona and Utah always send lovely brochures.
8. Friends in some states have invited us to their houses.
9. Sometimes we pitch a tent at a campsite.
10. Two summers ago we rented a cabin along a lake.
11. In the previous year, the whole family got salmonella.
12. Last summer we visited our aunt in San Francisco.
13. We stayed at a large hotel near the bay.
14. My room looked out over the city.
15. The other room had a beautiful mural painted on the wall.
16. We toured the area for seven days.
17. My family saw old homes in interesting neighborhoods.
18. One day we rented bikes and rode to a landmark in the city.
19. That night we ate dinner at a restaurant.
20. I ate shrimp cooked in a delicious sauce.
21. Next year we will drive to the mountains.

Exercise C
Make nouns out of the words listed below by adding the suffixes shown.

22. -ance   disappear, accept, appear, avoid, annoy

23. -er   teach, sing, write, play, dance

24. -ness   sloppy, wild, happy, lazy, fond

25. -or   investigate, detect, govern, translate, accelerate

Name _____ Class _____ Date _____

Lesson 18
Kinds of Nouns

Proper nouns name particular persons, places, or things. All other nouns are common names. Nouns may also be categorized as concrete or abstract.

Nouns may be grouped as common or proper. **Common nouns** name something general—a *book*, a *student*, a *river*. **Proper nouns** name something specific—*A Tale of Two Cities*, *Maria*, the *Nile River*. Only proper nouns, or the most important words in them, begin with capital letters. Common nouns do not, unless they are used to begin a sentence. Find the common and proper nouns in the following sentences.

> **Robert Christy** took a **ship** to **London** to see *The Sound of Music*. **People** in his **family** have taken the *Queen Elizabeth* 2 before.

Nouns may also be grouped as concrete or abstract. A **concrete noun** names something you can see, hear, taste, touch, or smell.

> **Robert** heard the **concert** given by the **orchestra** on the **ship**.

An **abstract noun** names an idea, quality, or state of mind. It does not name something that can be experienced with the senses. Abstract nouns often end with such suffixes as *-ism*, *-ness*, *-tion*, *-ty*, and *-ance*.

> He felt **joy** and **happiness** at hearing them play with such **dedication**.

Joy, happiness, and dedication are things that are real, but you cannot see, hear, taste, touch, or smell them. These words are abstract nouns. Here are some other examples.

Concrete nouns
house, onion, music, bell

Abstract Nouns
idea, belief, goodness, fear

Exercise A
Write the common and proper nouns in each sentence.

> **Example:** Arthur Goldschmidt is an importer and exporter.
> **Answer:** **Common Nouns**   **Proper Nouns**
> importer, exporter   Arthur Goldschmidt

1. He travels to Guam and Korea in his plane, *The Eagle*.

   common nouns: _____

   proper nouns: _____

2. He buys and sells goods all over the world, including India.

   common nouns: _____

   proper nouns: _____

Grade Eight SkillBook, Grammar, Usage, and Mechanics

3. He speaks many languages in his business.

   common nouns: _____

   proper nouns: _____

4. People buy medicines from him in Africa and Europe.

   common nouns: _____

   proper nouns: _____

5. His journeys have taken him up the Amazon River.

   common nouns: _____

   proper nouns: _____

Exercise B
Write the concrete and abstract nouns in each sentence. You should find nine concrete and four abstract nouns in all.

1. The idea for a book of records was acclaimed by everyone.

   concrete nouns: _____

   abstract nouns: _____

2. The authors must have had some intelligence.

   concrete nouns: _____

   abstract nouns: _____

3. Their belief was that all records should be recognized.

   concrete nouns: _____

   abstract nouns: _____

4. Their book contains many facts, figures, and comments.

   concrete nouns: _____

   abstract nouns: _____

5. It has a fascination for many readers.

   concrete nouns: _____

   abstract nouns: _____

Lesson 19
Plural Nouns

A singular noun names one. A plural noun names more than one.

Most nouns are made plural by adding *-s* or *-es*. Some nouns are made plural by making a spelling change. Study the chart. If you have questions about other nouns, check a dictionary.

Most nouns: add -s.	shoe—shoes; clock—clocks valley—valleys; roof—roofs
Nouns ending in **s, x, ch, z, sh, ss**: add -es	box—boxes; waltz—waltzes gas—gases; wish—wishes match—matches; glass—glasses
Nouns ending in a consonant and **y**: change **y** to **i** and add -es.	city—cities; story—stories party—parties; lady—ladies (But: alley—alleys)
Nouns ending in vowel plus **o**: add -s. Nouns ending in consonant plus **o**: some add -s, some add -es, some add either.	radio—radios; tattoo—tattoos alto—altos; piano—pianos veto—vetoes; potato—potatoes tornado—tornadoes or tornados volcano—volcanoes or volcanos
Some nouns ending in **f** or **fe**: change **f** to **v** and add -es. Others: add -s. A few: add either. Nouns ending in **ff**: add -s.	elf—elves; leaf—leaves life—lives; knife—knives roof—roofs; chief—chiefs scarf—scarfs or scarves cuff—cuffs; sheriff—sheriffs
Compounds of more than one word: add -s or -es to the main word.	sister-in-law—sisters-in-law ten-year-old—ten-year-olds car pool—car pools
Nouns that change spelling: add or change letters. Nouns that do not change.	ox—oxen; child—children stimulus—stimuli; crisis-crises deer—deer; series—series

Exercise A
Write the plural of each of these nouns: *tax, dish, echo, loaf, workman.*

Exercise B
Write the plural form of each noun below.

    Example: leaf   **Answer:** leaves

Name _____ Class _____ Date _____

1. donkey _____
2. switch _____
3. car pool _____
4. library _____
5. tariff _____
6. sheep _____
7. hatbox _____
8. boss _____
9. veto _____
10. calf _____

11. basis _____
12. stereo _____
13. fox _____
14. stepson _____
15. roof _____
16. woman _____
17. goose _____
18. child _____
19. knife _____
20. ox _____

Exercise C

Underline each misspelled plural. Write the correct form of the misspelled plural on the line.

21. Our canarys sing us lovely choruss each morning. _____
22. His daughter-in-laws had more crisises than anyone else. _____
23. The clownes with umbrellaes kept us in stitchs. _____
24. Rowes of neat pansys stood in front of the mulberrys. _____
25. Workmans opened the boat's hatchs and unloaded its freight. _____
26. Both designers' studioes were filled with dress dummys. _____

Exercise D

Rewrite the sentences below, changing each noun in parentheses to its plural.

27. All (generation) have their (hero) and (ideal).

_____

28. (Statesman) and (stateswoman) are admired for leadership.

_____

29. Some people envy the (lifestyle) of (actor) and (actress).

_____

30. Television (personality) and (musician) have their (follower).

_____

Grade Eight SkillBook, Grammar, Usage, and Mechanics

Lesson 20
Possessive Nouns

Possessive nouns show ownership. They are formed with an apostrophe and the letter *s* ('s) or with only an apostrophe.

A **possessive noun** is used to tell who owns, or possesses, something. Possessive nouns end with an apostrophe and -*s* or just an apostrophe.

Possessive nouns modify nouns. They describe or limit the nouns they precede. Look at the following sentences.

> The **athlete's** medal was gold.
> The **coach's** pride was great.

The possessive noun *athlete's* modifies *medal* by telling whose medal it is—the medal of the athlete. It limits the noun *medal* to the one belonging to the athlete. Find the word that *coach's* modifies.

When you form possessive nouns, follow the three steps below.

- See if the noun ends in the letter *s*.
- Decide if the noun is singular or plural.
- Use the rule below that applies.

Singular Possessive Nouns
If the noun is singular, add -'s.
skater's award   **class's** trip   **James's** decision
Plural Possessive Nouns
If the noun is plural and ends in s, add only an apostrophe.
player's awards   **classes'** trip   **the Smiths'** house
If the noun is plural and does not end in s, add -'s.
women's victory   **children's** toys   **mice's** squeaks

The possessive forms of compound nouns follow similar rules. Note the singular and plural forms below.

my **brother-in-law's** team   singular—add **'s** to end of word
my **brothers-in-law's** team   plural, no **s** at end—add **'s** to end

Exercise

On the next page, write the possessive form of each noun in parentheses. Use the guide to help you.

Example: the (dog) tail
Answer: the dog's tail

Grade Eight SkillBook, Grammar, Usage, and Mechanics

Name _____ Class _____ Date _____

1. the (student) pencils _____
2. the (class) teacher _____
3. the (foxes) den _____
4. the (policemen) pants _____
5. an eighth (grader) writing _____
6. my (sister-in-law) visit _____
7. our (ponies) pasture _____
8. (Charles) life _____
9. the (birds) song _____
10. our (women) baseball team _____
11. my (family) celebration _____
12. the (girls) uniforms _____
13. a (cat) paw _____
14. the (victim) scream _____
15. the (astronauts) spaceship _____
16. the (Millers) homes _____
17. the (neighbor) dog _____
18. the (mayor) election _____
19. the (crowd) reaction _____
20. the (ships) crews _____
21. the (rockets) glare _____
22. that (gentleman) hat _____
23. the (babies) playpen _____
24. this (story) ending _____
25. the (deer) antlers _____

Name _____ Class _____ Date _____

Lesson 21
Plural or Possessive

An apostrophe is used to form the possessive of a noun. It is not used to form the plural of a noun.

You usually change the spellings of words to make them plural, and you always change their forms to make them possessive. These changes can be confusing. The chart shows the form changes of some nouns.

Nouns		Possessive Nouns	
Singular	Plural	Singular	Plural
diamond	diamonds	diamond's value	diamonds' value
fox	foxes	fox's den	foxes' dens
canary	canaries	canary's song	canaries' songs
woman	women	woman's group	women's group
knife	knives	knife's blade	knives' blades

Plurals and possessives sound alike. If you read the words *inventors*, *inventor's*, and *inventors'* aloud, the words sound exactly the same. But, they have different forms.

Possessive nouns are used to show ownership. Plural nouns are used to show more than one. Study the sentences below.

All the **inventors'** works were small.
One **inventor's** tools were custom-made.
The **inventors** were elves.

The possessive nouns *inventors'* and *inventor's* in the first two sentences show ownership. The plural noun *inventors* in the last sentence tells that there was more than one inventor.

Exercise A
Write whether the underlined word in each phrase is plural or possessive. Two are plural possessives.

Example: <u>singers'</u> voices
Answer: plural possessive

1. the <u>gardeners</u> dug _____

2. the <u>butcher's</u> coat _____

3. a <u>banker's</u> desk _____

4. the <u>explorer's</u> journey _____

5. the <u>clerks</u> lunched _____

Grade Eight SkillBook, Grammar, Usage, and Mechanics

6. the President's speech _____
7. the senators spoke _____
8. the students' demands _____
9. woman's club _____
10. sailor's boat _____
11. the athletes scored _____
12. my mother's hobby _____
13. the book's cover _____
14. the bands performed _____
15. the judges decided _____
16. the package's ribbon _____
17. the book club's offer _____
18. the swimmers' times _____
19. the car's tires _____
20. the radios blared _____

Exercise B

On your paper rewrite each sentence, correcting the mistake. Some plural nouns should be made possessive, and some possessives should be made plural.

Example: Archaeologists discoveries provide many surprises.
Answer: Archaeologists' discoveries provide many surprises.

1. Word's have fascinated people for centuries.
2. Not all words were written with letter's.
3. Some words meanings took years to understand.
4. An archaeologists job is understanding the past.
5. Archaeologists have studied ancient Egyptians writing.
6. The Egyptians influenced the Greeks way of writing.
7. The shapes of letter's in alphabets have changed.
8. Different languages' have different alphabets.
9. Some languages do not even have alphabets'.
10. Archaeologists' investigations' concern other things too.

Name _____ Class _____ Date _____

Lesson 22
Personal Pronouns

Personal pronouns are used in place of nouns that name persons, places, or things. The antecedent of a pronoun is the word or words to which the pronoun refers.

Personal pronouns stand for, or take the place of, nouns. They are used in sentences in the same place nouns would appear. The word (or words) to which a pronoun refers is called its **antecedent**. The antecedent may be either a noun or a noun and a pronoun.

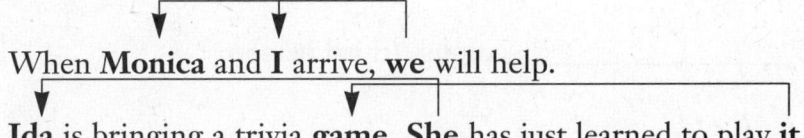

When **Monica** and **I** arrive, **we** will help.

Ida is bringing a trivia **game**. **She** has just learned to play **it**.

In the first sentence, the antecedents of the pronoun *we* are *Monica* and *I*. In the second sentence, the antecedent of *She* is *Ida*; the antecedent of *it* is *game*.

The chart below shows that personal pronouns have **number**; that means they can be singular or plural. It also shows that personal pronouns have **person**. They can be grouped according to first person (the speaker), second person (the one spoken to), or third person (the one spoken about).

	Singular	Plural
First person	I, me	we, us
Second person	you	you
Third person	he, she, it, him, her	they, them

Exercise A
Underline the personal pronouns once and their antecedents, twice.

1. Ana and Jean decided they would go hiking.
2. The girls invited Bob to join them.
3. Joel asked, "May I come too?"
4. Ana packed a lunch and brought it along.
5. Dom and I met the group and asked if we could accompany them.

Exercise B
Add a personal pronoun to each sentence. Use the person and number shown in parentheses for each pronoun.

Grade Eight SkillBook, Grammar, Usage, and Mechanics

Example: José and _____ went to wash the car. (first person, singular)
Answer: José and I went to wash the car.

1. I spoke up, "José, _____ will drive!" (first person, singular)

2. José insisted that _____ would drive. (third person, singular)

3. _____ tossed a coin to decide. (first person, plural)

4. _____ won and got behind the wheel. (third person, singular)

5. We met two pals and invited _____ along. (third person, plural)

6. The boys said _____ would help polish. (third person, plural)

7. José and I were glad they could help _____ (first person, plural)

8. Then _____ decided to wax the car. (first person, plural)

9. Our pals groaned as _____ worked. (third person, plural)

10. "_____ know, we should have walked." (second person, plural)

Exercise C
Circle the antecedent of each underlined personal pronoun.

Example: Our teachers say they will support Events Day.
Answer: teachers

11. Manny and Liz asked friends to join them in the sack race.

12. My friends and I think we will enter the downhill wagon race.

13. The race is dangerous because it is held on a steep hill.

14. If Bill and Jim enter, they must build a wagon.

15. If riders turn over, they are out of the race.

16. Rick believed that he would enter the potato race.

17. Rick's mother said she thought that event was safer.

18. Students from other schools may join us if they are invited.

19. Our principal said that she would invite one school this year.

20. Last year Oak School students were invited, and they attended.

Lesson 23
Possessive Pronouns

Personal pronouns have two possessive forms. These forms are used to show ownership, or possession.

Just as pronouns take the place of nouns, **possessive pronouns** take the place of possessive nouns. Notice the possessive pronouns in the sentences below.

> The motorcycle is in the **Jacksons'** garage.
> It is in **their** garage.
> The garage is **theirs**.

In the second sentence, *it* takes the place of *motorcycle* and *their* takes the place of *Jacksons'*. *Their* shows possession, or ownership. *Their* describes and limits the meaning of *garage*.

Now look at the pronoun *theirs* in the third sentence. It stands alone. *Theirs* is used to tell whose garage it is: the *Jacksons'*. *Their* is one possessive form and *theirs* is the other. *Theirs* has no apostrophe. Most other personal pronouns also have two possessive forms, as shown in the chart below.

Personal Pronouns	Possessive Forms	
I own this record.	It is **my** record.	It is **mine**.
We own this record.	It is **our** record.	It is **ours**.
You own this record.	It is **your** record.	It is **yours**.
He owns this record.	It is **his** record.	It is **his**.
She owns this record.	It is **her** record.	It is **hers**.
It owns this record.	It is **its** record.	
They own this record.	It is **their** record.	It is **theirs**.

Remember that personal pronouns do not use an apostrophe to show possession: *its* face (not *it's* face); it is *yours* (not it is *your's*).

Exercise A
Underline the possessive pronouns in these sentences. There are eight possessive pronouns in all.

1. Walter thought that his teacher was remarkable.
2. My teacher and his is Mr. Griffin, a professional weight lifter.
3. Our workouts are held in the basement of his family's house.
4. The weights are mine, but the basement is theirs.
5. What are some of your hobbies?

Grade Eight SkillBook, Grammar, Usage, and Mechanics

Name _____ Class _____ Date _____

Exercise B

Rewrite each sentence below twice. Use one possessive form in the first sentence and the other form in the second.

Example: Mickey and Janice own the building.
Answer: It is their building. The building is theirs.

6. Harold owns the shiny new folder.

   _____

7. Felice owns the fancy red notebook.

   _____

8. Molly and I own new yellow pencils.

   _____

9. You own the erasers.

   _____

10. Harold, Felice, and Molly own new book bags.

    _____

Exercise C

Complete each pair of sentences with the correct possessive form of the personal pronoun in parentheses.

Example: I bought a pair of skis. They are _____ (I).
Answer: I bought a pair of skis. They are <u>mine.</u>

11. The sports shop was crowded. _____ (It) customers had to wait.
12. We took a number. _____ (We) number was finally called.
13. Sally needs a new ski jacket. _____ (She) is worn out.
14. May had lent me some skis. But _____ (she) skis were way too short for me.
15. Skis should be the right height. Are _____ (you) skis right for you?
16. The clerk showed me some skis. They were just _____ (I) height.
17. My boots fit well. Do _____ (you)?
18. Sally and Joe bought matching jackets. _____ (They) are bright red.
19. They have blue hats. _____ (They) outfits are colorful.
20. The season starts soon. _____ (We) equipment is ready.

186   Grade Eight SkillBook, Grammar, Usage, and Mechanics

Lesson 24
Interrogative, Relative, and Demonstrative Pronouns

Interrogative pronouns introduce questions. Relative pronouns introduce groups of words that act as adjectives. Demonstrative pronouns point out persons or things.

The **interrogative pronouns** *who*, *whose*, *whom*, *which*, and *what* introduce questions. They always come at the beginning or close to the beginning of a sentence.

Who is at the door? **Whose** bicycle is outside?
What do you want? To **whom** do you wish to talk?
Which package is for me? **Who** sent this?

The **relative pronouns** *who*, *whose*, *whom*, *which*, and *that* introduce groups of words that act as adjectives. Notice how relative pronouns are used in the following sentences. Relative pronouns are in dark type.

The baseball game, [**which** we attended last night], was a cliffhanger.

Everyone [**who** watched] it felt the excitement.

The play [**that** decided the game] was brilliant.

The **demonstrative pronouns** *this*, *that*, *these*, and *those* point out persons or things. *This* and *these* refer to things near in time or place. *That* and *those* refer to things farther away. *This* and *that* are singular. *These* and *those* are plural.

This is Grover, and **that** is his house over there.
These are his parents, and **those** are his friends.

Exercise A
Underline the interrogative, relative, and demonstrative pronouns in each sentence.

1. Who gave you that?
2. Which of the vendors sold you these?
3. Any store that stocks this shouldn't be trusted.
4. These are too expensive for me.
5. I need a bike that is more in my price range.
6. To whom should I speak about my problem?

Grade Eight SkillBook, Grammar, Usage, and Mechanics

Name _____ Class _____ Date _____

Exercise B

Write whether the underlined pronouns are interrogative, relative, or demonstrative.

    Example: Who is the group's leader?
    Answer: Who is the group's leader?—interrogative

1. Which of the hikers was injured? _____
2. They tried to find their compass, which was lost. _____
3. Two boys searched for a trail that looked familiar. _____
4. Maria was the one who carried the map. _____
5. Who knew the reason that they were missing? _____
6. To whom did they tell their plans? _____
7. What could they do besides wait for help? _____
8. One of the boys found a path that he recognized. _____
9. Whose is that farmhouse at the end of the trail? _____
10. A man whom the hikers knew lived there. _____

Exercise C

Underline each interrogative, relative, and demonstrative pronoun in the sentences. Then write what kind each is.

    Example: Which is your favorite watercolor?
    Answer: Which is your favorite watercolor?—interrogative

11. This is very soft and delicate for an oil painting. _____
12. For whom are you buying the sketch? _____
13. Here is the canvas that won first prize. _____
14. Who painted the portraits of the royal family? _____
15. The artist who painted them does not want to sell. _____
16. Whose is the ink sketch of a sailboat? _____
17. Which do you think my sister would like? _____
18. Those are all made of fabric and string. _____
19. Have you looked at the drawings that are hanging upstairs? _____
20. What is the title of the large pastel drawing? _____

Lesson 25
Reflexive and Intensive Pronouns

A reflexive pronoun reflects the action back to the subject. An intensive pronoun intensifies, or emphasizes its antecedent.

Reflexive and intensive pronouns end in *-self* or *-selves*. Study the chart below showing the forms of these pronouns.

	Singular	Plural
1st person	myself	ourselves
2nd person	yourself	yourselves
3rd person	herself, himself, itself	themselves

Reflexive pronouns serve as mirrors or reflectors. They reflect the action of the verb back to the subject. Study these examples.

The picnickers helped **themselves.**

We were pleased with **ourselves.**

Sometimes we use a pronoun ending in *-self* or *-selves* to intensify, or emphasize, its antecedent. This pronoun is called an **intensive pronoun.** Look at these examples.

The coach **herself** set up the schedule.

Did he carry that box **himself**?

Remember these facts about reflexive and intensive pronouns.

- There are only eight reflexive and intensive pronouns. They are listed in the chart above. Never use incorrect forms like *hisself, ourself, theirself,* or *theirselves.*
- Reflexive and intensive pronouns should not be used in place of personal pronouns. (Not: Joe and **myself** went. But: Joe and **I** went.)

Exercise A
Write whether the underlined pronoun in each sentence is intensive or reflexive.

Example: Have you read that Dr. Jane Goodall <u>herself</u> did much of the chimpanzee research in Tanzania?
Answer: intensive

Grade Eight SkillBook, Grammar, Usage, and Mechanics

Name _____ Class _____ Date _____

1. Dr. Goodall began the important work almost by <u>herself</u>. _____
2. Dr. Louis S. B. Leakey <u>himself</u> gave her his support in the study of primates. _____
3. Dr. Leakey knew <u>himself</u> well enough to know he would love his work. _____
4. They prided <u>themselves</u> on their findings about primates. _____
5. If you students were to visit Gombe Stream, you might find <u>yourselves</u> among fifty or more chimpanzees. _____
6. A mother chimp occupies <u>herself</u> taking care of her baby until it is five or six years old. _____
7. The father does not care for it <u>himself</u> during its infancy. _____
8. You would find chimps of all ages living together, sharing food among <u>themselves</u>. _____
9. Dr. Goodall <u>herself</u> patiently studied the chimps. _____
10. They <u>themselves</u> knew the chimps as well as humans can. _____

Exercise B
Complete each sentence with the correct pronoun.

Example: Sue took the bracelet and thanked Jack _____.
(herself, itself)
Answer: Sue took the bracelet and thanked Jack <u>herself</u>.

1. He had designed the bracelet _____. (hisself, himself)
2. Tom and _____ gave it to the cat. (I, myself)
3. The cat chewed it up before cleaning _____. (itself, theirselves)
4. We couldn't forgive _____ for letting that happen. (ourself, ourselves)
5. Jack said he _____ would repair the bracelet. (himself, hisself)
6. He told Tom and _____ that the accident was our fault. (myself, me)
7. We promised _____ to be more careful. (ourself, ourselves)
8. We would make Tom a present _____. (ourself, ourselves)
9. I asked _____ what we could make for him. (me, myself)
10. Finally, Tom _____ said he would like a new keychain. (hisself, himself)

Name _____ Class _____ Date _____

Lesson 26
Indefinite Pronouns

An indefinite pronoun may or may not have a stated antecedent. Indefinite pronouns may be singular or plural.

The word *indefinite* means "vague, not certain." A pronoun that may refer to a noun but does not have a stated antecedent is called an **indefinite pronoun**. Notice the pronouns in dark type in the sentences below.

> The firefighters battled the blaze with courage, but **many** of them realized the building was doomed.
> **Everyone** suspected the fire had been set.

In the first sentence the indefinite pronoun *many* refers to its antecedent, *firefighters*. But the pronoun does not tell you how many firefighters realized the building was doomed. In the second sentence there is no antecedent for the indefinite pronoun *Everyone*.

Indefinite pronouns can be singular or plural. Some of the most commonly used indefinite pronouns are shown in the chart below.

Indefinite Pronouns		
Singular		Plural
another	neither	many
anybody	nobody	both
anyone	no one	few
anything	one	others
each	other	several
either	somebody	
everybody	someone	
everyone	something	
everything		

Some pronouns—*all, any, most, none,* and *some*—can be either singular or plural, depending on how they are used.

Exercise A
Underline the indefinite pronoun once and its antecedent twice.

Example: Buyers flocked to the flea market. Many bought expensive items.
Answer: <u><u>Buyers</u></u> flocked to the flea market. <u>Many</u> bought expensive items.

1. Antiques sell fast. Several are very expensive.

2. Old comic books are hot items too. Few are left.

Grade Eight SkillBook, Grammar, Usage, and Mechanics

3. I bought two books and enjoyed both.

4. My parents bought a vase, but neither really liked it.

5. Kevin and George found an old phonograph. Both wanted it.

6. Two more phonographs were there. Neither worked very well.

7. The buyers were anxious. All of them were looking around.

8. Kevin found two dictionaries. Each of them was very old.

9. Six books were nearly falling apart. Others, though, were new.

10. The new books were in boxes. Several were best sellers.

11. I bought two books. Both should be quite interesting.

12. I found a bookmark in a book. Something like that is priceless.

13. My friends are attending this show next week. Everyone is excited about all the antiques.

14. There is always a large crowd there, but everybody always sees a familiar face.

15. The variety is amazing. Everything looks interesting to me.

16. My mother looked at the teacups. She could buy only one.

17. She looked at the cups again. Many of them were beautiful.

18. I looked at the candlesticks. Few of them were what I wanted.

19. One booth sold antique radios. I found many that were more than fifty years old.

20. Depression glass plates are lovely. I bought several.

Exercise B

Underline the indefinite pronoun in each sentence and write whether it is singular or plural.

Example: Many of the students have junk to sell.
Answer: <u>Many</u> of the students have junk to sell.—plural

1. Several of the booths are open. _____

2. Everyone comes early for bargains. _____

3. Anybody who is in school is welcome. _____

4. Each of the sellers has marked-down items. _____

5. Many of the buyers appreciate a bargain. _____

Lesson 27

Subject and Object Pronouns

Personal pronouns can be in either the nominative case or the objective case.

The different forms of pronouns are called **cases.** When a pronoun is the subject of a sentence, it is in the **nominative case** and is called a **subject pronoun.** When a pronoun is used as a direct object, an indirect object, or the object of a preposition, it is in the **objective case** and is called an **object pronoun.**

Singular Pronouns		Object Pronouns	
Singular	Plural	Singular	Plural
I	we	me	us
you	you	you	you
he, she, it	they	him, her, it	them

Mark is a salesman. **He** travels a good deal. (subject)
He takes **us** along sometimes. (direct object)
He sends **them** post cards. (indirect object)
He also sends post cards to **her.** (object of a preposition)

When a single pronoun is used as a subject or object, people seldom have problems knowing which form to use. People do have problems using pronouns in a compound subject or object.

Mark and (**I, me**) like traveling.

When you are unsure which pronoun form to use in a compound subject or object, try the pronoun alone in the sentence. For example, if you say the sentence above without *Mark and*, your ear will tell you that *I* is the correct form to use—*Mark and I.*

Use the "pronoun alone" test to determine which forms are correct in the other three sentences above.

Exercise A
Underline the correct form of the pronoun in parentheses.

Example: Kiku and (he, him) have started a newspaper.
Answer: Kiku and (<u>he</u>, him) have started a newspaper.

1. Sue and (I, me) are reporters.

2. We asked Tom and (they, them) about their plans.

3. We get our news from the neighbors and (they, them).

4. (She, Her) and Li will edit the paper.

5. (We, Us) and Kiku will get the paper typed and copied.

6. The advertising will be handled by Li and (we, us).

Grade Eight SkillBook, Grammar, Usage, and Mechanics

Name _____ Class _____ Date _____

7. You can send classified ads to Sam and (she, her).

8. The editorials will be written by Kiku and (I, me).

9. We put Herb and (he, him) in charge of photography.

10. (She, Her) and Pat can write the headlines.

11. (He, Him) and Tom will deliver the papers.

12. (They, Them) and the neighbors have hopes for our success.

13. Send your advertising to (he, him) by the tenth of the month.

14. Design will be handled by my brother and (she, her).

15. (They, them) have already designed a sample copy.

16. We know we can trust (they, them) with the design.

17. I have never designed a paper, but (they, them) have.

18. Because I have reported before, you can trust (I, me) with that.

19. Some neighbors have said they would support (we, us).

20. We will not disappoint (they, them).

Exercise B
Underline the correct form of the pronoun in parentheses.

1. The Brands and (we, us) are going on vacation together.

2. It will be a lot of fun for (they, them) and (we, us).

3. (We, Us) and (they, them) enjoy doing things together.

4. Their son Tony and (I, me) are good friends.

5. (He, Him) and (I, me) will be the navigators.

6. New York City will be a new experience for (he, him) and (I, me).

7. Mom will take my sister and (I, me) to the art museum with Mrs. Brand and (she, her).

8. (She, Her) and my sister Gen are both painters.

9. I sometimes paint with Gen and (she, her).

10. (She, Her) and Mr. Brand also want to go to Philadelphia.

11. We'll go to Independence Hall and the Betsy Ross House with Tony and (they, them).

12. (They, Them) and (I, me) like to visit historical places.

13. (We, Us) look for historical places wherever we are.

14. Last year Dad took Gen and (I, me) to Plymouth Rock.

15. (He, Him) showed us the Puritan village there, too.

194 Grade Eight SkillBook, Grammar, Usage, and Mechanics

Lesson 28
Pronouns as Subject Complements

A subject pronoun is used as a subject complement.

A word that follows a linking verb and identifies the subject is called a **subject complement**. A pronoun that follows a linking verb such as *am, is, are, was,* or *were* and renames the subject is called a **predicate pronoun**. Study the pronouns in dark type.

She is the doctor. The doctor is **she**.
Bess and **I** are friends. Her friends are Bess and **I**.

In the sentences at the left, the subject complement *doctor* identifies the subject *She*, and the subject complement *friends* identifies the subject *Bess and I*. Since the subjects and subject complements refer to the same people, the sentences can be turned around as they are on the right without changing the meaning. The same pronoun forms—subject pronouns—are used as subjects and as subject complements.

A special case is the answer to the question "Who is it?" In informal situations, when talking to family or friends, you would most likely answer "It's me" or "It is me." This usage is acceptable in everyday conversation. But in writing or in formal speech, for example, say "It is I." In both formal and informal English, only subject pronouns are used in sentences like "It is she," "This is he," "It was we."

Exercise A
Underline the correct form of the pronoun in parentheses to use in formal situations.

1. It was (she, her) who won the contest.
2. It was (I, me) who came in second.
3. They congratulated Vinnie and (I, me).
4. It was (they, them) who congratulated us.
5. Then we all sang a victory song beginning with the words "We are champions, champions are (we, us)."

Exercise B
Write the answer to each question below. Use a pronoun in each sentence that is correct in formal situations.

    Example: OWNER: Who is Sherlock Holmes?
                   HOLMES: I am _____.
    Answer: I am he.

1. OWNER: Did my greedy nephew steal the jewels?

   HOLMES: It was not _____.

Grade Eight SkillBook, Grammar, Usage, and Mechanics

2. OWNER: Did the butler steal them?
   HOLMES: It couldn't have been _____.
3. OWNER: Did the maids steal them?
   HOLMES: It was definitely not _____.
4. OWNER: Did the detectives from your department steal them?
   HOLMES: It certainly wasn't _____.
5. OWNER: Did you steal them for the insurance money?
   HOLMES: I confess; it was _____.

Exercise C
Decide whether a subject or object pronoun is needed. Underline the pronoun that completes the sentence correctly.

Example: The host of the party was (he, him).
Answer: The host of the party was (<u>he</u>, him).

6. Albert invited Jack and (I, me) to the party at the farm.
7. It was (he, him) who thought of having the party there.
8. (He, Him) and his friends prepared most of the food.
9. The best cooks were Jack and (I, me).
10. It was (we, us) who made the salad and baked beans.
11. Albert took Jack and (I, me) horseback riding.
12. The first one to ride was (I, me).
13. Albert and (I, me) did just fine, but not Jack.
14. It was (he, him) who said not to be afraid.
15. Jack told (we, us) that horseback riding was easy.
16. It was (he, him) who claimed the horses were safe to ride.
17. It was (we, us) who had the frisky horses, not Jack.
18. Yet it was (he, him) who fell off the horse.
19. The luckiest of the riders was (I, me).
20. The sorest and most bruised was (he, him).
21. There (he, him) was, rubbing his wrist.
22. It must have hurt (he, him) very much.
23. "(I, me) am not as great a rider as you are," he said.
24. "The horse threw (I, me) before I knew what had happened."
25. "It was (I, me) who learned a lesson today!"

196 Grade Eight SkillBook, Grammar, Usage, and Mechanics

Lesson 29
Pronouns in Comparisons

Both subject and object pronouns can be used in incomplete comparisons.

Comparisons that begin with *than* or *as* followed by a pronoun are often incomplete comparisons. You must complete the comparisons before you can determine the appropriate pronouns to express your meaning. How might the following comparisons be completed?

> Hank can't swim as far as **she**.
> My Aunt Hillary is older than **I**.

The comparisons could be completed as follows.

> Hank can't swim as far as **she can (swim)**.
> My Aunt Hillary is older than **I am (old)**.

In the first sentence, the pronoun *she* is the subject of the verb in the clause *as far as she can swim*. In the second sentence, the pronoun *I* is the subject of the verb in the clause *than I am old*.

Pronouns can also function as objects in comparisons.

> The shirt looks better on José than **me**.
> The comparison would be completed as follows.
> The shirt looks better on José than **it looks on me**.

In this sentence the pronoun *me* is the object of the preposition *on* in the clause *than it looks on me*.

Sometimes the intended meaning of a sentence determines whether a subject or object pronoun is used. Read these sentences.

> Sasha knows Rick better than **we**.
> Sasha knows Rick better than **us**.

Both sentences are correct, but they are different in meaning.

> Sasha knows Rick better than **we know Rick**.
> Sasha knows Rick better than **Sasha knows us**.

In the first sentence, the pronoun *we* is the subject of the clause *than we know Rick*. What is the pronoun *us* in the second sentence?

Exercise A
Write the words on the line that show how you could complete the comparisons.

1. Sasha helped José more than I. _____

2. Sasha helped José more than me. _____

3. Fran is as good a dancer as he. _____

4. Lee annoyed Pat as much as us. _____

Grade Eight SkillBook, Grammar, Usage, and Mechanics

Exercise B
Underline the correct pronoun to complete each sentence.

Example: Few people swim faster than (she, her).
Answer: Few people swim faster than (<u>she</u>, her).

1. The high-school swim club practices as much as (they, them).
2. Coach Penn works more with Crista than with (I, me).
3. After swimming fifty laps, Jay was more tired than (we, us).
4. Sid will have to swim as fast as (he, him).
5. Sharon likes to dive more than (I, me).
6. Joe thinks that everyone is a better swimmer than (he, him).
7. More points were awarded to Nona than (she, her).
8. Ian has a much stronger stroke than (he, him).
9. Everyone wants to swim against Jessie rather than (she, her).
10. Do the junior swimmers get more practice time than (we, us)?

Exercise C
Read each sentence. Write *correct* if the pronoun comparison is correct. Rewrite the sentences that have mistakes, correcting the pronoun used in the comparison.

Example: Michael sent more letters to Dan than to I.
Answer: Michael sent more letters to Dan than to me.

11. I got more birthday cards than he.
_____
_____

12. Jerry likes to write letters more than I.
_____
_____

13. My sister Diana makes more telephone calls than me.
_____
_____

14. She talks on the telephone as much as him.
_____
_____

15. I don't talk as long as her.
_____
_____

Name _____ Class _____ Date _____

Lesson 30
Using *who* and *whom*

Who is generally used as a subject. Whom is used as a direct object or object of a preposition.

Who and *whom* are often misused. By studying a sentence, you can tell which pronoun form should be used in the sentence.

Who made the largest pizza?
The baker **who** made it lives in my town.

In each sentence above, *who*, the subject form, is used. In the first example, it is the subject of the sentence. In the second, *who* is the subject of the clause *who made it*.

The pronoun *whom* may be used as a direct object or as an object of a preposition, such as *for*, *from*, *to*, or *with*.

Whom do we thank for this delicious meal?
That is the woman **whom** I notified.
To **whom** did you speak on the telephone?

In the first sentence *whom* is used as direct object of the verb *do thank* (we do thank *whom*). In the second sentence *whom* is used as a direct object of the verb *notified*. In the third sentence *whom* is the object of the proposition *to*. Now read the following sentences. Notice how *who* and *whom* are used in these sentences.

Who went to the play?   **Whom** did they visit yesterday?
Those **who** went enjoyed it.   With **whom** did you come?

In everyday conversation you will sometimes hear *who* used in place of *whom*, especially at the beginning of questions. But in writing and formal speech, *who* should be used as a subject, and *whom* should be used as a direct object or object of a preposition, no matter where in a sentence it appears.

Exercise A
How is *who* or *whom* used in each sentence? Write *subject*, *subject of clause*, *direct object*, or *object of preposition* for each underlined word.

1. From <u>whom</u> did you get the silver bracelet? _____
2. My aunt <u>who</u> lives in Mexico sent it. _____
3. <u>Who</u> could have sent you the message in secret code? _____
4. <u>Whom</u> do you suspect? _____

Exercise B
Read each of the sentences on the next page. Decide if *who* or *whom* is used correctly in each sentence. If it is used incorrectly, rewrite the sentence.

Grade Eight SkillBook, Grammar, Usage, and Mechanics

Example: Whom wrote the letter?
Answer: Who wrote the letter?

1. Who bought the birthday present? _____
2. With who did you play softball? _____
3. His father taught whom? _____
4. Who was the first President of the United States? _____
5. Whom is coming to the meeting? _____

Exercise C
Complete each sentence, using *who* or *whom*. Tell how the pronoun is used in the sentence.

Example: She is the person _____ wrote the hit song.
Answer: She is the person <u>who</u> wrote the hit song.—subject of clause

6. With _____ did you go to the music awards? _____
7. _____, in your judgment, was the best singer? _____
8. Davey Sanchez, _____ wrote "Ballad for L. A.," was best. _____
9. Wilma preferred Karen Ching, _____ sang "My Side." _____
10. To _____ was the prize for best song awarded? _____
11. I also liked Jay King, _____ Wilma praised. _____
12. His songs are often sung by the Valdez Brothers, _____ are young Mexican-Americans from Fresno. _____
13. _____ did most people like best? _____
14. _____ sings better than Vera and Jay King? _____
15. Aren't they the ones _____ won the most awards last year? _____
16. Jay gave his gold records to his parents, _____ are delighted. _____
17. _____ can blame them for being pleased? _____
18. _____ did you really prefer? _____
19. I agreed with the judges, with _____ I usually disagree. _____
20. He was the one _____ I would vote for too. _____

Grade Eight SkillBook, Grammar, Usage, and Mechanics

Lesson 31
Pronoun Agreement

A pronoun should agree with its antecedent.

An antecedent is the word to which a pronoun refers. Read the sentences below.

Kay returned **her** books to the library.
Andy completed **his** homework before dinner.
Kiku and Les returned **their** books to the library.

In the first sentence the singular pronoun *her* is feminine and agrees with its antecedent, *Kay*. Find the antecedents of the pronouns in the second and third sentences. Notice if they are singular or plural.

Read the following sentence. Think of a pronoun to complete it.

Before a person signs a contract, _____ should read it.

In formal English the pronoun *he* or *she*, not *they* or *you*, is used. Some people use the phrase *he or she* or *she or he*. To avoid too much repetition, however, the sentence might be rewritten.

Before people sign contracts, they should read them.

Singular indefinite pronouns like *anyone*, *each*, *either*, and *someone* must agree with other pronouns in the sentence that refer to the same person.

Each of the boys paid **his** dues promptly. (Not: their dues)
Neither of the girls did **her** lessons. (Not: their lessons)

In the first sentence *each* is singular and agrees with *his*. What are the pronouns in the second sentence? Why is the pronoun *her* singular?

Plural indefinite pronouns like *few*, *several*, and *both* must also agree in number with other pronouns that refer to the same persons.

Both of the construction workers wore **their** helmets.
Several of the women drive **their** cars to work each day.

In each of the above sentences, the indefinite pronouns are plural; therefore, the plural form *their* is used.

Exercise A
Underline the correct pronoun or pronouns in each sentence.

1. Authors want (his, their) works to be widely read.
2. Michele Sim wants (her, their) client's work published.
3. Publishers produce books (he, they) can sell.
4. Kristy Lee often helps publicize (her, their) own books.
5. Each reader knows what books (he or she, they) will enjoy.

| Name | Class | Date |

6. Librarians buy books (his, their) towns will read.

7. Neither of the boys brought (his, their) own book to read.

8. Did either of the students write (his or her, their) own story?

9. Several of the women wrote (her their) autobiographies.

10. Not one of the boys had finished (his, their) story.

Exercise B

In the sentences below, find and correct the errors in pronoun agreement. Write the sentence on the line. If the sentence is correct, write *correct*.

Example: Each of the men cleaned their camera lens.
Answer: Each of the men cleaned his camera lens.

1. Neither of the girls wants their picture taken.

2. When everyone arrived, they began work on the mural.

3. All of the boys are trying out for their class play.

4. Each typist was rated on their speed and accuracy.

5. Someone in this line has asked for his money back.

Lesson 32
Identifying Verbs

Action verbs tell what action is taking place. Linking verbs join the subject to a word or words in the predicate.

In a sentence, a **verb** either expresses action or it links the subject to a word or words in the predicate. An **action verb** tells what action is taking place and can show either physical or mental action.

> The jogger **ran** around the block.
> The girl **remembered** her appointment book.

In the first sentence, the action verb *ran* shows physical action. In the second sentence, the action verb *remembered* shows mental action.

A **linking verb** does not show action; it joins a word or words in the predicate to the subject. Some of the more common linking verbs are forms of *be: am, are, is, was, were*. Other linking verbs include *seem, appear, feel, look, taste, smell, sound,* and *become*.

Notice how the linking verbs are used in these sentences.

> Mr. Boda **is** a baker.   Mr. Boda **is** successful.
> His doughnuts **taste** delicious.   His bread **smells** fresh.

Exercise A
Underline each verb and write whether it shows action or is a linking verb.

1. Ned bought tickets for the baseball game. _____
2. He was a fan of the Jersey Jaguars. _____
3. The Jaguars won all their games last year. _____
4. Now they appeared ready for another successful season. _____

Exercise B
Underline the action verb of each sentence and tell whether it expresses a mental or physical action.

> **Example:** Henry dreamed of being the fastest runner in his school.
> **Answer:** Henry <u>dreamed</u> of being the fastest runner in his school.—mental action

1. A year ago he ran last in his division. _____
2. He thought about his goal for this year. _____
3. During the summer he jogged every day. _____
4. He remembered his poor physical condition last year. _____
5. He and his teammates participated in daily workouts. _____

Grade Eight SkillBook, Grammar, Usage, and Mechanics

6. Sometimes they swam as a part of their conditioning. _____
7. Soon Henry noticed an improvement in his speed. _____
8. He cut several seconds off last year's time. _____
9. The coach marveled at Henry's improvement. _____
10. This fall the team raced against some stiff competition. _____

Exercise C
Underline the action verbs once and the linking verbs twice.

   Example: The *Odyssey* is a great poem. Homer created it long ago.
   Answer: The *Odyssey* is a great poem. Homer created it long ago.

11. Its hero Odysseus started on his voyage home from Troy.
12. He was also a great Greek warrior like Achilles.
13. Odysseus's voyage home to Greece seemed simple enough.
14. In the end, Odysseus journeyed over twenty years.
15. Some of Odysseus's adventures were dreadful.
16. One time, he endured the unearthly screams of the Sirens.
17. Their irresistible cries almost drove him mad.
18. His men tied him to the mast of the boat for his own sake.
19. Another time, his party wandered into the giant Cyclops's cave.
20. The eye in the middle of the giant's head looked monstrous.
21. He trapped the men with a boulder in the cave's entrance.
22. Then he hungrily devoured two of the men.
23. The rest of the crew were afraid for their lives.
24. However, the clever Odysseus was calm as always.
25. He quickly thought of a clever escape.
26. Odysseus tricked the Cyclops with a powerful liquid.
27. Within a short time, the Cyclops felt sleepy.
28. Then they blinded the sleeping giant with a fiery stake.
29. The furious Cyclops searched in vain for the men.
30. The next day, Odysseus and his men escaped to their ship.

Name _____ Class _____ Date _____

Lesson 33
Action or Linking Verb

Some verbs can be either action verbs or linking verbs.

You may sometimes have trouble deciding whether the verb in a sentence is an action verb or a linking verb. A good test is to replace the verb with a form of *be*. If the sentence still makes sense, the verb you've replaced is probably a linking verb.

   Lucia **looks** restless during the play.

   Can *looks* be replaced by *is* without destroying the meaning? The answer is yes. In this sentence *looks* is a linking verb. It joins *Lucia* to *restless*—a word in the predicate that describes her. Now consider the word *looks* in the sentence below.

   Lucia **looks** for her books each morning.

   In this sentence, *looks* cannot be replaced by *is*. Here *looks* is an action verb. It describes an action performed by Lucia.

   Some verbs can be used as either linking or action verbs. Some common verbs of this kind are *look, feel, appear, grow, smell, remain, become, sound,* and *taste.* Notice how some of these verbs are used in the chart below.

Action verbs	Linking verbs
The child **looked** at the watch.	The child **looked** curious.
He **felt** the glass mirror.	It **felt** cold and hard.
Suddenly a figure **appeared**.	The child **appeared** anxious.
The figure **grew** in size.	He **grew** more curious.
He **smelled** the air.	It **smelled** sweet.
He **tasted** the salt water.	It **tasted** terrible.

Exercise A
Underline the verbs in the sentences, and write whether they are action verbs or linking verbs.

   Example: We tasted their coffee cake.
   Answer: We <u>tasted</u> their coffee cake.—action

   Example: It tasted better than ours.
   Answer: It <u>tasted</u> better than ours.—linking

   1. Ann looked ill. _____

   2. She felt a pain in her side. _____

   3. Ann's mother looked at her. _____

   4. Ann appeared pale. _____

   5. Ann smelled the medicine. _____

Grade Eight SkillBook, Grammar, Usage, and Mechanics

Name _____ Class _____ Date _____

6. It smelled strange. _____

7. She tasted it cautiously. _____

8. Soon Ann felt better. _____

Exercise B
Underline the verbs in the sentences, and write whether they are action verbs or linking verbs.

1. This probably sounds a little strange. _____
2. I never feel lazy about one kind of errand. _____
3. One time mother felt too busy for a visit to the bakery. _____
4. This errand remains my favorite. _____
5. The aroma of freshly baked bread smells wonderful to me. _____
6. I even smelled it blocks away from the bakery. _____
7. I grew more ravenous by the minute. _____
8. Soon I felt hunger pangs in my stomach. _____
9. Finally, I appeared in front of the shop. _____
10. It looked busier than usual. _____
11. I remained calm nevertheless. _____
12. I looked for some standing room near the counter. _____
13. I remained close to the door with my number in my hand. _____
14. My anticipation grew because of the long wait. _____
15. Finally, my number sounded above the noisy voices. _____
16. The clerk looked at me curiously. _____
17. She appeared very friendly, however. _____
18. I felt in my pocket for my money. _____
19. I remained there long enough for my order. _____
20. Once outside the door, I looked into my bag. _____
21. The rolls still felt warm from the oven. _____
22. They smelled delicious. _____
23. I tasted one with a buttery crust. _____
24. It tasted moist and rich. _____
25. I looked into the bag often. _____
26. The rolls looked better with each step. _____

Grade Eight SkillBook, Grammar, Usage, and Mechanics

Name _____ Class _____ Date _____

Lesson 34
Verb Phrases

A verb phrase contains a main verb and one or more auxiliary, or helping, verbs.

The **main verb** tells what is happening. It is always the last word in the verb phrase. The **auxiliary verb** or verbs precede the main verb and help it express meaning and tense. Study the verb phrases below.

Alan **had bought** his equipment weeks ago.
He **might have been watching** for sales before that time.

Here are some of the most commonly used auxiliary verbs. Some of these verbs may be used alone, as main verbs.

Auxiliary Verbs
do, does, did, have, has, had
am, are, is, was, were, be, being, been
can, could, will, would, shall, should, must, may, might

We **are** happy. (*Are* is the main verb.)
We **are** singing. (*Are* is an auxiliary verb.)

In a statement, one or more auxiliary verbs may come before the main verb. Sometimes the auxiliary verb is separated from the main verb by an adverb or adverbial phrase. In a question, the auxiliary verb usually comes first and is separated from the main verb by a subject.

Statement: She **is teaching** history.
Statement: She **is** still **teaching** history.
Question: **Is** she **teaching** history?

Exercise A
Underline the verb phrase in each sentence.

1. Al had climbed that mountain before.

2. Al has been climbing for four years.

3. He will soon climb a new mountain.

Exercise B
Underline the verb phrase in each sentence.

Example: Do you enjoy the outdoors?
Answer: <u>Do</u> you <u>enjoy</u> the outdoors?

Grade Eight SkillBook, Grammar, Usage, and Mechanics

1. Our class will soon be going on a nature walk.
2. We may hike through Jensen Nature Preserve this time.
3. Several teachers might lead us.
4. Mr. Hilton has been a well-known naturalist for many years.
5. His nature tours should interest us.
6. Can we join his group?
7. Bird watchers should have registered with Ms. Dee's tour.
8. Does she know all of the nesting areas?
9. Many rare birds have been seen on her tour.
10. Would you bring your field glasses with you?
11. Fiona McGee is lecturing on wildflowers again.
12. Her lecture will take about thirty minutes.

Exercise C

Underline each auxiliary verb once and each main verb twice.

   Example: Have you ever gone to the mountains?
   Answer: Have you ever gone to the mountains?

13. Mountaineering could eventually grow in popularity.
14. The conquest of Mt. Everest in 1953 may well have increased interest in the sport.
15. Climbers have now reached the summit dozens of times.
16. The Nabisco Wall has always been regarded as Mt. Everest's most difficult face.
17. Bad weather has often caused trouble for climbers.
18. They must surely be conditioned properly for the task.
19. One man had actually fallen over one mile without injury!
20. Climbers should always use the best gear available.
21. Experts would never climb alone either.
22. Did you hear about the Mt. Everest skier?
23. Luckily for him, he did not kill himself!
24. Most people can hardly imagine a five-mile-high mountain.
25. Someone might possibly be climbing it right now.

Lesson 35
Simple Tenses

Verbs have simple present, past, and future tenses.

The **tense** of a verb helps to tell the time something takes place. Both action and linking verbs have tenses. The **simple tenses** of a verb are the present, past, and future tense.

Look at the forms of the simple tenses in this chart.

Present Tense	Past Tense	Future Tense
jump	jumped	will jump
cry	cried	will cry
care	cared	will care
jog	jogged	will jog
prefer	preferred	will prefer
am, is, are	was, were	will be

The past tense of most verbs is formed by adding -ed to the present form. Review the following spelling rules:

- For verbs ending in a consonant plus *y*, the *y* is changed to *i* before -ed is added.
- For verbs ending in *e*, the *e* is dropped before -ed is added.
- For one-syllable verbs ending in one vowel followed by one consonant, the final consonant is doubled before -ed is added.
- The final consonant is also doubled for two-syllable verbs ending in one vowel and one consonant and having the accent on the second syllable.

Exercise A
Underline each verb and tell what tense it is.

1. Dana and Sean are junior mountain climbers from our school. _____

2. They climb Mt. Baldy at least once every year. _____

3. Last summer they climbed it twice. _____

4. They and their group will scale it again tomorrow. _____

5. Francis, their guide, trained the whole group well. _____

6. He instructed them in the latest rescue techniques. _____

7. Dana excelled as a group leader. _____

8. Sean completes his last lesson with Francis today. _____

Grade Eight SkillBook, Grammar, Usage, and Mechanics

9. All group members conditioned themselves for instructions.
_____

10. Some of the group departed at four o'clock this morning.
_____

11. They left early to set up their base camp. _____

12. They have the first-aid supplies also. _____

13. They will wait there until the others arrive. _____

14. The second group brought all the food. _____

15. They shopped for all the food last night. _____

Exercise B
Change each underlined verb, if necessary, to make it the tense given in parentheses.

   Example: The duet <u>practice</u> their music daily. (past)
   Answer: The duet <u>practiced</u> their music daily.

1. Jon and Tina <u>study</u> their parts alone and together. (past)
_____

2. They still <u>needed</u> a few more hours of practice. (present)
_____

3. Tina <u>sings</u> her solo for an audience tonight. (future)
_____

4. Jon <u>accompanies</u> her on the piano. (future)
_____

5. They <u>hope</u> to know their music by this evening. (present)
_____

6. They <u>stop</u> their rehearsal. (past)
_____

7. This recital <u>is</u> their first since last year. (future)
_____

8. Both <u>appear</u> confident earlier this afternoon. (past)
_____

210   Grade Eight SkillBook, Grammar, Usage, and Mechanics

Lesson 36
Principal Parts of Verbs

Verbs have four basic forms called principal parts. These principal parts are used to build tenses.

The principal parts of a verb are its four basic forms. They are the present, the present participle, the past, and the past participle. You must know these forms in order to build tenses.

Present	Present Participle	Past	Past Participle
jump	(is) jumping	jumped	(have, has, had) jumped
move	(is) moving	moved	(have, has, had) moved
tap	(is) tapping	tapped	(have, has, had) tapped
carry	(is) carrying	carried	(have, has, had) carried
play	(is) playing	played	(have, has, had) played

The first form is the **present**. The second form, the **present participle**, is formed by adding *-ing* to the present. The present participle is used with present tense forms of the auxiliary verb *be*, as in the verb phrases *is playing* and *are dancing*.

Verbs formed from the present participle are sometimes said to be in the **progressive tense**. Notice the spelling changes that can occur when *-ing* is added.

The **past** and the **past participle** are usually made by adding *-ed* to the present form. Verbs forming their past and past participles in this way are called **regular verbs**. The past participle always requires an auxiliary verb, one of the forms of *have*. Verbs whose principal parts are formed in other ways, such as *fall, falling, fell,* and *fallen,* are called **irregular verbs**. The dictionary shows principal parts of irregular verbs.

Exercise A
Underline the verb in each sentence. Then write the principal parts of the verb.

Example: We used a sailboat on our vacation.
Answer: We <u>used</u> a sailboat on our vacation.—use, (are) using, used, (have) used

1. We vacationed in Wisconsin. _____
2. Mother visits there often. _____
3. My uncle lives on an island. _____
4. He stays there all year. _____
5. Our family likes tours. _____
6. Some hurry to the beaches. _____

Grade Eight SkillBook, Grammar, Usage, and Mechanics

7. They skip in the sand. _____

8. They fish in the lake. _____

9. They pack picnic lunches. _____

10. Everyone loves it there. _____

Exercise B
Rewrite each question. Change the underlined verb from the past to a form using the past participle.

   Example: Which friends <u>called</u> me?
   Answer: Which friends have called me?

1. Who <u>asked</u> you? _____

2. Which ones <u>baked</u> bread? _____

3. What <u>started</u> the fire? _____

4. Who <u>consulted</u> you? _____

5. Which one <u>seemed</u> sleepy? _____

6. Who <u>answered</u> the phone? _____

7. Who <u>patched</u> this coat? _____

8. Which stars <u>appeared</u>? _____

9. Who <u>watched</u> the play? _____

10. Which ones <u>acted</u> in it? _____

Exercise C
Underline the verb in each sentence. Then write what principal part it was formed from: *present*, *past*, *present participle*, or *past participle*.

   Example: Kate has measured four yards of wool.
   Answer: Kate <u>has measured</u> four yards of wool.—past participle

11. Donna cares for someone. _____

12. Tom had mixed the paint. _____

13. They have used their brains. _____

14. Sam showed his medals. _____

15. Meg is laughing out loud. _____

16. Amy has fixed the stove. _____

17. My pay included a bonus. _____

18. She is starting a trend. _____

19. He operates a tractor. _____

20. Who is playing the piano? _____

Name _____ Class _____ Date _____

Lesson 37
Perfect Tense

Verbs have present, past, and future perfect tenses.

The **perfect tenses** of a verb are made by using forms of the auxiliary verb *have* with the past participle. They express actions that were completed or will be completed by a certain time.

Look at the forms of the perfect tenses in this chart.

Present Perfect	Past Perfect	Future Perfect
has, have jumped	had jumped	will have jumped
has, have batted	had batted	will have batted
has, have been	had been	will have been
has, have made	had made	will have made

The **present perfect** tense expresses an action that began at some time in the past and may still be going on.

Sue **has exercised** daily for twelve weeks.
I **have finished** with exercise for now.

The **past perfect** tense shows an action that began and was completed in the past.

I **had walked** every day until yesterday.
Until then, I **had** never **experienced** a leg cramp.

The **future perfect** tense describes an action that began in the past or present and will end at a definite time in the future.

Todd **will have finished** his job by tonight.
Will you **have started** your work by then?

Exercise A
Underline the ten perfect tense verbs in the sentences, and write what tense forms they are.

1. Have you heard of the lost city of Atlantis? _____
2. I had not thought about it for years. _____
3. Soon I will have read almost everything on the subject. _____
4. They say that Atlantis had been a rival of Athens. _____
5. There have been many references to this strange place in myths. _____
6. Perhaps Atlantis had sunk during an earthquake. _____
7. Since then, many adventurers and scholars have looked for it. _____

Grade Eight SkillBook, Grammar, Usage, and Mechanics

Name _____ Class _____ Date _____

8. By now, they will have searched both seas and oceans. _____

9. They will have discovered many lost cities in the process. _____

10. No one has ever found any evidence of Atlantis's existence. _____

Exercise B
Using the predicates and verb tenses given below, write five sentences about your morning. Use your own paper.

  Example: exercise (past perfect)
  Answer: Before breakfast, I had exercised by jogging a mile.

11. fix my lunch (past perfect)

12. brush my teeth (past perfect)

13. dress myself (present perfect)

14. prepare breakfast (present perfect)

15. walk to school (future perfect)

Exercise C
Write answers to these questions. Use the same verb tenses.

  Example: Have you ever played backgammon?
  Answer: I have never played backgammon.

16. Had you planned to attend a concert this year?
   _____

17. Has your family decided on plans for vacation?
   _____

18. Will you have finished sixty books by your sixteenth birthday?
   _____

19. Have you tried skydiving yet?
   _____

20. Have you studied for your science exam?
   _____

Grade Eight SkillBook, Grammar, Usage, and Mechanics

Name _____ Class _____ Date _____

Lesson 38
Transitive and Intransitive Verbs

Action verbs with direct objects are transitive. Action verbs without direct objects are intransitive, as are linking verbs.

Some action verbs are followed by **direct objects** — nouns or pronouns that complete a verb's meaning. A **transitive verb** is an action verb that is followed by a direct object. The verb passes the action from the subject to the object.

      S   V   DO   S   V   DO
The girls **painted** the room. Lisa **scraped** the windows.

Find the transitive verbs in these sentences. Then locate the direct objects.

An action verb is **intransitive** when it does not need an object to complete its meaning. Look at the verbs in these sentences.

      S   V   S   V
The girls **painted** until dark. Lisa **scraped** under the sills.

In these examples, there are no direct objects to receive the actions of the verbs. Therefore, the verbs are intransitive. Notice that verbs like *painted* and *scraped* can be transitive or intransitive, depending on whether they have direct objects.

Linking verbs are always intransitive. They never have direct objects.

      S V   S   V
Lisa **was** the slowest worker. She **seemed** weary by six o'clock.

Exercise A
Write whether each underlined verb is transitive or intransitive.

1. Karen <u>made</u> a poster about the art show. _____

2. First she <u>planned</u> her design. _____

3. Then she <u>colored</u> with her finest markers around the edges of the poster.
_____

4. She <u>colored</u> the center orange and blue. _____

5. At last she <u>was</u> happy with her poster. _____

Exercise B
Draw one line under each transitive verb or verb phrase and two lines under its direct object.

    Example: The hockey team has won its game.
    Answer: The hockey team <u>has won</u> its <u>game</u>.

1. Juanita plays field hockey on a team in her neighborhood.

2. She plays a forward position.

Grade Eight SkillBook, Grammar, Usage, and Mechanics

3. Her team beat Overton in the semifinals last week.
4. Overton lost the game in the last two minutes.
5. Juanita scored two important goals for her team.
6. She and her teammates play Clifton in the finals on Friday.
7. Clifton won the championship last year.
8. As a result, their games always attract a crowd.
9. Two coaches accompany Clifton's team to the playing field.
10. The better team will win the match.

Exercise C
If a sentence is intransitive, write *intransitive*. If it is transitive, write *transitive*. Then underline its verb or verb phrase once and its direct object twice.

   Example: The beginning swimmers started class today.
   Answer: The beginning swimmers started class today.—transitive

11. Expert swimmers helped them with their lessons. _____
12. First they floated for a short time on their stomachs. _____
13. Then they dog-paddled awkwardly across the pool. _____
14. Their bodies moved in a crouching position. _____
15. A guard helped Inez with the motions. _____
16. With help she learned quickly. _____
17. Each foot kicked in turn. _____
18. Once she kicked the wall of the pool by mistake. _____
19. She finally learned the correct movements for the dog paddle. _____
20. Inez was happy at the end of the class period. _____
21. The guard had complimented her on her abilities. _____
22. Inez will be a fine swimmer some day. _____
23. She might teach others about techniques and movements in a pool. _____

Lesson 39
Principal Parts of Irregular Verbs

The past and past participle forms of irregular verbs do not end in -ed.

All verbs have four principal parts. They are the present, the present participle, the past, and the past participle. The past and past participle forms of regular verbs end in -ed — for example, *jumped, have jumped*.

The past and past participle of irregular verbs are not formed in the same way. An **irregular verb** is any verb that doesn't follow the -ed pattern for forming the past and past participle.

The chart below shows the principal parts of several commonly used irregular verbs.

Present	Present Participle	Past	Past Participle
run	(is) running	ran	(has, have, had) run
come	(is) coming	came	(has, have, had) come
become	(is) becoming	became	(has, have, had) become
go	(is) going	went	(has, have, had) go
begin	(is) beginning	began	(has, have, had) begin
see	(is) seeing	saw	(has, have, had) see

Two guidelines will help you use the past and past participle forms of irregular verbs correctly.

- Don't use the past participle form without an auxiliary verb such as *have, has,* or *had.*

    I **have seen** that movie several times. (Not: I seen)
    He **has begun** writing his book again. (Not: He begun)

- Don't use the past form with an auxiliary verb.

    You **have gone** there many times. (Not: You have went)
    She **had run** the marathon before. (Not: she had ran)

As you study the chart of irregular verbs on the following pages, look for patterns in groups of verbs. (Since the present participle presents no problem, it is not included in the chart.)

Present	Past	Past Participle
ring	rang	(has, have, had) rung
drink	drank	(has, have, had) drunk
shrink	shrank, shrunk	(has, have, had) shrunk
sing	sang, sung	(has, have, had) sung
sink	sank, sunk	(has, have, had) sunk
spring	sprang, sprung	(has, have, had) sprung
swim	swam	(has, have, had) swum

Grade Eight SkillBook, Grammar, Usage, and Mechanics

Present	Past	Past Participle
grow	grew	(has, have, had) grown
know	knew	(has, have, had) known
throw	threw	(has, have, had) thrown
blow	blew	(has, have, had) blown
fly	flew	(has, have, had) flown
draw	drew	(has, have, had) drawn
wear	wore	(has, have, had) worn
tear	tore	(has, have, had) torn
swear	swore	(has, have, had) sworn
break	broke	(has, have, had) broken
speak	spoke	(has, have, had) spoken
steal	stole	(has, have, had) stolen
freeze	froze	(has, have, had) frozen
choose	chose	(has, have, had) chosen
weave	wove	(has, have, had) woven
drive	drove	(has, have, had) driven
eat	ate	(has, have, had) eaten
fall	fell	(has, have, had) fallen
ride	rode	(has, have, had) ridden
write	wrote	(has, have, had) written
hide	hid	(has, have, had) hidden
take	took	(has, have, had) taken

Study the pattern for each group of verbs above when shifting from the present to the past to the past participle. In the top group of verbs, find the exception with the verbs *shrink*, *sing*, *sink*, and *spring*.

Present	Past	Past Participle
bring	brought	(has, have, had) brought
say	said	(has, have, had) said
think	thought	(has, have, had) thought
buy	bought	(has, have, had) bought
catch	caught	(has, have, had) caught
lose	lost	(has, have, had) lost
teach	taught	(has, have, had) taught
lead	led	(has, have, had) led
lend	lent	(has, have, had) lent
leave	left	(has, have, had) left
find	found	(has, have, had) found
sting	stung	(has, have, had) stung
swing	swung	(has, have, had) swung
let	let	(has, have, had) let
bet	bet	(has, have, had) bet

Present	Past	Past Participle
bid	bid	(has, have, had) bid
burst	burst	(has, have, had) burst
hit	hit	(has, have, had) hit
read	read	(has, have, had) read
put	put	(has, have, had) put

Study the pattern for each of the above groups of verbs when changing from the present to the past to the past participle.

Exercise A
Write the present, past, and past participle forms of the underlined verbs in the following sentences.

1. Marsha has begun to make a wall hanging.

2. Before she started, she drew a design on paper.

3. Marsha knew farm life would be her theme.

4. She has driven many places to gather her materials.

5. I have become interested in farm life too.

Exercise B
Underline the correct form of the verb to complete each sentence.

Example: Carrie (knew, knowed) her lines for the school play.
Answer: Carrie (knew, knowed) her lines for the school play.

1. Rehearsal time for the performance has (flew, flown).
2. All of the students have (grew, grown) in their acting abilities.
3. Tess (wore, worn) her costume to school.
4. On stage Russ (freezed, froze).
5. A stagehand (speaked, spoke) the cue for his next line.
6. The actors have (took, taken) many curtain calls.
7. The "acting bug" has (stang, stung) Carrie and Tess.

Grade Eight SkillBook, Grammar, Usage, and Mechanics

8. Some students have (chose, chosen) their favorite activity.

9. Everyone (rid, rode) home after the play.

10. A local critic has (wrote, written) of the play's success.

Exercise C

Read the sentences below. Write the correct past tense or past participle of the verb in parentheses.

Example: Winston (take) his brother Henry to the zoo.
Answer: Winston took his brother Henry to the zoo.

11. Before leaving home, Henry (put) peanuts in his pocket.

12. At the zoo a monkey suddenly (hit) the bars near him.

13. Henry (shrink) back in amazement.

14. I have never (see) Henry look so surprised.

15. His peanuts (fall) inside the cage.

16. The smallest monkey (steal) them.

17. Quickly he (eat) a peanut.

18. Meanwhile other monkeys have (swing) from tree to tree.

19. Henry has (lose) peanuts in this manner before.

20. The last time he went to the zoo, he had (bring) more peanuts.

Lesson 40
Forms of *be*, *have*, and *do*

Use the forms of the verbs *be*, *have*, and *do* correctly.

Focus
The verbs *be*, *have*, and *do* can be used both as main verbs and as auxiliary verbs.

Main verb:	Dr. Smith **is** a dentist.
Auxiliary verb:	He **is adjusting** my braces.
Main verb:	Kim **has** a collection.
Auxiliary verb:	She **has collected** stamps.
Main verb:	Kevin **does** many household chores.
Auxiliary verb:	He **does repair** appliances.

The principal parts of *be*, *have*, and *do* (except the present participle) are formed irregularly. Study the charts and examples below and on the following page.

	Pronoun	Present	Past	Past Participle
Singular	I	am	was	(have, had) been
	you	are	were	(have, had) been
	he, she, it	is	was	(has, had) been
Plural	we	are	were	(have, had) been
	they	are	were	(have, had) been

I **am** here. (Not: I is)   You **were** also here. (Not: You was)

Use the form *being* with the auxiliary verbs *am*, *is*, *are*, *was*, and *were*. Use the form *been* with the auxiliary verbs *has*, *have*, and *had*.

She **is being** paid for her summer job. (Not: She being)
She **has been** there before. (Not: She been)

The form *be* should not be used in place of *am*, *is*, or *are*.

It **is** time to go. (Not: It be)

The form *ain't* should not be used.

Paul **isn't** old enough to go. (Not: Paul ain't)

	Pronoun	Present	Past	Past Participle
Singular	I	have	had	(have, had) had
	you	have	had	(have, had) had
	he, she, it	has	had	(has, had) had
Plural	we	have	had	(have, had) had
	they	have	had	(have, had) had

Grade Eight SkillBook, Grammar, Usage, and Mechanics

Megan **has** the answer. (Not: Megan have)
We **have heard** it. (Not: We has heard)
I **had** several more questions. (Not: I has)
You **have** more too. (Not: You has)

Do not write the word *of* in place of the word *have* in phrases like *would have, should have, could have,* and *must have.*

Jeremy **must have heard** of him. (Not: Jeremy must of heard)
We **could have told** him more (Not: We could of)

	Pronoun	Present	Past	Past Participle
Singular	I	do	did	(have, had) done
	you	do	did	(have, had) done
	he, she, it	does	did	(have, had) done
Plural	we	do	did	(have, had) done
	they	do	did	(have, had) done

Our friends **did** all the work. (Not: Our friends done)
He **has done** the best job. (Not: He done)
He **has done** all of it by himself. (Not: He has did)
He **doesn't want** to do it again. (Not: He don't want)

Exercise A
Circle the correct form of each verb.

Example: The man (was, were) sure of his facts.
Answer: The man was sure of his facts.

1. Marjorie Kinnan Rawlings (is, be) the author of *The Yearling*.
2. Her home in Florida (been, has been) preserved.
3. She and her husband (was, were) farmers.
4. Her first success as a writer was the story of a boy.
5. The book, *The Yearling*, (been, has been) read worldwide.
6. Frank (ain't, isn't) planning to read this book.
7. I told him he (being, is being) silly.
8. "I (am, is) not interested in her books," he said.
9. "You (was, were) never interested in reading anything," I said.

Exercise B
On your own paper, rewrite the paragraph, correcting the forms of *have* if necessary. You will make six corrections.

    (1) I has begun to wish that I knew more about other lands. **(2)** Most people have little knowledge about other countries. **(3)** My friends and I

222   Grade Eight SkillBook, Grammar, Usage, and Mechanics

has started to learn more. **(4)** We should of learned about large and small countries long ago. **(5)** Some small, independent countries have names I have never heard before. **(6)** Has you heard of Nauru or Liechtenstein? **(7)** Liechtenstein is a tiny country and has no army. **(8)** Jody have decided to go there someday.

Exercise C
Insert the correct form of the verb *do* for each sentence.

Example: She _____ n't know where her brother is right now.
Answer: She doesn't know where her brother is right now.

9. The interviewer said, "What kind of work have you _____?"

10. I said that I like to _____ some kind of work each summer.

11. "What _____ you do last summer, for instance?" she asked.

12. "I _____ n't remember all the jobs that I _____ then," I said.

13. "Why _____ n't you?" the interviewer asked.

14. "It _____ n't matter because I like many kinds of jobs."

15. "_____ you remember the odd job you liked best?" she asked.

16. "Rescuing a cat is the most interesting thing I have _____ so far."

Lesson 41
Troublesome Verb Pairs

Some pairs of verbs are confusing because they have similar forms, similar meanings, or similar spellings.

Compare the verb pairs below and notice the similarities and differences in the principal parts of each pair.

Present	Past	Past participle
lay	laid	(have, has, had) laid
lie	lay	(have, has, had) lain
set	set	(have, has, had) set
sit	sat	(have, has, had) sat
let	let	(have, has, had) let
leave	left	(have, has, had) let
lend	lent	(have, has, had) lent
borrow	borrowed	(have, has, had) borrowed
teach	taught	(have, has, had) taught
learn	learned	(have, has, had) learned
bring	brought	(have, has, had) brought
take	took	(have, has, had) taken
rise	rose	(have, has, had) risen
raise	raised	(have, has, had) raised

Exercise A
Study the pairs of definitions. Write the correct verb for each sentence.

1. *Lay* means "put or place." *Lie* means "rest or recline or be at rest."

   a. _____ the book on the table.   b. _____ on the couch.

2. *Set* means "put something somewhere." *Sit* means "sit down."

   a. _____ down over there.   b. _____ it down over there.

3. *Let* means "allow." *Leave* means "depart."

   a. _____ me go home.   b. _____ the room at once.

4. *Lend* means "give with the idea of getting back." *Borrow* means "take with the idea of giving back."

   a. Please _____ me the book.   b. _____ it from him.

5. *Teach* means "give lessons or knowledge." *Learn* means "gain knowledge."

   a. I'll _____ my lesson later.   b. Can you _____ me to dance?

6. *Bring* means "carry something toward." *Take* means "carry something away."

   a. _____ him away from here.   b. _____ your game here.

7. *Rise* means "get up or move up." *Raise* means "lift or put up or raise something higher."

   a. Please _____ the window.   b. Watch the temperature _____.

Exercise B
Underline the correct verb in parentheses to complete the sentence.

   Example: Where have you (set, sat) the camera?
   Answer: Where have you set the camera?

1. Yesterday the workers (laid, lay) all the tools on the bench.
2. I have (learned, taught) you everything I know.
3. (Let, Leave) me show you the way out.
4. He (laid, lay) down to rest before the game.
5. Paul (brought, took) his bike here with him.
6. The student (raised, rose) his hand in class.
7. I think I'll (set, sit) down here in this chair.
8. She (rose, raised) to her feet before speaking.
9. We shall (let, leave) for our vacation next week.

Exercise C
Underline the correct verb in parentheses to complete the sentence.

10. I (lent, borrowed) her that book last Tuesday.
11. Will your mother (leave, let) you go?
12. (Sit, Set) your packages in the corner.
13. She (lent, borrowed) the skirt from me.
14. (Take, Bring) this with you when you go.
15. Maggie (has lain, has laid) on that rug for hours.
16. Why don't you (lay, lie) in the shade?
17. Jane taught her parakeet to (set, sit) on her head.
18. (Leave, Let) him buy his own ticket.
19. I have to (bring, take) this trash out to the incinerator.
20. Mom (learned, taught) us how to make hollyhock dolls.
21. Mrs. Suarez asked me to (bring, take) her cake to the bake sale.

Grade Eight SkillBook, Grammar, Usage, and Mechanics

Name _____ Class _____ Date _____

Exercise D
Underline the correct verb in parentheses to complete the sentence.

22. (Lie, Lay) down and be quiet.
23. Did the doctor say that you could (set, sit) up?
24. As soon as the company left, Mother (laid, lay) down again.
25. Someone with muddy shoes had (laid, lain) on the sofa.
26. Someone had (laid, lain) a muddy shoe on the sofa.
27. Pat (lie, lay) awake for hours, worrying about the test.
28. Where should I (set, sit) this orange crate?
29. I won't (borrow, lend) him my skates again.
30. Please (raise, rise) the window shade all the way up.
31. He wanted the bread to (raise, rise) for one more hour.
32. Once it (raised, rose), he put it in the oven.
33. He (laid, lay) there for at least ten minutes.
34. Mr. McPherson (raised, rose) all our salaries.
35. His temperature (raised, rose) too.
36. Please (leave, let) the light on for me.
37. Don't let the cat (lay, lie) on the bed.
38. Will you (bring, take) these clothes over to the rummage sale?
39. Please don't (bring, take) any other used items back home.

Exercise E.
On your paper rewrite the following sentences using correct verbs.

40. Just as she laid down, the telephone rang.
41. Did Ronnie remember to bring his watch to the jeweler?
42. The temperature has raised ten degrees in one hour.
43. Do you think that I could learn my dog to set up and beg?
44. My friend learned his dog to lay down and roll over.
45. After I bring my book back to the library, I'll lay down and take a nap.
46. I'll leave you borrow my ax if you'll borrow me your saw.
47. Mother was furious when she found out that I had laid around the house all day.

Lesson 42
Active and Passive Verbs

Active verbs are used most often because they express action in a natural and direct way. Passive verbs are used less often.

A verb is **active** when the subject performs the action.

   Kristen **bounced** the ball.

Kristen performed the action and is the subject of the sentence. *Bounced* is the active verb. *Ball* receives the action and is the direct object of the sentence.

A verb is **passive** when the subject receives the action, as in the sentence below.

   The ball **was bounced** by Kristen.

Ball received the action, but now it is the subject of the sentence. *Was bounced* is the passive verb. Notice that passive verbs have some form of *be* as an auxiliary verb, followed by a past participle.

Normally writers prefer to use active verbs because they express action in a natural, direct way. Passive verbs are usually preferred only in these two cases:

- When you want to emphasize the receiver of the action

The only meet record **was set** by a runner from Carver.

- When the doer of the action is unknown or unimportant

The stadium walls **were vandalized** sometime Thursday night.

Exercise A
Which of the sentences below have active verbs? Which have passive verbs? Write your answers on the lines.

1. Tony *lifted* the stone. _____
2. He *hit* the hockey puck. _____
3. The medal *was won* by Sue. _____
4. The song *was sung* by Flora. _____
5. The stone *was lifted* by Tony. _____
6. The hockey puck *was hit*. _____
7. Sue *won* the medal. _____

Exercise B
Read each of the following sentences. Underline each verb and write whether it is active or passive.

   Example: Eve travels west each year.
   Answer: Eve <u>travels</u> west each year.—active

Grade Eight SkillBook, Grammar, Usage, and Mechanics

1. My brother Hank cooks like a pro. _____
2. Pies and cakes are prepared at our place for any occasion. _____
3. Yesterday he made "Cheesecake à la Hank" for Mrs. Elroy. _____
4. Eggs were beaten by him. _____
5. Flour was sifted before he began. _____
6. Graham crackers were crushed by hand. _____
7. Hank slaved away in the kitchen for hours. _____
8. Finally, the cake was delivered to Mrs. Elroy. _____
9. Mrs. Elroy remarked, "How nice of your mother!" _____
10. Poor Hank didn't even correct her. _____

Exercise C
Rewrite the sentences below, changing the passive verbs to active verbs.

11. The movie had been advertised by the theater as a kiddie matinee.

    _____

12. The children had been taken to the movie by their parents.

    _____

13. Popcorn and candy were bought in abundance by the children.

    _____

14. The boys and girls were shown to their seats by the ushers.

    _____

15. The theater lights were darkened by the owner.

    _____

16. The movie was shown by the projectionist.

    _____

17. High-pitched cries were screamed by some audience members.

    _____

18. Piercing yelps were shrieked by others.

    _____

Lesson 43
Consistent Verb Tenses

The tenses of the verbs in a paragraph should be consistent.

Compare the tenses in these two groups of sentences.

He **finishes** practicing.	He **finished** practicing.
He **puts** down the flute.	He **put** down the flute.
He **goes** to the window.	He **went** to the window.

All the verbs on the left are in the present tense. On the right, the verbs are in the past. Either style—past or present—is acceptable for a narrative passage. The key to correct usage is to keep the tenses within a piece of narrative writing consistent.

You should shift tense only when you mean to show a change in the time of the action. Notice what happens in this paragraph when the writer shifts tense unintentionally.

> Cautiously Janet **approached** her mare. She **strokes** the rough hair on the horse's forehead. She **talks** soothingly to the horse. "Easy, girl. You **were** the best horse I **knew**."

What is the effect of the shifting tenses? Here is one way the paragraph could be written correctly.

> Cautiously Janet **approached** her mare. She **stroked** the rough hair on the horse's forehead. She **talked** soothingly to the horse. "Easy, girl. You **are** the best horse I **know**."

Notice that the words Janet speaks are in the present tense. Sometimes you will have to shift tenses, as in the above example, for a direct quotation. If you made the tenses the same, the quote would not make sense.

You can also shift to the present tense in the case of a statement that is always true.

> On seeing the snake, the horse **wanted** to run, since a horse's best defense **is** its speed.

The present tense is used in the second half of the sentence because the statement describes a fact that is always true.

Exercise A
Study each underlined verb. Then rewrite the sentence or sentences so that the other verbs match the underlined verb.

Example: The jugglers <u>appear</u> on stage and took their places.
Answer: The jugglers appear on stage and take their places.

1. Miranda took off her hat and <u>bows</u> deeply to the audience.

Name _____ Class _____ Date _____

2. She <u>lifts</u> her clubs into the air and began juggling.
   _____

3. The clubs <u>fly</u> through the air; they never fell.
   _____

4. But wait. Here <u>comes</u> Phil and he had another club.
   _____

5. He <u>throws</u> it in too, so now there were five.
   _____

6. She <u>is</u> doing it! Now she takes off her hat and threw it in too.
   _____

7. Phil <u>catches</u> the hat and tossed it back.
   _____

Exercise B
On your paper rewrite the story so it is told in the past. Change the verb tenses to past tense; some sentences need more than one change.

   Example: Jim takes my hand and shook it.
   Answer: Jim took my hand and shook it.

1. We knew there was some kind of carnival at the shopping center, but we don't expect to see an elephant there.
2. The sign read "Elephant rides for $1.00." At the time it seems a reasonable price for an unusual five-minute ride.
3. The face of the man by the sign looked as wrinkled as the elephant's face was. He assures me, "It's an experience."
4. My friends urge me to try a ride, and I get my courage up as much as I can while the elephant man begins to instruct me.
5. "You are a brave young woman," the elephant man says when he led me to the stepladder for the ascent.

Name _____ Class _____ Date _____

Lesson 44
Subject-Verb Agreement

The subject and verb of a sentence must agree in number.

In grammar, **agreement** of subject and verb means that those two parts of the sentence match. A singular verb is used with a singular subject. A plural verb is used with a plural subject.

A chime clock **is** a nuisance. (singular subjects—singular verb)
Chime clocks **are** too loud. (plural subject—plural verb)

Most pronoun subjects follow this rule. The pronouns *I* and *you*, however, always take plural verbs.

She **sews**. *We* **weave**. *I* **cook**. *You* **leave**.

When the subject of a sentence is compound, two rules will help you decide whether the verb should be singular or plural.

Rule 1 Subjects joined by *and* or *both . . . and* generally require a plural verb.

Both motorcycles and trailers **were banned** from the highway.
A bicycle and a motorcycle **have** many things in common.

Rule 2 If both parts of a compound subject joined by *or, either . . . or,* or *neither . . . nor* are singular, use a singular verb. If both parts are plural, use a plural verb. If one is singular and one is plural, the verb agrees with the subject nearer the verb.

Barb or Les **is** riding here. *His dogs or his cats* **are** there.
Neither her friends nor her teacher **knows** her plans.

Some subjects are considered singular even though they consist of more than one word. Study the subjects below that are singular.

Macaroni and cheese **tastes** good.
Two years **seems** a long time.
The Three Cats **is** an entertaining film.

Exercise A
Read the sentences below. Choose the form of the verb that agrees with each compound subject. Underline your answer.

Example: Both you and your friends (know, knows) the way to the park.
Answer: Both you and your friends (<u>know</u>, knows) the way to the park.

1. Either Tim or Debbie (is, are) supervising the cleanup.
2. Both Rob and Fred (are, is) bringing trash bags.
3. Neither the students nor the counselor (understand, understands) how the park got so messy.
4. Both Tim and Bart (has, have) begun painting benches.

Grade Eight SkillBook, Grammar, Usage, and Mechanics

5. Either Lisa or Margo (is, are) planting flowers.
6. Barry and Pam (is, are) picking up cans, bottles, and papers.
7. Neither Rob nor Fred (know, knows) the way to the recycling center.
8. Either Mr. Malone or Tim (has, have) a map.
9. Both Rob and Fred (want, wants) to celebrate with a cookout.
10. Both the neighbors and the park department (is, are) pleased with the way the park looks now.

Exercise B
Underline the form of the verb that agrees with the simple subject.

1. A debate (is, are) an event in a speech contest.
2. Four weeks (is, are) the usual time spent in preparation.
3. I (studies, study) the arguments for both sides.
4. Ten minutes (is, are) the limit for a beginning speech.
5. We (listens, listen) carefully to the opponent.
6. Debaters (discusses, discuss) all issues that arise.
7. A second speech (argues, argue) against an opponent's remarks.
8. Debate rules (allows, allow) time for a rebuttal.
9. Judges (gives, give) points for skill in delivery and logic.
10. Persuasive and emotional appeals (is judged, are judged).
11. Five hundred dollars (is, are) the prize.
12. *Watch Those Arguments* (gives, give) guidelines for debaters.
13. Smith and Sons (carries, carry) books on debating.

Name _____ Class _____ Date _____

Lesson 45
Subjects Separated from Verbs

Agreement between subject and verb is not affected by words or phrases that come between the subject and the verb.

In a sentence in which the subject and the verb are separated, the subject and the verb should still agree. Look at the sentence below, paying attention to the subject and the verb.

          S   V
    The *briefcase* behind those coats **is** mine.

The subject of the sentence is the singular noun *briefcase*, which agrees with the singular verb *is*. The prepositional phrase *behind those coats*, which comes between the subject and the verb, does not affect the form of the verb. Although the plural noun *coats* appears near the verb, it has no effect on the number of the verb because it is not the subject.

    Here are some other examples.

    A *leader* with many devoted followers **has** the power to change history.
    The *choice* of the audience and of the three judges **was** the golden retriever.
    That *box* with snapshots and various other mementos **belongs** to Aunt Harriet.
    The *books* on the top shelf **have needed** dusting for some time.

Exercise A
Write why the underlined verb in each sentence is singular or plural.

    Example: The box of books next to the stairs <u>is</u> for the rummage sale.
    Answer: The subject *box* is singular; it must agree in number with the verb.

1. A bundle of the twins' outgrown clothes <u>seems</u> a good donation.

    _____

2. The prices of some items of clothing <u>seem</u> high to me.

    _____

3. The table with vases and knickknacks <u>has</u> some interesting items.

    _____

4. The worker behind the table with kitchen utensils <u>looks</u> busy.

    _____

Exercise B
For each of the following sentences, underline the subject once and the verb twice. Put parentheses around any words that come between the subject and the verb.

Example: The center for theater arts is awarding scholarships.
Answer: The <u>center</u> (for theater arts) <u>is awarding</u> scholarships.

1. That man with the huge radio in his arms is rude.
2. This bench in the park has been an island of peace for me.
3. The voice of the disk jockey now jars my peace.
4. The radio with a thousand knobs and dials blares.
5. The thoughtlessness of some people makes me furious.

Exercise C
Underline the correct form of the verb in parentheses.

6. The members of the most successful hockey team in the history of the school (has, have) thanked the coach for his help.
7. A grapefruit with brown spots probably (is, are) rotten.
8. The woman's story about hearing the howling of wolves (sends, send) shivers up my spine.
9. The moonlight on the river and on the trees (makes, make) everything around look snowbound.
10. That friend of my parents (is, are) waving at us.
11. The dog with the newborn puppies (was, were) protective.
12. The holidays on the calendar in my room (has, have) been printed in red.
13. The man with the shiny shoes and gray pants (is, are) singing.
14. Your plaid jacket of black, red, and yellow (looks, look) great with black slacks.
15. The small craft on the angry waves (bob, bobs) up and down.

Name _____ Class _____ Date _____

Lesson 46
Sentences in Inverted Order

The position of a subject in a sentence has no effect on the agreement between subject and verb.

In most sentences the subject comes before the verb. In some sentences, though, and in questions, the verb or part of the verb comes first. When the subject follows the verb, the sentence is said to be in **inverted order**. To make sure inverted order sentences have subject-verb agreement, reverse the order.

Out from the path **jumps** *Bill*.   *Bill* **jumps** out from the path.
Are *you* ready for the test?   *You* **are** ready for the test.
With whom **does** *Jenny* **go**?   *Jenny* **does go** with whom?

In the first sentence pair the verb *jumps* agrees with the singular subject *Bill*. The verb *are* in the second pair agrees with the plural subject *You*. In the third pair the verb phrase *does go* agrees with the singular subject *Jenny*.

Subject-verb order is also usually reserved in sentences that begin with *here* or *there*.

There **are** three *chairs* left.   Three *chairs* **are** left.
Here **is** my favorite *book*.   My favorite *book* **is** here.

In the first sentence pair the plural verb *are* agrees with the plural subject *chairs*. Find the subject and the verb in the second sentence pair.

Pay special attention to subject-verb agreement in sentences with *here's* or *there's*. *Here's* is the contraction for *here is* and *there's* is the contraction for *there is*.

Incorrect: There's the *trucks*. Here's the *cars*.
Correct: There **are** the *trucks*. Here **are** the *cars*.

Exercise A
Underline the subject once and the verb twice. Write whether they agree.

Example: There go the best team in the league.
Answer: There <u>go</u> the best <u>team</u> in the league.—don't agree

1. Is Gerald coming to the parade too? _____
2. There is a good place to stand on the sidewalk. _____
3. Here comes the Boy Scouts on the left. _____
4. Down the street marches our baton twirlers. _____
5. Isn't that music stirring? _____

Exercise B
In the sentences on the next page, find the subject and then underline the correct form of the verb in parentheses.

Grade Eight SkillBook, Grammar, Usage, and Mechanics

Name _____ Class _____ Date _____

Example: Here (comes, come) my aunt and uncle.
Answer: Here (comes, <u>come</u>) my aunt and uncle.

1. Under the old coats (hides, hide) the cat.
2. Among the exhibits (was, were) a collection of famous drawings.
3. At the bottom of the box (was, were) the flash cubes.
4. Then around the corner (comes, come) two more fire trucks.
5. After the cheerleaders and the team (comes, come) the floats.
6. (Is, Are) Matt and Miguel tennis partners for the tournament?
7. (There's, There are) thirty days in April.
8. Down the staircase (creeps, creep) the cat and kittens.
9. Here (comes, come) the twins.
10. Hidden in the mattress (was, were) three diamond rings.
11. There (isn't, aren't) enough potato chips.
12. (Does, do) the girls sing in the play?
13. (Here's, Here are) the balloons for the party.
14. Where (was, were) your parents last night?
15. (There's, there are) still a few copies left.

Exercise C

Use the phrases below to write sentences beginning with either *here* or *there* plus a verb in the present tense. Capitalize *here* or *there*.

Example: . . . someone looking over my shoulder.
Answer: There is someone looking over my shoulder.

16. . . . a list of groceries that we need.

_____

17. . . . the copies of the bylaws of our club.

_____

18. . . . neither a piece of bread nor a roll in the house.

_____

19. . . . many reasons for the decline of the Roman Empire.

_____

Lesson 47
Agreement with Special Subjects

Collective nouns and some other nouns present special agreement problems.

Nouns that name single groups made up of several people or things are called **collective nouns**. Study these collective nouns.

army	club	family	herd	panel
audience	committee	fleet	jury	public
band	crew	flock	mob	school
cast	crowd	gang	orchestra	team
class	faculty	group	pack	troop

A collective noun can take either a singular or a plural verb, depending on the meaning intended. When a writer intends a group to be thought of as a unit that acts as one, a singular verb is used. When a writer intends a group to be thought of as individuals, a plural verb is used. Compare the following sentences.

In a single voice the *committee* **shouts**, "No! No! No!"
The *committee* **work** on individual projects one day a week.

Find the sentences in which the writer intends the group to be thought of as a unit and as individuals.

Some nouns that end in *-s* are singular in meaning and take singular verbs.

Measles **is** contagious. (one disease)
Economics **was** not **required**, was it? (one subject)

Other nouns that end in *-s* and are singular in meaning take plural verbs.

| eyeglasses | pants | shorts | pliers | tweezers |

The *pliers* **are** on the bottom shelf.
Her *eyeglasses* **have been lost** for a week.

Exercise A
Underline the correct verb form for each sentence.

1. The team (is, are) playing a game of baseball.
2. At the end of every show, the audience quickly (moves, move) toward the exit.
3. The troop (has, have) established new rules for membership.
4. The panel (is, are) arguing heatedly with each other about the issue.
5. The crowds (stands, stand) back to let the queen pass.
6. The crew of the ocean liner (has, have) scattered to tell the guests about the storm.

Grade Eight SkillBook, Grammar, Usage, and Mechanics

7. My class (has, have) held a debate.

8. The cast of the play (has, have) performed for the mayor.

9. The jury (has, have) gone to the courthouse.

10. The rancher's family (has, have) all helped him round up the cattle.

11. The band (is, are) taking the school bus when they tour the United States this year.

12. The army (was, were) on maneuvers for several days and nights during this past month.

13. The orchestra (has, have) played each weekend in this city for over twenty years.

14. The junior high school faculty (has, have) all reported to the principal on the proposed addition to the school.

Exercise B

Write six sentences using the following nouns as the subjects of the sentences. Use only present tense verbs.

Example: diabetes
Answer: Diabetes strikes people of all ages.

1. mathematics
2. trousers
3. tweezers
4. shorts
5. mumps
6. economics

Lesson 48
Agreement with Indefinite Pronouns

When an indefinite pronoun is used as a subject, the verb in the sentence must agree with it.

Indefinite pronouns are words such as *anybody, someone, few,* and *most.* An indefinite pronoun can be singular or plural.

Below are some common singular indefinite pronouns. When they are subjects, they take singular verbs, as the sentences show.

anybody	either	neither	one
anyone	everybody	nobody	somebody
each	everyone	no one	someone

Everyone **has** a seat   *No* one **talks** much

Some indefinite pronouns, such as *few, several, both,* and *many,* are always plural and require plural verbs. Look at the sentences.

Few of them **were** interested in their projects.
Several **take** their assignments seriously.

Other indefinite pronouns, such as *some, all, most, any,* and *none,* can be either singular or plural, depending on their meaning.

Some of the **work** was hard.   *Some* of the **jobs** were easy.
Most of the **action** is over.   *Most* of the **actions** are done.

In sentences on the left, the indefinite pronouns *some* and *most* tell how much (of the work, of the action). They are used with singular verbs. In the sentences on the right, the same pronouns are used with a plural meaning. They tell how many.

Often a phrase following a subject like *some* and *most* gives a clue. If the phrase ends with a singular noun, the subject usually takes a singular verb. If the phrase ends with a plural noun, the subject usually requires a plural verb.

Exercise A
Write the form of the verb in parentheses that belongs in the sentence. Use the present tense.

1. Anyone in the class _____ free to ask a question. (be)
2. Some of the questions _____ difficult. (seem)
3. Most of the orchard _____ to Mr. Ott. (belong)

Exercise B
Underline the correct form of the verb for each sentence.

1. Both of my parents (has, have) interesting jobs.
2. Anyone with a mitt (is, are) welcome to be the catcher.

Grade Eight SkillBook, Grammar, Usage, and Mechanics

3. Few of the forecasters' predictions (has, have) come true.
4. Some of us with responsibilities (has, have) to work hard.
5. Several of the squirrels (has, have) moved into our attic.
6. Nobody in my family (thinks, think) the house has ghosts.
7. Everybody in my classes (likes, like) to raise questions.
8. Neither of the planes from Canada (has, have) landed yet.
9. Many of my best ideas (occurs, occur) to me before sleep.
10. Each of the stories (ends, end) happily.
11. Everyone on the teams (thinks, think) the umpire is wrong.
12. One of the paintings (was, were) damaged in the flood.
13. Many of the teachers (has, have) finished their grades.
14. All of my friends (is, are) going to the concert.
15. No one in any of my study halls (wastes, waste) time.

Exercise C

Complete each sentence with *has* or *have*.

   Example: No one _____ given me a ticket.
   Answer: No one has given me a ticket.

16. Everyone on the track team _____ improved.
17. Many on our team _____ worked hard this year.
18. Several of the players in the game _____ broken a golf club.
19. Few of the scores _____ been recorded.
20. No one from Minneapolis _____ left a phone number.
21. Neither of us _____ seen the results yet.
22. Most of the tournament _____ been played now.
23. Both of them _____ gained recognition for achievement.
24. Somebody _____ cleaned the room thoroughly.
25. Each of the children _____ bright red hair and freckles.
26. Neither of the twins _____ the slightest fear of water.
27. _____ any of the facts been studied?
28. Anybody on the two teams _____ time to practice.

Lesson 49
Identifying Adjectives

An adjective modifies a noun or pronoun.

Adjectives are words that modify nouns and pronouns, making the meaning of nouns or pronouns more exact. Adjectives usually come before, but may come after, the words they modify.

> **Four** boys from **that** school bicycled to the **old, run-down** mill.
> They were **nervous** about the **broken** gears on the **green** bike.

Notice that in the second example **nervous** modifies the pronoun *They*. What words do the other adjectives modify?

An adjective gives specific information about a noun or pronoun by telling what kind, how many, or which one.

> **What kind: new** buildings, **clever** students, **fancy** bicycle
> **How many: some** words, **two** racers, **many** girls
> **Which one: this** song, **that** competition, **those** plants

Adjectives can be formed from certain words when suffixes such as -ful, -able, -less, or -ish are added to them.

peace + -ful = peaceful   help + -less = helpless
remark + -able = remarkable   self + -ish = selfish

A word that is ordinarily a noun may be used as an adjective: *table lamp, lion tamer*. Some proper nouns can also be used as proper adjectives: *Flag Day parade, California sunshine*. A **proper adjective** is an adjective formed from a proper noun. It is always capitalized and may contain more than one word.

Proper Noun	**Proper Adjective**
Ireland	**Irish** stew
Latin America	**Latin American** dances

Articles are special kinds of adjectives. These words—a, an, and the—appear before many nouns.

Exercise A
Write the adjective. Tell whether it is proper.

1. graceful horses _____
2. two small puppies _____
3. Shetland pony _____
4. English setter _____
5. few giraffes _____
6. that Siamese cat _____

Grade Eight SkillBook, Grammar, Usage, and Mechanics

Name _____ Class _____ Date _____

Exercise B
Underline the adjectives in the sentences below. Do not underline the articles.

1. Fossils provide a record of past life forms.
2. Soft rocks, such as sandstone and shale, preserve many fossils.
3. Some coal contains the delicate outlines of extinct plants.
4. Certain dead organisms are the source of valuable fossil fuels.
5. The muddy bottoms of lost rivers eventually dried to sandstone.
6. This sedimentary rock trapped animal bones and shells.
7. Fossil hunters find whole impressions of extinct fish skeletons in the soft rock.
8. In these searches, geological maps and hammers are useful.
9. In June I found Petoskey stone on a Michigan beach.
10. For a million years, dead coral had piled up in a shallow sea.

Exercise C
Underline each adjective and proper adjective in the sentences.

11. We had a United Nations party at school.
12. A student from Ireland brought Irish stew and soda bread.
13. Another student prepared a colorful platter of Mexican tacos.
14. Our teacher is Italian, and she cooked a spaghetti casserole.
15. I enjoyed the warm French bread and onion soup.
16. Another classmate brought Swedish meatballs from home.
17. Doug taught us an old Scandinavian board game.
18. Kiku wore a silk kimono, and Carla read us African legends.
19. Four students demonstrated several Polish dances.
20. Everyone learned some characteristics of other cultures.

Lesson 50
Comparative Forms of Adjectives

Most adjectives have a positive, a comparative, and a superlative form.

Many adjectives have three forms, two of which are used in making comparisons. Notice the endings or words that are added to the forms below. Sometimes, multisyllabic words use *more* or *most* rather than adding endings to the positive form. Notice also the spelling changes that can occur.

Positive	Comparative	Superlative
short	shorter	shortest
red	redder	reddest
weary	wearier	weariest
noticeable	more (or less) noticeable	most (or least) noticeable

The different forms of the adjectives above are called **degrees of comparison**. The **positive degree** shows no comparison; it only describes. The **comparative degree** shows a comparison between two people, things, or ideas. The **superlative degree** shows a comparison between three or more people, things, or ideas.

Some adjectives have irregular forms. Study this chart.

Positive	Comparative	Superlative
good	better	best
bad	worse	worst
much	more	most
little	less	least
far	farther	farthest

Avoid double comparisons with regular or irregular adjectives.

Don't write: This card is **more prettier** than those.
Write: This card is **prettier** than those.

Note, as in the correct example, that *than* often signals the comparative form.

Exercise A
Beside each adjective on the next page, write its comparative and superlative forms.

Example: bulky
Answer: bulky, bulkier, bulkiest

Grade Eight SkillBook, Grammar, Usage, and Mechanics

Name	Class	Date

1. small _____   11. delicious _____
2. green _____   12. fat _____
3. lively _____   13. pretty _____
4. humorous _____   14. curious _____
5. bad _____   15. clear _____
6. late _____   16. windy _____
7. rough _____   17. unusual _____
8. slim _____   18. much _____
9. large _____   19. little _____
10. good _____   20. beautiful _____

Exercise B
Complete the sentences below. Use the correct form of the adjective in parentheses. You will not need to change some.

   Example: Judy is (easy) to get along with than Sam.
   Answer: Judy is easier to get along with than Sam.

1. The _____ (interesting) of all stories about Niagara Falls tells about Charles Blondin.

2. Charles Blondin was the _____ (daring) of all acrobats.

3. He was _____ (imaginative) than other acrobats of his time.

4. Blondin's feats were also _____ (funny) than those of most acrobats.

5. He performed the _____ (astonishing) feats of his life in 1859.

6. He walked across Niagara Falls on a tightrope _____ (thick) than wire.

7. Each new stunt was _____ (dangerous) than the last.

8. Next he rolled a _____ (heavy) wheelbarrow across the tightrope.

9. A _____ (fearful) crowd watched this stunt in horror.

10. His very _____ (good) stunt of all also involved Niagara Falls.

11. This time Blondin made the walk even _____ (difficult) by crossing on stilts.

12. Then he gave the crowd the _____ (bad) scare of their lives by actually repeating this stunt blindfolded.

Name _____ Class _____ Date _____

Lesson 51
Identifying Adverbs

Adverbs can modify verbs, adjectives, and other adverbs. An adverb modifies a verb by telling how, where, or when.

An **adverb** is a word that can modify a verb. When it does so, the adverb tells *how*, *where*, or *when* the action of the verb takes place. Notice the adverbs in the following sentences.

The lion walks **slowly** into the clearing.
There he notices a herd of Antelopes.
The antelopes will **immediately** flee at the predator's approach.

Slowly in the first example tells how the lion walks. *There* and *immediately* in the next two examples tell where and when. Notice that the adverb can occur after the verb, at the beginning of a sentence, or even in the middle of a verb phrase.

Adverbs can also modify adjectives or other adverbs by telling how much or to what extent.

A **very** noisy crowd watched. The lion roared **quite** fiercely.

The adverb *very* modifies the adjective *noisy*. It tells to what extent the crowd was noisy. The adverb *quite* modifies the adverb *fiercely*. It tells to what extent the lion roared fiercely.

Some adverbs are formed by adding the suffix *-ly* to adjectives.

Adjectives	+	**Suffix**	=	**Adverb**
eager		-ly		eagerly
quiet		-ly		quietly

However, not all words that end in *-ly* are adverbs. Some are adjectives: *curly, lonely, lovely, friendly.*

Exercise A
Underline each adverb and write which word it modifies.

1. Gina studied for a very difficult history test. _____

2. She began early in the evening. _____

3. First she listed the important events. _____

4. She reviewed her notes carefully. _____

5. She studied quite hard until eleven o'clock. _____

6. Afterwards she slept soundly. _____

Grade Eight SkillBook, Grammar, Usage, and Mechanics

Name _____ Class _____ Date _____

Exercise B
For each sentence, underline the adverb once and the word it modifies twice. Then tell whether the adverb indicates how, when, or where.

Example: Greg wrote the newspaper article yesterday.
Answer: Greg <u>wrote</u> the newspaper article <u>yesterday</u>. —when

1. The crash happened suddenly. _____
2. Lights flashed outside. _____
3. The police came instantly. _____
4. Then the ambulance arrived. _____
5. A man promptly received aid. _____
6. His arm was badly hurt. _____
7. The traffic moved slowly. _____
8. An officer soon fixed that. _____
9. Trucks pulled the cars away. _____
10. Finally everyone left. _____

Exercise C
For each underlined adverb, put two lines under the word that the adverb modifies. Write whether the word you have written is an adjective or an adverb.

Example: Clowns work <u>very</u> hard.
Answer: Clowns work <u>very</u> <u>hard.</u>—adverb

11. <u>Almost</u> all clowns go to a special school. _____
12. Making people laugh can be a <u>very</u> difficult job. _____
13. Clowns <u>quite</u> often study acrobatics. _____
14. Many of them are <u>rather</u> good actors and make-up artists.
 _____
15. The work they do is <u>extremely</u> precise and requires discipline.
 _____
16. Clowns dress <u>somewhat</u> oddly, but that is part of their charm.
 _____

246 Grade Eight SkillBook, Grammar, Usage, and Mechanics

Name _____ Class _____ Date _____

Lesson 52
Functions of Adverbs

Adverbs that modify verbs can function as adverbs of time, place, or manner. Adverbs that modify adjectives or other adverbs function as intensifiers.

You have learned that adverbs modify verbs by telling *when*, *where*, or *how*. An **adverb** that tells *when* is called an *adverb of time*. An **adverb** that tells *where* is called an *adverb of place*. An **adverb** that tells *how* is called an *adverb of manner* and usually ends in *-ly*. Which kind of adverb is each word in dark type?

> The party **tonight** will be **outside**. Please dress **casually**.

Here are come other examples of these kinds of adverbs.

Adverbs of time:	soon, today, now, always, then, later, never
Adverbs of place:	above, below, down, inside, here, there, over
Adverbs of manner:	softly, neatly, poorly, well, eagerly, slowly

Adverbs that modify adjectives and other adverbs are called **intensifiers**. They function by increasing or decreasing the intensity of the words they modify, and they come right before the words they modify. In the following sentences, which intensifier modifies an adjective? Which modifies another adverb?

> In her **first** performance Susan danced **extremely** well.
> **Surprisingly**, she was **hardly** nervous at all.

Here is a list of adverbs commonly used as intensifiers: *very, so, too, really, almost, nearly, extremely, somewhat, hardly, quite, rather, slightly, barely, especially*. To decide if a word is an intensifier, see how it is used in the sentence. It should tell *how much* or *to what extent*.

Exercise A
Write how each adverb functions in these sentences: time, place, manner, intensifier.

1. We had an extremely heavy rainfall today. _____

2. Everyone stayed inside during the storm. _____

3. Then my little sister happily hurried outside. _____

4. She and her friend splashed happily in the puddles. _____

Exercise B
Rewrite each sentence on the next page. Add the kind of adverb or adverbs indicated in parentheses.

Grade Eight SkillBook, Grammar, Usage, and Mechanics

Name _____ Class _____ Date _____

Example: Daniel drove. (intensifier, manner)
Answer: Daniel drove quite carefully.

1. Our family stayed at home for a change. (time)
   _____

2. We sat by the fire in the living room. (manner)
   _____

3. Dad made hot chocolate for us. (time)
   _____

4. It tasted good, but bitter. (intensifier)
   _____

5. Judith asked to play a game. (manner)
   _____

6. "Let's go," she suggested. (place, time)
   _____

Exercise C
Underline the adverbs in the sentences. Then write whether each one is an adverb of time, place, or manner or an intensifier.

Example:: One station has carried a very interesting show lately.
Answer: One station has carried a <u>very</u> interesting show <u>lately</u>.— intensifier, time

7. Recently, Ramona's radio show has been extremely popular. _____
8. She cleverly interviews rather unusual guests. _____
9. Tonight her program should be quite informative. _____
10. An extremely shy star finally agreed to an interview. _____
11. A mayoral candidate will be there. _____
12. Her guests usually answer her personal questions frankly. _____
13. Next, Ramona will cover some really important issues. _____
14. Listeners may then call in with their questions. _____
15. Later, she will graciously thank her guests for their visit. _____
16. Ramona never disappoints her very loyal audience. _____

248 Grade Eight SkillBook, Grammar, Usage, and Mechanics

| Name | Class | Date |

Lesson 53
Comparative Forms of Adverbs

Many adverbs have a positive, a comparative, and a superlative form.

Like adjectives, adverbs have three forms to show degrees of comparison. These are called the **positive degree,** the **comparative degree,** and the **superlative degree.** Notice the endings or words that are used with each of these forms.

Positive	Comparative	Superlative
loud	louder	loudest
soon	sooner	soonest
neatly	more or less neatly	most or least neatly
fearfully	more or less fearfully	most or least fearfully

The positive degree simply describes. The comparative degree compares two, and the superlative degree compares three or more.

Some adverbs have irregular comparative forms. Study the chart.

Positive	Comparative	Superlative
well	better	best
badly	worse	worst
much	more	most
little	less	least
far	farther	farthest

Avoid double comparisons with regular or irregular verbs.

Don't write: The job went **more faster** than I expected.
Write: The job went **faster** than I expected.
Don't write: He spent the **leastest** of anyone.
Write: He spent the **least** of anyone.

Exercise A

On your own paper, use each adverb on the next page in a sentence. Use the form of the adverb indicated in parentheses. (C) = Comparative; (S) = Superlative.

Example: frequently (C)
Answer: Mary writes more frequently than her sister.

Grade Eight SkillBook, Grammar, Usage, and Mechanics

1. strangely (C)
2. late (S)
3. brightly (S)
4. badly (C)
5. speedily (S)
6. clearly (C)
7. loosely (C)
8. far (C)
9. well (S)
10. tightly (C)
11. much (S)
12. little (C)
13. eagerly (S)
14. softly (C)
15. clumsily (S)
16. roughly (S)
17. completely (C)
18. hopefully (S)
19. selfishly (C)
20. gently (S)
21. well (C)
22. excitedly (S)
23. truthfully (C)
24. far (S)
25. comically (C)
26. badly (S)
27. little (S)

Exercise B

Rewrite the sentences below. Use the correct form of the adverb in parentheses. In some sentences, the adverb will not change.

Example: John cleaned the yard (thoroughly) than his room.
Answer: John cleaned the yard more thoroughly than his room.

1. Rachel shopped (carefully) at the record store than Vernon.

2. She walked (slowly) down each aisle than he.

3. She looked (closely) for special sales than other shoppers.

4. Vernon cared (little) about sales than Rachel.

5. He enjoys rock and roll (much) than jazz.

6. Vernon likes the blues (well) of all.

7. Classical music interests him (little) of all.

8. One record (quickly) caught his eye as he browsed.

Name _____ Class _____ Date _____

Lesson 54
Adjective or Adverb

Use adjectives to modify nouns and pronouns. Use adverbs to modify verbs, adjectives, and other adverbs.

How do you know whether to use an adjective or an adverb with the verb in a sentence? Your choice depends on what word is being modified and what kind of verb is used. Read these sentences.

    The fox **was quick.**   The fox **ran quickly.**

The verb *was* in the first sentence is a linking verb. It is followed by the predicate adjective *quick*, which modifies the noun *fox*. In the second sentence *ran* is an action verb. *Quickly* is an adverb that describes how the fox ran.

Be sure you know which word is being modified before you choose between an adjective or an adverb following a verb. Use an adjective after a linking verb to modify nouns and pronouns used as subjects.

    Nothing **smells** more **delicious** than fresh-baked bread. (Not: deliciously)
    It **tastes wonderful** too. (Not: wonderfully)

Use an adverb to modify an action verb.

    Zim **tasted** the hot soup **carefully.** (Not: careful)
    You **take** their joking too **seriously.** (Not: serious)
    That costume **fits** Juanita **perfectly.** (Not: perfect)

Two troublesome pairs are the adjective *sure* and the adverb *surely* and the adjective *real* and the adverb *really*. Notice the way these modifiers are used in the following sentences.

    My brother was **sure.**   He was **surely** stubborn about it.
    The story was **real.**   The story was **really** suspenseful.

In the first sentence on the left, the adjective *sure* is a predicate adjective. It follows the linking verb *was* and modifies the noun *brother*. In the sentence on the right, the intensifier-type adverb *surely* modifies the predicate adjective *stubborn*. In the second pair of sentences, the adjective *real* modifies the noun *story*. The adverb *really* modifies the word *suspenseful*.

Exercise A
Tell if the underlined word is correct or incorrect.

1. Locusts' songs are <u>real</u> shrill.
2. John always walks <u>slowly</u>.
3. The roses smelled <u>sweetly</u>.
4. Don't speak so <u>sarcastic</u>.
5. This milk tastes <u>sour</u>.
6. She is <u>sure</u> unhappy.

Exercise B
Some of the sentences on the next page are correct, but six of them are incorrect. Rewrite the incorrect sentences correctly. Write *correct* for the others.

Grade Eight SkillBook, Grammar, Usage, and Mechanics

Name _____ Class _____ Date _____

Example: My science grades are real low.
Answer: My science grades are really low.

1. Martin and I are really close friends.
_____

2. I've been doing poor in science.
_____

3. Martin is sure he can help me improve my grade.
_____

4. I chose my research-paper topic careful.
_____

5. Martin and I are researching the topic of insects thoroughly.
_____

6. He can identify most insects very quick.
_____

7. He has a real large collection of books about insects.
_____

8. My report will be really complete.
_____

9. One insect is sure different from another.
_____

10. I think my report will be real excellent.
_____

Exercise B
Underline the word in parentheses that completes the sentence correctly.

1. Cicadas, or seventeen-year locusts, grow (slow, slowly).
2. Their development underground is (slow, slowly).
3. Their time aboveground is (quick, quickly), though.
4. You should look (close, closely) at a locust sometime.
5. You can see them (clear, clearly) without a magnifying glass.
6. Swarms of locusts can be (real, really) large.
7. They damage crops (terrible, terribly) by feeding on them.
8. Farmers don't feel (sad, sadly) that cicadas are short-lived.

252 Grade Eight SkillBook, Grammar, Usage, and Mechanics

Name _____ Class _____ Date _____

Lesson 55
Good, well, bad, and *badly*

Good and **bad** are adjectives. **Well** and **badly** are adverbs.

Do not confuse the modifiers *good* and *well* or *bad* and *badly*. The adjective *good* is used to modify a noun or pronoun. Do not use it to modify a verb. Use the adverb *well* to modify a verb.

Don't write: Dolores sings **good.**
Write: Dolores sings **well.**
Don't write: She also plays the harp **good.**
Write: She also plays the harp **well.**

In the first pair of sentences, the adverb *well* modifies the verb *sings*. What does *well* modify in the second pair of sentences?

The modifiers *bad* and *badly* can also be troublesome. Use the adjective *bad* to modify a noun or pronoun. Use the adverb *badly* to modify a verb.

Don't write: Lou's car was smashed **bad** in an accident.
Write: Lou's car was smashed **badly** in an accident.
Don't write: Was Lou or the other driver hurt **bad?**
Write: Was Lou or the other driver hurt **badly?**

What does the adverb **badly** modify in the first pair of sentences? What does it modify in the second pair of sentences?

Remember that the adjectives *good* and *bad*, not the adverbs *well* and *badly*, are used after linking verbs.

She looked **good** in her gypsy costume. (Not: well)
He felt **bad** about missing the play. (Not: badly)

One exception: After a linking verb such as *feel*, the word *well* is used as an adjective to mean "in good health": *I feel well.* Use the adjective *good* after *feel* to mean "in good spirits": *I feel good.*

Exercise A
Underline the correct adjective or adverb from the choices in parentheses, and tell what word or words it modifies.

Example: Our bowling team looks (good, well) this year.
Answer: Our bowling team looks (<u>good</u>, well) this year.—team

1. Kim Lee always bowls (good, well). _____

2. Until he helped me with my delivery, I bowled pretty (bad, badly). _____

3. I felt (bad, badly) about my poor game. _____

4. Now I am doing (good, well). _____

Grade Eight SkillBook, Grammar, Usage, and Mechanics

Name _____ Class _____ Date _____

5. I feel (good, well) when I get a strike. _____
6. Andy doesn't do too (bad, badly) either. _____
7. Our team bowled (good, well) last night. _____
8. Only once this season have we lost because we bowled (bad, badly). _____
9. Anyone who bowls (good, well) enough can join the team. _____
10. How (bad, badly) do you want to be on the team? _____
11. Since you're not (bad, badly) run-down, you can learn to bowl. _____

Exercise B
Add an appropriate modifier—*good, well, bad, badly*—in the blank.

Example: Everyone is _____ at some sport.
Answer: Everyone is <u>good</u> at some sport.

1. Lonnie plays basketball _____ for being so short.
2. Yesterday she got over twenty points, even though the rest of her team played _____.
3. Can Lonnie play baseball as _____ as she plays basketball?
4. I felt _____ for Sara when she didn't make the team.
5. Our baseball team usually doesn't play _____.
6. Ron and I can hit _____, but we don't often hit home runs.
7. No matter how hard he tries, Fred fields _____.
8. Fred's chances of being a starter don't look too _____.
9. My brother swims _____ enough to win almost every meet.
10. Unlike my brother, the champion, I swim _____.

Lesson 56
This, *that*, *these*, and *those*

The demonstrative adjectives *this* and *that* are singular. *These* and *those* are plural.

The adjectives *this*, *that*, *these*, and *those*, which point out which one or which ones, are called **demonstrative adjectives.** *This* and *these* refer to things that are near in time or space. *That* and *those* refer to things that are at some distance in time or space.

> **This** orchestra playing now sounds better than **that** orchestra we heard last week.
> **These** musicians in the studio are more skilled than **those** musicians waiting outside.

As the examples show, *this* and *that* are used with singular nouns. *These* and *those* are used with plural nouns.

Since *this* adds the meaning "here" to the word it modifies, and *that* adds the meaning "there," do not unnecessarily use the words *here* and *there* with them.

> **This** aisle seat is mine. (Not: This here aisle seat)
> **That** seat is yours. (Not: That there seat)

Avoid using the pronoun *them* in place of the adjective *those*.

> **Those** songs are silly. (Not: Them songs)

Use the singular demonstrative adjectives *this* and *that* to modify the singular nouns *kind* and *sort* in sentences like the following.

> Did you want **this kind** of juice oranges? (Not: these kind)
> I wouldn't buy **that sort** of apples. (Not: those sort)

Use the plural *these* and *those* only when the nouns are plural.

> **These kinds** of plants need sunlight.
> **Those sorts** of plants need shade.

Exercise A
Underline the correct word or words in parentheses.

1. (Them, Those) pans are just the right size.
2. What do I need besides (this, these) kind of pots?
3. (Those, Those there) tomatoes are ripe enough to eat now.
4. Do you like (this, these) sort of recipe?
5. For (that, that there) dish we need potatoes and onions.
6. Joyce wants (that, those) kind of dessert.

Grade Eight SkillBook, Grammar, Usage, and Mechanics

7. (Them, Those) grapes need to be washed.
8. According to (this, this here) recipe, honey can be used.
9. Use (this, these) sort of scissors to cut the celery leaves.
10. We can't use (this, these) kind of apples for baking.
11. When you chop (these, these here) onions, be ready to cry.
12. Elmer bought both of (them, those) kinds of berries.
13. Have you tasted (that, that there) fruit punch?
14. (This, This here) new cookbook is a big help.
15. (That, Those) kinds of food are very appetizing.

Exercise B

Use *this*, *that*, *these*, and *those* to complete the following sentences.

Example: Dale is looking at _____ maps over there.
Answer: Dale is looking at those maps over there.

1. _____ atlas isn't as good as this one.
2. _____ atlas on my lap contains maps of the solar system.
3. Did you renew all of _____ books sitting here on the table?
4. Yes, but I forgot _____ two upstairs in my room.
5. On _____ map I have here you can see the Ohio River.
6. Turn the page and you will see _____ mountain I described.
7. _____ lakes you mentioned are about 300 miles south of here.
8. We still enjoy living in _____ city.
9. How many of _____ islands out on the bay are inhabited?
10. How far is it to _____ ranger tower over there?

Lesson 57
Using Negative Words

Use only one negative word when you mean "no."

The use of two negative words in the same clause to convey the meaning "no" or "not" is called a **double negative.** Only one negative word is needed. Negative words include the words *neither, never, no, not, nothing, nobody, none, nowhere,* and the contraction *n't,* the shortened form of *not.*

Read the examples below to see ways to correct double negatives.

Incorrect:	He **couldn't** do **nothing** right.
Correct:	He could do **nothing** right.
Correct:	He **couldn't** do anything right.
Incorrect:	We **haven't** had **no** rain for a month.
Correct:	We have had **no** rain for a month.
Correct:	We **haven't** had any rain for a month.

As you can see, the sentences were corrected by dropping one of the negative words or by changing one negative word to a positive word. Positive words that can be substituted for negative words include *any, anything, anybody, anywhere, either,* and *ever.*

Negative words that do not begin with the letter *n,* like *hardly, barely, scarcely,* and *without,* are somewhat harder to catch. But they should not be used with another negative word.

Incorrect:	**Hardly nobody** wanted to have a picnic.
Correct:	**Hardly anybody** wanted to have a picnic.

Occasionally three negatives are incorrectly used together.

Incorrect:	Mitch **shouldn't never** count on **nothing** at all.
Correct:	Mitch **shouldn't** count on anything at all.
Correct:	Mitch should **never** count on anything at all.
Correct:	Mitch should count on **nothing** at all.

Exercise A
Decide which word in parentheses would correctly complete each sentence. Underline the correct word.

1. I (couldn't, could) scarcely say no.
2. Ruth and I don't know (nothing, anything) about soccer rules.
3. How can you eat cold beef without (no, any) horseradish?
4. Didn't (neither, either) of the two want the job?
5. She (couldn't, could) barely lift that heavy suitcase.
6. There wasn't (nobody, anybody) collecting tickets.
7. I would have drunk some milk, but there wasn't (none, any).

8. Weren't there (no, any) guards around?

9. Dad won't let (none, any) of us use his new camera.

10. We didn't have (no, any) snow until the end of December.

11. I (can't, can) hardly wait for spring vacation!

12. Sam won't go (nowhere, anywhere) without that rabbit's foot.

13. But you haven't (never, ever) had the mumps!

Exercise B

Rewrite the sentences to eliminate double and triple negatives.

   Example: I called twice, but there wasn't no one home.
   Answer: I called twice, but there was no one home.

1. Stuart won't direct neither production this year.

2. He doesn't have no time because of his new job.

3. The drama club doesn't have hardly enough people for no play.

4. Nobody knows nothing about stage work.

5. None of the costumes are ready neither.

6. We can't put on this play without no props.

7. I can't find no one nowhere who can work the lights.

8. He worked his way through college without no help.

9. We were so scared we couldn't hardly breathe.

10. Don't you never go bowling?

Name _____ Class _____ Date _____

Lesson 58
Placement of Modifiers

Place modifiers as close as possible to the words they modify.

A modifier should be placed in a sentence where it will clearly show what word it modifies. Read the following sentence, paying close attention to the modifier in dark type.

    Instructions are given on how to plant the dahlias **in the seed catalog.**

The sentence seems to suggest that someone would plant dahlias in a catalog. That cannot be the meaning the writer intended. To help a reader immediately understand the meaning, the modifying phrase should be placed next to *instructions*, the noun it modifies.

    In the seed catalog, instructions are given on how to plant the dahlias.

A modifier not placed close to the word it modifies is called a **misplaced modifier.** Misplaced modifiers can confuse a reader for a moment and cause unintended amusement. Now read this sentence.

    A farmer gave us the collie **who had put an ad in the paper.**

The modifiers *only* and *just* should always be placed immediately before the words they modify. Notice how the placement of *only* affects the meaning of these two sentences.

    Only she helped me. (No one else helped.)
    She helped **only** me. (She helped no one else.)

What would be the meaning if *only* were placed between *she* and *helped*?

Exercise A
Rewrite each sentence, placing the misplaced modifier close to the word it modifies. Be sure to change capital letters as necessary.

    Example: People missed a good skit that came late.
    Answer: People that came late missed a good skit.

1. The lion ignored the crowd that was pacing in his cage.

2. Martha opened the door of the new house with a broad smile.

3. Sal appointed a committee to count the ballots before the voting began.

4. The explorer told about his many adventures at a meeting of the Optimists Club.

Grade Eight SkillBook, Grammar, Usage, and Mechanics

5. We took the bicycle wheel to a repair shop that was bent out of shape.

6. They watched the whale dive through their binoculars.

7. After they were rounded up, the cowhands branded the cows.

8. A groundskeeper found the lucky coin in the park that Inez had lost last week.

9. The ferocious dog barked at the mail carrier with bared teeth.

10. Kenji and I put the ripe apples into a bushel basket that had fallen off the tree.

Exercise B
On your paper rewrite each sentence in two ways. Place the word in parentheses in two different positions in each sentence to show how sentence meaning changes.
Be sure to change capital letters as necessary.

Example: The fort is over the hill. (just)
Answer: Just the fort is over the hill.
The fort is just over the hill.

1. Pierre can carry one canoe. (only)
2. He will take us as far as the next fort. (just)
3. Our choice is to stay for three days. (only)
4. The trapper exchanged pelts for food. (only)
5. Those people grow vegetables inside the fort. (just)

Lesson 59
Participles and Participial Phrases

A participle is a verb form that can be used as an adjective. It may appear by itself or with other words in a participial phrase.

A **participle** is a form of a verb. You may recall that present participles end with *-ing* and most past participles end with *-ed*. The past participles of the first three verbs in the chart have regular endings. The last three do not; they are irregular.

Present Tense	Present Participle	Past Participle
jump	jumping	jumped
talk	talking	talked
anticipate	anticipating	anticipated
bite	biting	bitten
blow	blowing	blown
hold	holding	held

A participle can be used with an auxiliary verb to form a verb phrase. A participle is also used without an auxiliary verb, as an adjective to modify a noun or pronoun. Study these sentences.

The runner **is jumping** the hurdles.
The **jumping** runner tripped.
The **shaken** runner got to her feet.

In the first sentence the present participle *jumping* is part of the verb phrase *is jumping*. In the second sentence *jumping* is used as an adjective to describe the noun *runner*. What is the past participle in the third sentence? How is it used?

Since participles are verb forms, they can take objects, complements, and modifiers. A participle together with these other words forms a **participial phrase**.

Jumping over a hurdle, the runner tripped.

In this sentence *Jumping over a hurdle* is a participial phrase that modifies the noun *runner*.

Now study these sentences with participial phrases.

Jan, **seeing the accident,** grabbed my binoculars.
Being her friend, I let her have them.
Worried about the runner, she watched him anxiously.
The runner, **moving slowly,** began to run again.
The spectators, **concerned for the runner,** sighed in relief.

What participial phrases are used in these sentences? What noun or pronoun does each modify?
Many participial phrases can come before or after the words they modify.

Grade Eight SkillBook, Grammar, Usage, and Mechanics

When a participial phrase comes at the beginning of a sentence, it must modify the subject.

Crossing the finish line, even the first runners looked tired.
Even the first runners **crossing the finish line** looked tired.

Another term for a verb form that can be used as an adjective or noun is a verbal. In the next two lessons you will learn about two other kinds of verbals, verb forms that are used as nouns.

Exercise A
Underline the participle in each sentence. Tell whether it is a present participle or a past participle and what word it modifies.

1. The barking dog alerted them. _____

2. The cracked windowpane made them suspicious. _____

3. They hurried into the darkened house. _____

4. Holding their breath, they tiptoed from room to room. _____

5. Which sentence has a participial phrase? _____

Exercise B
Read each sentence. Then write what word the underlined participle modifies.

Example: The <u>excited</u> explorers dug for relics.
Answer: explorers

1. The <u>burning</u> sun slowed their progress. _____
2. Each <u>sunburned</u> explorer dug carefully. _____
3. A <u>forgotten</u> people once lived here. _____
4. Searchers sifted the <u>mounded</u> earth for relics. _____
5. Sometimes <u>beating</u> rain flooded the site. _____
6. Everyone welcomed the <u>cooling</u> breezes. _____
7. Someday each <u>hidden</u> relic will be uncovered. _____

Name _____ Class _____ Date _____

Exercise C

Underline each participle in the sentences below. If the participle is part of a participial phrase, put parentheses around the phrase.

   Example: The puppy wandering the streets was looking for a friend.
   Answer: The puppy (<u>wandering</u> the streets) was looking for a friend.

8. The biting wind licked at his heels.
9. Frozen snow crunched under his feet.
10. Looking alarmed, the puppy ran into an alley.
11. A siren, screeching loudly, caused him to hide in a box.
12. The sound came closer to the terrified animal.
13. A lady taking a walk saw him.
14. Rushing to him, she gathered him in her arms.
15. Her comforting embrace soothed his nerves.
16. A dogcatcher driving a van waved to the lady.
17. Feeling secure, the puppy barked at the van.

Exercise D

Underline each participial phrase. Then draw two lines under the noun or pronoun that the phrase modifies.

   Example: Laughing with glee, Rosa entered the sack race.
   Answer: <u>Laughing with glee,</u> Rosa entered the sack race.

18. Motivated by the prizes, everyone entered the contests.
19. Pedro, carrying an egg in a spoon, beat Lisa.
20. Being a runner, she expected to win.
21. The crowd cheered the contestants hopping in the one-leg race.
22. The winners, exhausted form their efforts, got their prizes.
23. Looking pleased, Mike won a ticket to the movie.
24. Willa, soaking wet, beat Ed at the loop toss.
25. Resting between games, contestants compared scores.

Name _____ Class _____ Date _____

Lesson 60
Gerunds and Gerund Phrases

A **gerund** is a verb form ending in *-ing* that is used as a noun. It may be used by itself or in a gerund phrase.

When a verb form ending in *-ing* is used as a noun, it is called a **gerund**. A gerund can be used in any way that a noun can be used. Compare the uses of nouns and gerunds in the following sentences:

Subject:	**Photography** is my hobby. (noun)
Subject:	**Cooking** is my hobby. (gerund)
Predicate noun:	Her favorite sport is **tennis**. (noun)
Predicate noun:	Her favorite sport is **surfing**. (gerund)
Direct object:	She enjoys **handball** too. (noun)
Direct object:	She enjoys **swimming** too. (gerund)
Object of preposition:	That music is good for **aerobics**. (noun)
Object of preposition:	That music is good for **exercising**. (gerund)

A gerund and any object, complement, or modifiers that go with it form a **gerund phrase**. A gerund phrase may also be used just as a noun is used.

They started **dancing to the music**. (direct object)
Their goal was **dancing smoothly**. (predicate noun)
Taking lessons improved their form. (subject)
They dream of **winning a trophy**. (object of preposition)

Remember that, unlike participles, gerunds end only in *-ing*.

Exercise A
Write how each underlined gerund or gerund phrase is used in the sentence: direct object, predicate noun, subject, or object of a preposition.

1. A good exercise is <u>walking</u>. _____

2. We were tired after <u>hiking for two hours</u>. _____

3. <u>Jogging</u> is not for some people. _____

4. I like <u>working out at the gym</u>. _____

5. <u>Walking the dog</u> is Frannie's only exercise. _____

6. Maybe she enjoys <u>running with the dog</u>. _____

7. What's your opinion of <u>swimming</u>? _____

Exercise B
Use a gerund to complete each sentence. Remember that gerunds are made by adding *-ing* to the present tense form of a verb.

Example: A glass is used for _____ water.
Answer: A glass is used for drinking water.

Name _____ Class _____ Date _____

1. A knife is used for _____ potatoes.
2. Use a spoon for _____ soup.
3. _____ the cake took almost all afternoon.
4. Ellen forgot about _____ her homework.
5. I enjoy _____ her with her work.
6. Greg's favorite recreation is _____ basketball.
7. _____ the game was a big thrill.
8. _____ to records is not my favorite evening activity.
9. I am tired of _____ country music.
10. _____ her hair in braids makes Barbara look like one of my favorite country singers.
11. Celia thought she might look more like a country singer by _____ a bouffant wig.
12. My favorite singers, Clare Cassidy and the Downhomers, are sure of _____ an award this year.

Exercise C
Underline the gerund in each sentence. If the gerund has an object, a complement, or modifiers, put parentheses around the gerund phrase.

Example: We will enjoy touring the museum.
Answer: We will enjoy (<u>touring</u> the museum.)

13. Visiting museums is educational.
14. Does touring appeal to you?
15. Learning is easier this way.
16. Do you enjoy walking so much?
17. Studying exhibits is educational.
18. The guide is an expert in lecturing.
19. Here are some earphones for listening.
20. Seeing a movie is next.
21. The museum theater is for showing educational films.
22. Here is a good spot for viewing.
23. I hate to think of leaving the museum.
24. Walking slowly helps us see more.
25. Observing the exhibits carefully is important.

Grade Eight SkillBook, Grammar, Usage, and Mechanics

Name _____ Class _____ Date _____

Exercise D

Underline the gerund or the gerund phrase in each sentence. Tell whether it is used as a subject, predicate noun, direct object, or object of a preposition.

Example: Doing pushups is tiring.
Answer: <u>Doing pushups</u> is tiring. subject

26. The team started exercising early each morning. _____
27. One of the most difficult tasks is doing sit-ups. _____
28. Some students dislike climbing up ropes. _____
29. The objective is climbing to the top in less than a minute. _____
30. Sliding down afterwards is fun. _____
31. Tumbling makes me dizzy sometimes. _____
32. Several persons have signed up for tumbling next month. _____
33. Some people prefer lifting in the weight room. _____
34. Working out regularly is important. _____
35. A big mistake is resting too much between exercises. _____
36. Exercising is really good for you and a lot of fun. _____

Exercise E

On your own paper, write sentences using the following gerunds and gerund phrases. Tell how the gerund or gerund phrase is used in each sentence—as a subject, direct object, predicate noun, or object of a preposition.

Example: running in a marathon
Answer: Running in a marathon is strenuous. subject

37. taking a test
38. buying clothes
39. learning karate
40. complaining
41. reading the directions
42. helping a friend
43. hang gliding
44. hitting a home run
45. ice skating

266 Grade Eight SkillBook, Grammar, Usage, and Mechanics

Name _____ Class _____ Date _____

Lesson 61
Infinitives and Infinitive Phrases

An **infinitive** is a present tense verb, usually preceded by *to*. It can be used as a noun, either by itself or with other words in an infinitive phrase.

Infinitives are verb forms that can be used as adjectives, adverbs, or nouns. This lesson will concentrate on infinitives used as nouns. An infinitive often is easy to recognize because it usually begins with the word *to* immediately followed by a present tense verb. *To go*, *to play*, and *to run* are all infinitives. Notice how infinitives are used in these sentences.

A good hobby is **to bicycle**. (predicate noun)
To race is my ambition. (subject)
I very much want **to win**. (direct object)

An infinitive and the object, complement, or modifiers that go with it form an **infinitive phrase**. An infinitive phrase may also be used as a noun.

To enter the Cassidy Class Race is my first goal. (subject)
My chief task is **to practice daily**. (predicate noun)
I want **to achieve perfect condition.** (direct object)

What is the infinitive used in each phrase?
When infinitives follow certain verbs, the *to* may be understood and need not be written. *Dare* and *help* are among those verbs.

I never dared (to) skip training sessions.
My friends helped (to) keep me on schedule.

Exercise A
Write how the underlined infinitive or infinitive phrase in each sentence is used—as subject, direct object, or predicate noun.

1. We hoped <u>to travel this summer</u>. _____
2. <u>To visit Alaska</u> was our first choice. _____
3. The whole family wants <u>to see Mount McKinley</u>. _____
4. Our purpose would be <u>to photograph the highest mountain in North America</u>. _____

Exercise B
Use an infinitive to complete each sentence. Remember that an infinitive is a present tense verb preceded by *to*, unless it follows a verb like *dare* or *help*.

Example: My first assignment is _____ about Abraham Lincoln.
Answer: My first assignment is <u>to write</u> about Abraham Lincoln.

Grade Eight SkillBook, Grammar, Usage, and Mechanics

1. When Lincoln was a boy, his family decided _____ from Kentucky to Indiana.
2. When he was eight years old, he helped _____ a log cabin.
3. _____ books to read was difficult on the frontier.
4. Lincoln promised _____ any borrowed books.
5. People liked _____ in the general store in his community.
6. A popular pastime was _____ to Lincoln's stories.
7. In 1830, the Lincoln family decided _____ in Illinois.
8. Lincoln helped _____ logs for a new cabin.
9. One of his early jobs was _____ a boat down the Mississippi.
10. When he returned, he began _____ in a store.
11. _____ daily was one of Lincoln's goals.

Exercise C
Underline the infinitive or the infinitive phrase, whichever the sentence contains. (One sentence has two infinitive phrases.) Tell whether the infinitive is used as a subject, direct object, or predicate noun.

Example: Francine Patterson decided to study gorillas.
Answer: Francine Patterson decided <u>to study gorillas</u>. —direct object

12. Francine helped raise the young gorilla Koko. _____
13. She decided to teach the gorilla sign language. _____
14. To teach Koko 375 signs took six years. _____
15. Koko uses signs when she wants to "talk." _____
16. Koko eventually learned to ask questions. _____
17. She wouldn't dare tell lies. _____
18. Koko has learned to understand many directions. _____
19. Koko's new task is to use a computer. _____
20. The computer helps translate her thoughts. _____
21. To know Koko is to love her. _____

Name _____ Class _____ Date _____

Lesson 62
Placement of Participial Phrases

A participial phrase should be placed as close as possible to the word that it modifies.

A **participial phrase** is a group of words introduced by a present or past participle. A participial phrase modifies a noun or pronoun.

Read the following sentences. Notice the placement of the participial phrases.

> Janine saw two lions and a tiger **visiting the zoo**.
> **Buried under a pile of papers**, Joshua found his library card.

As you read the first sentence, what does the participial phrase seem to modify? What does the phrase in the second sentence modify?

The placement of the participial phrases confuses the meanings of the sentences above. Modifiers that are not placed close to the words they modify are called **misplaced modifiers**.

To correct these sentences, decide who or what the participial phrase modifies. The first sentence suggests that the two lions and a tiger are visiting the zoo. Since that does not make sense, the phrase must be intended to modify another word—*Janine*. What is the meaning suggested in the second sentence? What word is the participial phrase intended to modify?

When the participial phrases are placed next to the word they modify, the sentences make sense.

> **Visiting the zoo**, Janine saw two lions and a tiger.
> Joshua found his library card **buried under a pile of papers**.

Exercise A
The participial phrase in each of the following sentences is incorrectly placed. Rewrite each sentence and move the participial phrase so the sentence will make sense.

1. We found a patch of ripe strawberries coming down the hill.

_____

2. Stealing second base, the umpire almost didn't see Rob.

_____

3. Wrapped in bacon strips, my uncle likes chicken livers.

_____

4. Rachel saw three rosebushes watering the plants.

_____

Grade Eight SkillBook, Grammar, Usage, and Mechanics

Exercise B
Underline the sentence in each pair that contains the correctly placed participial phrase.

1. Tied with a red ribbon, the package sat on the table.
   The package sat on the table tied with a red ribbon.

2. Camping out last summer, we saw a bear.
   We saw a bear camping out last summer.

3. The plane startled the onlookers coming in for a landing.
   Coming in for a landing, the plane startled the onlookers.

4. We couldn't see the birds perched on the topmost branches.
   Perched on the topmost branches, we couldn't see the birds.

5. Climbing in a window, Cara saw a burglar.
   Cara saw a burglar climbing in a window.

Exercise C
Rewrite each sentence to correct the position of the misplaced modifier. Be sure to change capital letters as necessary.

Example: I was relieved to see my house turning the corner.
Answer: Turning the corner, I was relieved to see my house.

6. Herb found a rare book browsing through the library.

7. The detective watched the house hidden in a truck.

8. Fred could hear the music running down the stairs.

9. Lying under a pile of leaves, Sybil found the lost shovel.

10. Breathing with difficulty, the nurse comforted the patient.

11. The explorers found an oasis crossing the desert.

12. Setting over the lake, Ira thought the sun looked beautiful.

Name _____ Class _____ Date _____

Lesson 63
Prepositions and Prepositional Phrases

A preposition is used with a noun or pronoun to form a prepositional phrase.

Prepositions are words such as *in*, *by*, and *from*. Study the list. Notice that some prepositions contain more than one word.

about	behind	except	on	toward
above	below	for	onto	under
across	beneath	from	out	underneath
after	beside	in	outside	until
against	between	inside	over	up
along	beyond	into	past	with
among	but	like	through	according to
around	by	near	throughout	in addition to
at	down	of	till	in spite of
before	during	off	to	instead of

A **prepositional phrase** is a group of words that begins with a preposition and ends with a noun or pronoun. This noun or pronoun is called the **object of the preposition** and may have modifiers. Prepositions can have compound objects, as in the first example below. Notice also that prepositional phrases can occur at various places in a sentence, including right after each other.

1. Steve works **in dirty fireplaces and chimneys.**
2. **With modern equipment** he removes soot **from clogged areas.**
3. A job **like his** was much harder **for workers in the past.**

Notice in the third example that two prepositional phrases come right after each other.

Exercise A
Complete each sentence by adding a preposition.

    Example: Good books _____ children are now receiving recognition.
    Answer: Good books <u>for</u> children are now receiving recognition.

1. Have you heard _____ the Newbery and Caldecott medals?
2. They are awarded annually _____ outstanding children's books.
3. The Newbery Award is named _____ John Newbery, a bookseller.
4. Newbery was one _____ the first publishers of children's books.

Grade Eight SkillBook, Grammar, Usage, and Mechanics

5. The Caldecott Medal is given _____ distinguished picture books.

6. Children's authors are in competition for awards _____ these.

7. To them, the Newbery and Caldecott rank _____ all others.

8. The best books _____ the world are useless if not read, though.

9. Award winners frequently become popular _____ word of mouth.

10. Tell a friend of yours today _____ an outstanding book!

Exercise B

Underline each preposition or prepositional phrase and write **O** over its object.

Example: Steve Berg has an unusual occupation for an American.

Answer: for an American
          O

1. Steve is a chimney sweep and goes around town in a green van.

2. He knocks on doors and explains his work to people.

3. Until his visit many people didn't know about sweeps.

4. Steve's services sound strange to them, but in spite of their surprise they make contracts with him for work.

5. Steve arrives in his tall black hat and black clothes.

6. First, he pushes a long brush up the walls of the chimney.

7. Next he loosens the soot and ashes along the chimney walls.

8. The dirt and debris fall into the fireplace and sometimes spread across the room.

9. Steve runs his giant vacuum cleaner over the floor and rugs.

10. Then he climbs into his van and drives to his next job.

Name _____ Class _____ Date _____

Lesson 64
Preposition, Adverb, or Infinitive

Some words can be used both as prepositions and as adverbs. The word *to* can be a preposition, or it can begin an infinitive.

Many words can function as either prepositions or adverbs. It depends on how they are used. Look at these examples.

> Ellen walked **down** the steps to her car.
> Suddenly she fell **down** on the ice.

In the first sentence the word *down* is a preposition. Its object is *steps*. In the second sentence *down* is an adverb. It is not followed by an object. How are the words in dark type used in the sentences below?

> Ellen walked **outside**. She strolled **around** and thought. She stepped **outside** the school and jogged **around** the track.

The word *to* can also be confusing. Sometimes it is used to begin a prepositional phrase and other times to make the verb form called an infinitive. Study the examples.

> Prepositional phrase: *to* + noun or pronoun
>   Ellen went **to** the dentist.
> Infinitive: *to* + verb
>   She really wanted **to** swim.

The first *to* begins the prepositional phrase *to the dentist*. The second *to* begins the infinitive *to swim*. Remember, when *to* comes before a noun or pronoun, it begins a prepositional phrase; when *to* comes before a verb, it begins an infinitive.

Exercise A
Tell how each underlined word is used. You will find prepositions, infinitives, and adverbs.

1. Yesterday I decided <u>to</u> go <u>to</u> town. _____
2. I planned <u>to</u> look <u>around</u> in all the shops. _____
3. I drove <u>around</u> the block three times but couldn't find parking. _____
4. I waited <u>in</u> line <u>to</u> park inside a garage. _____
5. Finally someone pulled <u>out</u> from a spot and I pulled <u>in</u>. _____

Exercise B
Tell whether the underlined phrases on the next page are infinitives or prepositional phrases.

> **Example:** Sue ran <u>to the window</u> <u>to see</u> the new car.
> **Answer:** to the window—prepositional phrase; to see—infinitive

Grade Eight SkillBook, Grammar, Usage, and Mechanics

1. My friend called me to talk to someone about her problem. _____
2. But I had to leave to go to a doctor's appointment. _____
3. I had to hurry to the doctor's office. _____
4. To join school athletic teams you need to have a physical. _____
5. So on the phone I said some hard words to my friend. _____
6. To tell the truth, I told her to jump in the lake. _____
7. I even told her that I would drive her to the lake. _____
8. Normally, I would not say that to anyone. _____
9. When I lose my patience though, I say crazy things to people. _____
10. Later on, I have to apologize to them. _____

Exercise C
Tell whether the underlined words are adverbs or prepositions.

   Example: Yesterday I had lunch inside with my friend.
   Answer: inside—adverb; with—preposition

11. We argued over lunch about our quarrel on the phone. _____
12. She was angry at me for several reasons. _____
13. My friend and I waited outside for a few minutes. _____
14. Then we went in and chatted in the lobby. _____
15. Inside the restaurant, we sat down and talked some more. _____
16. Then my friend stood up and began pacing around. _____
17. She was so angry that she almost walked out of the restaurant. _____
18. For a long time, we talked about the situation. _____
19. When I apologized to her, she calmed down. _____
20. After lunch, we walked over to a pond near the restaurant. _____

Name _____ Class _____ Date _____

Lesson 65
Adjective and Adverb Prepositional Phrases

A prepositional phrase can be an adjective prepositional phrase or an adverb prepositional phrase.

Prepositional phrases may modify such words as nouns, pronouns, and verbs. An adjective prepositional phrase is a phrase that modifies a noun or pronoun. It functions much like a one-word adjective.

Adjective: A **colorful** parrot drank the water.
Phrase: A parrot **with colorful feathers** drank the water.

In the first example, the adjective *colorful* modifies *parrot*, telling what kind of parrot. The adjective phrase *with colorful feathers* in the second example also modifies *parrot*. Like *colorful*, it tells what kind of parrot.

One-word adjectives generally come just before the nouns they modify. Adjective prepositional phrases, however, nearly always come just after the nouns they modify. This is one clue for locating them in a sentence.

Adjective phrases may also follow each other, as in the following example. Then the second phrase usually modifies the object of the first phrase.

Those trees **behind the fence in the yard** are Japanese elms.

Behind the fence is an adjective prepositional phrase that modifies *trees*, telling which trees. *In the yard* modifies *fence*, telling which fence.

An **adverb prepositional phrase** generally modifies a verb. Like a one-word adverb, an adverb phrase may tell where, how, or when an action takes place.

The macaw watched **from its cage.** (where)
It screeched **in a harsh voice.** (how)
It scolded us **throughout the day.** (when)

Notice in the third example that an adverb phrase does not always come immediately after the verb it modifies.

Sometimes the two adverb phrases come right after each other. Then they often tell different things about the verb they modify.

The bird flew **into the elms with graceful movements.**

Into the elms tells where the bird flew, and *with graceful movements* tells how it flew.

Adverb phrases may come in various places in a sentence, including the beginning. To decide whether a phrase functions as an adverb, see if it tells *when*, *where*, or *how* about the verb.

By the next morning, everyone was searching for the lost bird.

Grade Eight SkillBook, Grammar, Usage, and Mechanics

Name _____ Class _____ Date _____

Exercise A

In the sentences below, draw two lines under the word or words that each underlined prepositional phrase modifies. Use **N** or **V** to show if it is a noun or a verb. Some sentences have more than one prepositional phrase.

    Example: The Grand Canyon of Arizona is 277 miles long.

                                    N
    Answer: The Grand Canyon of Arizona is 277 miles long.

1. The Colorado River flows <u>through the gorge</u>.
2. Forests grow <u>along the canyon's rims</u>.
3. The rocks <u>in the canyon</u> are more than a million years old.
4. <u>Over the years</u>, the river has cut a deep gorge.
5. Thousands <u>of mule deer</u> range <u>throughout the canyon</u>.
6. The waters <u>of the river</u> swarm <u>with trout</u>.
7. Preservation <u>of the canyon's natural beauty</u> is the responsibility <u>of the National Park Service</u>.
8. Some brave tourists raft <u>through the rapids</u>.
9. Visitors can tour <u>on a boat</u> or travel <u>by mule</u>.
10. Rock carvings <u>by ancient Indians</u> sometimes remain <u>on the canyon walls</u>.
11. Many people worry <u>about the area's future</u>.
12. Pollution and erosion concern thousands <u>of park visitors</u>.

Example B.

Underline the prepositional phrases in the sentences, and write whether they are adjective or adverb phrases. Some sentences have more than one phrase.

    Example: Many birds in North American migrate twice during the year.
    Answer: in <u>North America</u>—adjective; <u>during the year</u>—adverb

1. During the spring, ducks and geese arrive in large numbers at our local park.

_____

2. The small pond inside the park becomes their haven in the city.

_____

3. People in the blocks around the park enjoy their aerial antics.

_____

4. With great concentration, imagine a nearby pair of ducks.

_____

5. One lost mallard stands outside a hamburger stand and begs for food.

   _____

6. For its own sake, I shoo it back toward the park.

   _____

7. Within a minute, the duck is flying over the buildings.

   _____

8. Fortunately, the keepers at the nearby zoo feed the ducks and geese during the warm months.

   _____

9. Throughout the summer, residents of the neighborhood enjoy the adorable ducklings and goslings.

   _____

10. By autumn, they will migrate like their parents to some other pond.

    _____

Exercise C
Complete each sentence with the kind of prepositional phrase indicated in parentheses. Use a variety of prepositions.

11. In the morning they hiked _____. (adverb phrase)

12. They took pictures _____. (adjective phrase)

13. Wild animals _____ ran as they approached. (adjective phrase)

14. At noon the hikers stopped _____. (adverb phrase)

15. Someone _____ (adjective phrase) ate _____. (adverb phrase)

16. After ten minutes everyone continued _____. (adverb phrase)

17. Flowers _____ (adjective phrase) grew _____. (adverb phrase)

18. A tiny stream rippled _____. (adverb phrase)

Grade Eight SkillBook, Grammar, Usage, and Mechanics

Name _____ Class _____ Date _____

Lesson 66
Two Kinds of Conjunctions

A conjunction is used to join words or groups of words. Two kinds of conjunctions are coordinating and correlative.

The word *conjunction* comes from Latin *com-*, meaning "together," and *jungere*, meaning "to join." Conjunctions are used to join words or groups of words. There are different kinds of conjunctions.

A **coordinating conjunction** is used to join words or groups of words of equal value in a sentence. For example, it may join two or more nouns, adjectives, phrases, or sentences.

The most common coordinating conjunctions are *and*, *but*, and *or*. *And* shows the addition of one thing to another. *But* shows a contrast between two things. *Or* shows a choice. What kinds of elements are joined by these conjunctions in the examples below?

> I sent an invitation **and** a map to the guests.
> The party will end after dinner **but** before dark.
> Will the late arrivals be happy **or** angry?

Other coordinating conjunctions include *so*, *yet*, *for*, and *nor*.

> Pedro has been to my house before, **so** he knows the way.
> Lorinda enjoys parties, **yet** she didn't come to this one.
> Akira did well in the treasure hunt, **for** he knew the area well.
> He didn't team up with Mark, **nor** did he join anyone else.

Conjunctions that are used in pairs are called **correlative conjunctions**. Some correlative conjunctions are *both . . . and*, *either . . . or*, and *neither . . . nor*. A pair of correlative conjunctions is always separated by a word or group of a words.

> **Both** the scissors **and** the book were on the table.
> They went to the store **either** in a car **or** in a truck.
> **Neither** the telephone on the wall **nor** the light worked.

Exercise A
Underline the coordinating and correlative conjunctions from the sentences below. Tell if they are coordinating or correlative.

> **Example:** My favorite movies are both comedies and mysteries.
> **Answer:** My favorite movies are <u>both</u> comedies <u>and</u> mysteries.—correlative

1. I go to either matinees or early evening shows to avoid crowds.

   _____

2. Both Roger and Gene liked this movie, so I know I will too.

   _____

278 Grade Eight SkillBook, Grammar, Usage, and Mechanics

3. The movie was humorous yet suspenseful. _____

4. I couldn't guess the ending, nor could my friend. _____

5. He thought the music was loud and distracting, but I didn't. _____

6. I enjoyed both the acting and the special effects. _____

7. Neither the long wait for tickets nor the noisy little children could spoil the movie for me. _____

8. I see almost every movie, for I plan to be a film critic. _____

Exercise B
Complete these sentences with coordinating or correlative conjunctions that fit the meaning of the sentences.

Example: The first motorcycles were slow _____ uncomfortable.
Answer: The first motorcycles were slow <u>and</u> uncomfortable.

1. In 1855, an inventor tested one with a wooden frame _____ wheels.

2. Unfortunately, motorcycles were _____ lightweight _____ powerful for many years.

3. Armies used them for carrying _____ messages _____ ammunition.

4. Motorcycles were expensive, _____ not many people owned them.

5. By the 1960s, motorcycles were _____ heavy _____ powerful.

6. Motorcycles may be used _____ for business _____ for pleasure.

7. Heavy bikes are best for traveling long distances, _____ light bikes are better for off-road riding.

8. Police officers use heavy, powerful motorcycles, _____ they often need to reach high speeds on highways quickly.

9. Dirt bikes have knobby tires, _____ they can get good traction.

10. Motorcycles are no longer slow, _____ are they uncomfortable.

Grade Eight SkillBook, Grammar, Usage, and Mechanics

Name _____ Class _____ Date _____

Lesson 67
Identifying Interjections

Interjections are words that express strong emotion.

Interjections are used to stand for a sound or a strong feeling, such as surprise, excitement, fear, or joy. Some commonly used interjections are listed below.

| Ugh | Ouch | Phew | Ah | Oops | Hey | Shh |
| Yuk | Wow | Oh | Alas | Bam | Psst | Eek |

Interjections may appear at the beginning or at the end of a sentence, or they may stand alone. They are generally followed by a comma or an exclamation mark. Do not overuse interjections.

Exercise A
Underline the interjection in each sentence below. The list of interjections above will help you.

Example: Ouch, you stepped on my toe.
Answer: <u>Ouch</u>, you stepped on my toe.

1. Ah, I apologize.
2. Phew! The traffic was bad.
3. Oh, I know. It's terrible.
4. You can say that again. Oops!
5. Shh! The show has started.
6. Psst, is that Albert?
7. Ugh, I think it is.
8. Wow! Did you see that jump?
9. My! What a performer she is!
10. Alas, there's none like her.
11. Whee! What a day it was!
12. Wow! That was great.
13. Super! It really was.
14. I'll drive. Ugh!
15. Hey! Did you hear that?

280   Grade Eight SkillBook, Grammar, Usage, and Mechanics

Lesson 68
Combining Sentences with Modifiers

Combine sentences with adjectives, adverbs, or phrases to make smoother, more readable sentences.

When two or more sentences contain the same subject or predicate, their modifiers can often be combined.

The bear is **brown**.	The bear is **brown, shaggy, and clumsy**.
The bear is **shaggy**.	The **clumsy brown** bear is **shaggy**.
The bear is **clumsy**.	The **shaggy brown** bear is **clumsy**.

When the three adjectives *brown*, *shaggy*, and *clumsy* are combined in the first sentence on the right, they have equal emphasis. Commas are used to separate adjectives in a series.

The second and third sentences on the right show that adjective modifiers can be combined in other ways. When they are separated, the one that follows the linking verb is usually emphasized.

Adverb modifiers can also be combined.

The bear moved **slowly**.	The bear moved **slowly, awkwardly, and heavily**.
It moved **awkwardly**.	
It moved **heavily**.	

Phrases can also be combined as modifiers. Notice how the prepositional phrases are combined in the following sentences.

The bear lumbered **through the woods**.	The bear lumbered **through the woods** and **into the campground**.
The bear lumbered **into the campground**.	

An adverb can also be combined with a preposition.

The bear stood **alertly**.	The bear stood **alertly beside a tent**.
The bear stood **beside a tent**.	

Exercise
Write one sentence for each numbered item below.

Example: Elizabeth Cochrane lived in Pittsburgh. She lived near the end of the nineteenth century.
Answer: Elizabeth Cochrane lived in Pittsburgh near the end of the nineteenth century.

1. She was young. She was intelligent. She was well-educated.

2. Under the name Nellie Bly, she wrote about factory workers. She wrote for the *Pittsburgh Dispatch*.

3. She wrote honestly. She wrote sympathetically.

4. Then she moved from Pittsburgh. She moved to New York.

5. Her first assignment for the *New York World* was difficult. It was dangerous. It was exciting.

6. Her story proved that mental patients were treated cruelly. They were treated unfairly. They were treated thoughtlessly.

7. To get the story, she lived in the mental hospital. She lived among the patients.

8. Her most famous adventure was a trip around the world. It was also her most enjoyable adventure.

9. She traveled by ship. She also traveled by special train.

10. People bought the *World* to read her entertaining stories. Her stories were light. They were informative.

Name _____ Class _____ Date _____

Lesson 69
Capitalizing Proper Nouns and Adjectives

Proper nouns and proper adjectives formed from proper nouns are always capitalized.

A **proper noun** names a particular person, place, or thing. All other nouns are **common nouns.** Compare the lists of common nouns and proper nouns below. Note that the common nouns name general categories while the proper nouns are specific.

Common Nouns	Proper Nouns
player	Jeremy Ellis
city	Los Angeles
team	Tigers

Study the seven categories of proper nouns below.

Rule 1. Names of persons, initials, and words that show family relationships.

    Luella A. Watts   Uncle Ted   Father   Grandpa Lewis

Note: Do not capitalize a word showing a family relationship when it is preceded by a possessive pronoun or an article: *a cousin; my mother; our aunt.*

Rule 2. Planets, geographic regions, continents, countries, states, provinces, cities, towns, streets, buildings, and monuments.

Earth	the Middle East	Water Tower Place	Spain
Asia	Morse Avenue	Museum of Modern Art	Ontario
Utah	North Carolina	Statue of Liberty	Springfield

Rule 3. Bodies of water, islands, mountains, parks, and other particular geographic features.

Indian Ocean	Baffin Island	Rocky Mountains
Grand Canyon	Mississippi River	Continental Divide
Great Lakes	Bay of Fundy	Gulf of California

Rule 4. Clubs, companies, organizations, institutions, and government departments and agencies.

| Red Cross | Ace Realty Agency | Department of Labor |
| Salem Hospital | Lions Club | Senate |

Rule 5. Historic periods, events, special occasions, holidays, months, and days.

| Middle Ages | American Revolution | Chinese New Year |
| September | Wednesday | Valentine's Day |

Note: Do not capitalize the seasons: *spring, summer, fall, winter.*

Rule 6. Nationalities and languages.

    Mexican   Swahili   French   Dutch   South African

Grade Eight SkillBook, Grammar, Usage, and Mechanics

Rule 7. Brands, particular cars, ships, trains, planes, spacecraft and other vehicles, and special awards.

Orient **E**xpress	**O**range **S**hocker	*Titanic*
Pulitzer **P**rize	**C**ampbell's tea	*Mariner 4*

Note: Only product names and brand names are capitalized. In *Campbell's tea*, Campbell's is a brand name, so only Campbell's is capitalized.

A **proper adjective** is an adjective formed from a proper noun. Like a proper noun, a proper adjective may consist of more than one word. It also is capitalized, but the noun it modifies is not capitalized. Study the examples.

Proper Noun	**Proper Adjective**
Canada	**C**anadian sunset
Congress	**C**ongressional lobbyist
Latin **A**merica	**L**atin **A**merican novel
Shakespeare (**W**illiam)	**S**hakespearean comedy

Sometimes a word that would be a proper adjective by itself combines with another word to become a proper noun.

American **L**eague (name of a particular group)
British **C**olumbia (name of a particular place)
Congressional **R**ecord (name of a particular thing)

Sometimes a proper noun takes the place of a proper adjective, as in these examples.

Senate debate	**S**upreme **C**ourt decision
Texas cattle	**U**nited **S**tates policy

Exercise A

Underline each word that should be capitalized in the sentences below.

Example: These are the tickets that mary eng gave me.
Answer: These are the tickets that <u>mary eng</u> gave me.

1. This spring carver school will host sportarama, a national sport competition.

2. It will begin on monday, march 17, which is st. patrick's day.

3. There will be teams from such states as west virginia, nevada, florida, and new hampshire, as well as jamaican and puerto rican teams.

4. One team is coming from as far north as winnepeg, canada.

5. They will fly into montclare airport on a boeing 727.

6. My cousin, hans jorgen, is here as a west german exchange student.

7. My school asked cousin hans to be on our soccer team.

8. Because he was so happy, he went to bennet's department store and bought a special pair of whoopee soccer shoes.

9. A committee is planning entertainment, which will include a performance by a group of irish dancers at the agora theater.

10. If we can get enough tickets, mom, dad, and my sister patti all plan to go.

11. My older brother frank won't be able to attend sportarama.

12. He is going to be at a reunion of his graduating class at the university of vermont.

13. Mom says frank is one of several vermont alumni trying to locate members of the class that graduated in 1990.

14. Frank says members of his class have gone in all directions—north, south, east, and west—since they left vermont.

15. I know it's true because I've seen his list with addresses from anchorage, alaska; coral gables, florida; and several towns from the midwest and southeast.

16. One of the envelopes went to a woman who works at a mount rushmore souvenir shop in south dakota.

17. Frank's best friend in college is now stationed at fort benning, georgia.

18. A girl frank used to date ran st. rita's orphanage in southeast asia.

19. His old roommate, rafael santana, now is an atlanta executive for creighton industries, where he designs all the ads for olympia tractors.

20. Frank can hardly wait to go to new england in march to see all his old friends.

Exercise B
Each numbered pair below contains a two-word proper noun and a proper adjective modifying a common noun. Capitalize each item correctly.

Example: a. korean war b. korean soldier
Answer: a. Korean War b. Korean soldier

1. a. american revolution   b. american history

2. a. english countryside   b. english channel

3. a. kentucky derby   b. kentucky people

4. a. roman empire   b. roman architecture

Grade Eight SkillBook, Grammar, Usage, and Mechanics

5. **a.** irish setter   **b.** irish sea

6. **a.** indian food   **b.** indian ocean

7. **a.** mississippi river   **b.** mississippi tributary

8. **a.** ferris avenue   **b.** ferris wheel

Lesson 70
Capitalizing Titles

Capitalize the first word, the last word, and all important words in a title.

All titles are capitalized according to the same rule, whether they are titles of books, films, articles, songs, or other works. Capitalize the first word, the last word, and every important word in a title. (Unimportant words include *and*, *the*, and prepositions of fewer than five letters.) Study the following.

book: *Heart of Darkness*
newspaper: *The Town Crier*
magazine: *National Geographic*

poem: "The Raven"
story: "To Build a Fire"
song: "Take Me Out to the Ball Game"

play: *Let Me Hear You Whisper*
film: *Breaking Away*
work of art: *Distant Thunder*

TV series: *Nightly News*
article: "Canine Capers"

Notice that some titles are printed in italic type. Underline the titles of books, newspapers, magazines, plays, films, works of art, and TV shows to indicate italics. Use quotation marks when writing the title of a poem, story, song, or article.

Another kind of title is used with names of persons or in addressing persons. These titles, some of which are abbreviated, are capitalized when they precede the names of persons.

President Truman   **Mr.** and **Mrs.** Mays   **Dr.** Abernathy

Titles not followed by names are capitalized when used in direct address in place of a name, and also when they substitute for the names of high government officials and other important persons. In all other cases, they are not capitalized when used alone.

"Yes, **Officer**, I own the car you just ticketed."
The **President** met with the **Secretary of Defense**.
Has anyone tried to call the **doctor**?
The company **president** met with her new **secretary**.

Exercise A
Rewrite the following titles so they are capitalized correctly. You will capitalize fifty-four letters.

Example: *following the equator*
Answer: *Following the Equator*

1. *joan of arc* _____

2. *roughing it* _____

3. "woman with flower" _____

Grade Eight SkillBook, Grammar, Usage, and Mechanics

4. *sixty minutes* _____
5. *reader's digest* _____
6. *i am the cheese* _____
7. *evanston review* _____
8. *the gilded age* _____
9. *christina's world* _____
10. *the adventures of tom sawyer* _____
11. *"a man who had no eyes"* _____
12. *"the day the sun came out"* _____
13. *"this land is your land"* _____
14. *"president cleveland, where are you?"* _____
15. *the prince and the pauper* _____
16. *a connecticut yankee in king arthur's court* _____

Exercise B
Underline the titles that should be capitalized.

Example: The pope held an audience.
Answer: The <u>pope</u> held an audience.

1. The president planned a reception at the White House.
2. The reception was in honor of prince Charles.
3. Unfortunately, the guest of honor caught a bad cold.
4. His doctor advised him to stay in bed.
5. "I will follow your orders, doctor," Charles said.
6. The secretary of state came to see how he was.
7. The vice president also dropped by.
8. Charles's mother, queen Elizabeth, heard that he was ill.
9. The queen called long distance and spoke to dr. Longford.
10. "Your majesty, it's just a cold," the doctor reassured her.
11. princess Anne and prince William cheered him up.
12. Even mrs. Longford sent him some chicken soup.

Lesson 71
Commas in Sentences

Use commas to set off certain words, phrases, or clauses.

Commas are punctuation marks used to indicate pauses between words or groups of words. They are also used to clarify meaning. Study the rules about comma use that follow.

Rule 1. Use commas to separate words or phrases in a series.

> The play had **lively, funny,** and **entertaining** stories.
> Sign your name **at the top, on the line,** and **at the bottom.**

Rule 2. Use a comma before the conjunction in a compound sentence. Generally, omit the comma in a short compound sentence.

> I stopped by to pick you up, **but you had already left.**
> Jim came by but I wasn't home.

Rule 3. Use commas after introductory words and to set off interrupting words or expressions. Use one comma if the interrupter comes at the beginning or the end of the sentence. Use two commas if it comes in the middle.

Rule 4. Use commas to set off a noun of direct address. Use one comma if the noun is the first or last word in the sentence. Use two commas if the noun is in the middle.

> Please join us, **Ann.**   I'm sorry, **girls,** but my feet hurt.

Rule 5. Use commas to set off appositives. Use one comma if the appositive is at the end of the sentence. Use two commas if it comes in the middle.

> Did you buy the fruit at Fruits and Veggies, **the produce shop?**
> My favorite fruit, **peaches,** was on sale.

Rule 6. Use commas to set off long introductory phrases and dependent clauses that are not essential to the sentence.

> **Sparkling in the light of the sun,** the ocean looked beautiful.
> **After they built a sand castle,** they had a picnic.

Exercise

Insert commas as needed in the following sentences.

> **Example:** What is your favorite sport Clive?
> **Answer:** What is your favorite sport, Clive?

1. Baseball basketball and ice hockey are my favorite sports.

2. Personally I prefer swimming the greatest sport of all.

3. Ellen do you still run or do you prefer some other activity?

Grade Eight SkillBook, Grammar, Usage, and Mechanics

4. Jogging in my opinion is still the way to stay fit.
5. After Tim Gene and I took up yoga I felt so relaxed and limber.
6. Believe it or not I used to do calisthenics every day but now I ride a bike instead.
7. Ms. Cusick our English teacher and Mrs. Lane the principal's secretary walk three miles together every morning.
8. Though he gets no exercise Jerry looks better than any of us.
9. What's your secret old pal?
10. I eat balanced meals take vitamins and get enough sleep.
11. Will you help us Glen to set up an exercise program?
12. It should contain simple average and challenging activities.
13. You don't really need a rigid program but I'll help you anyway.
14. Sy's health club by the way has a new program for teenagers.
15. It's inexpensive and it looks like fun.
16. Lisa Karen and Karen's little brother went to a baseball game.
17. They sat in the bleachers ate popcorn and cheered.
18. Frank Karen's little brother's friend sat five rows away.
19. At the end of the third inning the two boys noticed each other.
20. Luckily they saw a few empty seats so they got closer together.

Lesson 72
Other Uses of Commas

Commas are used in addresses, dates, numerals, and letters.

You have already learned how commas can be used to divide sentences into logical word groups. Commas are also useful in punctuating parts of an address, a date, a numeral, or a letter.

Rule 1. Use a comma to set off the parts of a date. Use a comma between the day and the month. Also use a comma between the date and the year. Within a sentence, put a comma after the year as well.

My nephew was born on Friday, August 7, 1987, in New York.

Rule 2. In an address, use a comma to separate the city and the state or country. If an address is within a sentence, use a comma after the name, the street address, and the town or city. Use a comma after the state or the ZIP Code, whichever comes last within a sentence.

Dale Granger   Mr. John E. Baker
450 Scott Court   7 Maple Street
Roselle, IL 60172   Andover, NY 14806

Mail the letter to Meg Foster, 10 Landview, Pittsburgh, Pennsylvania 15318.
I moved from Detroit, Michigan, to Milan, Ohio, two years ago.

Rule 3. Use a comma to separate numerals greater than three digits.

$1,500,000 $16,666 $14,787,629.35

Rule 4. Use a comma to set off a person's last name when it comes before the first name.

The names on the list were Bender, Terry and Caldwell, Steve.

Rule 5. Use a comma after the greeting in a friendly letter and after the closing in all letters.

Dear Uncle Carlo,   Your friend,

Exercise A
Read the sentences. Write *Correct* if the sentence is correctly punctuated. Write *Incorrect* if the sentence is not punctuated correctly. Then write the sentence correctly, adding a comma or commas as necessary.

Example: Josh entered school on September 8 1996.
Answer: Incorrect. Josh entered school on September 8, 1996.

1. Mary and Diane attend a college in Boise Idaho.

Grade Eight SkillBook, Grammar, Usage, and Mechanics

2. Their car has over 80000 miles on the odometer.

3. There are about 11,000 students in their school.

4. Mary will graduate on May 26 1996 in an outdoor ceremony.

5. She will live at 23 Oak Road Provo Utah after graduation.

Exercise B
Add commas where necessary in the letter below.

47 Fifth Avenue
New York NY 10003

March 27, 1999

Dear Glenda
    I finally received your letter dated Friday December 1. We have moved from Hoosick Falls New York to New York City. Dad is now working at 850 Park Avenue his company's main office.
    As you can imagine I wasn't too happy about moving. I knew I would miss Tanya Dave Shirley and my other good friends. I miss them but I am having an exciting time here. Come visit me this summer. I'll show you the Statue of Liberty the Empire State Building and the World Trade Center. We can ride bikes row on the pond and visit the zoo. Write soon Glenda so we can make plans.

Your friend

Lesson 73
Semicolons and Colons

A semicolon is used to separate parts of a sentence. A colon is another punctuation mark that can separate items.

You have learned that a **semicolon** can be used to correct a run-on sentence. A semicolon can also be used to combine two closely related sentences into a compound sentence.

> **Run-on:** I'll play first base you can watch.
> **Correct:** I'll play first base; you can watch.
>
> **Two sentences:** Sue tossed the ball. It bounced off the tree.
> **Combined:** Sue tossed the ball; it bounced off the tree.

Sentences are usually closely related if the second one begins with a term such as *nevertheless, for example, however, therefore,* or *in fact.* Notice how semicolons and commas are used in combining such sentences.

> Chisa ran a good race; **however,** she finished second to Jay.
> This was a terrible snowstorm; **in fact,** it set a record.

Semicolons are used to separate sentence parts that already contain commas. For instance, they may be used to separate compound sentences or items in a series that already have commas in them.

> Submit your report to Bob, Anne, or Nolan; and I, needless to say, will put in a good word for you.
> Last week Dad traveled to Springfield, Illinois; Boston, Massachusetts; and Austin, Texas.

A **colon** is used after the greeting in a business letter. It is also used after expressions that introduce a list.

> Dear Sirs: Dear Brinks, Watson and Company:
> The box had the following: rocks, marbles, shoes, and rope.

A colon is used between the numbers for hours and minutes and between volume and page numbers in magazines.

> The club meetings are at 6:00 P.M. or 7:30 P.M.
> *Time,* 108: 40-41   *People,* 42: 14-17

Exercise A
Use a semicolon to combine each pair of sentences into one sentence. Then rewrite the sentence.

1. This was the heaviest snowfall in years. It broke all records.

Grade Eight SkillBook, Grammar, Usage, and Mechanics

2. People couldn't get to work. However, no one complained.

3. Some went skiing on Main Street. Others rode on sleds.

4. Snow stood in ten-foot drifts. It amazed everyone.

5. The children grew fidgety. The parents grew impatient.

Exercise B
Rewrite the following sentences. Use colons and semicolons where they are needed.

1. This letter confirms your reservation for 830 on June 14.

2. I love tennis in fact, I play four times a week.

3. Branch offices are located in San Francisco, Los Angeles, and Oakland, California Dallas and Houston, Texas and Springfield and Chicago, Illinois.

4. Lee, rake the yard Al, wash the car Fritz, clean the basement.

5. One week he travels on Monday, Wednesday, and Friday and the next week he travels on Tuesday, Thursday, and Saturday.

6. Add these things to your list soap, flour, and bread and come back as quickly as you can.

Lesson 74
Quotation Marks

Quotations marks are used to enclose a speaker's exact words. Quotation marks are also used to enclose certain titles.

When you use a direct quotation, place quotation marks before and after the speaker's exact words. Compare the following.

"I was offered the job," Rita said to Mark.
Rita told Mark that she was offered the job.

The first sentence is a **direct quotation.** It quotes Rita's exact words. They are enclosed in quotation marks. The second sentence does not quote Rita's exact words. It is an **indirect quotation.** Indirect quotations are not enclosed in quotation marks.

Study these rules for using quotation marks.

Rule 1. Enclose all directly quoted words within quotations marks.

After he congratulated her, she said, "Thanks, Mark."

Rule 2. If the direct quotation is interrupted, both parts are enclosed in quotation marks. When are capital letters used?

"Incidentally," Mark said, "you don't sound too happy."
"I am," Rita said. "College was my first choice, though."

Rule 3. Periods, commas, and usually question and exclamation marks are placed inside quotation marks. Notice also in the second example below that a comma follows *Mark said*.

"I wanted to go so badly!" Rita cried.
Mark said, "I didn't know that."

Rule 4. Quotation marks are also used to enclose the titles of songs, stories, poems, articles in magazines and newspapers, and the chapters in books.

"Jabberwocky"   "Home on the Range"   Chapter 2, "Verbs"

Exercise A
Add quotation marks to the direct quotations in the following sentences. If a sentence is correct, write *Correct*.

Example: It's a good day to go shopping, Mike said.
Answer: "It's a good day to go shopping," Mike said.

1. Mike told Emmy Lou about the sale at Ace Sporting Goods.
2. Look, Mike said, Ace Sporting Goods is having a super sale.
3. Jogging shoes are marked down fifty percent, he continued.
4. Mike suggested that they visit the store after school.
5. I could use a new pair of shoes, Emmy Lou admitted.

Grade Eight SkillBook, Grammar, Usage, and Mechanics

Exercise B
Add quotation marks and capital letters where necessary.

   Example: What is that strange-looking vehicle? she squealed.
   Answer: "What is that strange-looking vehicle?" she squealed.

1. Ben Franklin whistled yankee doodle as he emerged from his time machine, saw a woman, and asked, can you help me?

2. He said, Franklin's the name. Can you tell me what that is?

3. That, the woman replied, is an electric light.

4. But there's no storm, he said. also we have no kite.

5. You have an uncanny resemblance, she said, to someone.

6. She asked, have you ever appeared on late-night TV?

7. I don't know what TV is, he exclaimed, but I believe in going to bed early.

8. Franklin continued, is that a stove?

Name _____ Class _____ Date _____

Lesson 75
Other Punctuation Marks

Other punctuation marks help make your writing clear.

There are various punctuation marks used in writing besides those you have already learned. Here are some rules to remember.

Period A period is used to end declarative and imperative sentences. In addition, it is used after abbreviations and initials.

Declarative: Mr. Alan J. Smith and Ms. A. Suarez are the delegates.
Imperative: Tell Dr. T.G. Roovers to arrive at 3:15 P.M.

Other End Marks A question mark ends an interrogative sentence. An exclamation mark ends an exclamatory sentence.

Interrogative: Why haven't you called Willie McGee, Jr.?
Exclamatory: What heavy cord you used on this package!

Underlining Underline the titles of books, plays, magazines, films, and TV series.

<u>The Wizard of Oz</u>   <u>Sports Illustrated</u>   <u>The Dying Detective</u>

Underline letters, figures, and words used as words. Also underline foreign words and phrases.

Remember that there are two <u>e</u>'s in <u>noticeable</u>.
"<u>Au revoir</u>," said the child as she waved good-by.

Hyphen Hyphens are commonly used in writing to divide a word at the end of a line. They are also used in some compound words.

That person is a **roly-poly stick-in-the-mud**.

Use a hyphen in numbers from twenty-one to ninety-nine.

The halfback's number was **thirty-two** or **thirty-four**.

Dash Use a dash to show a sudden change of thought or to set off words that interrupt the main thought of a sentence.

The picnic today—**it can't rain**—is at Welles Park.
The Jets—**they're ahead by ten points**—should win.

Parentheses Use parentheses to enclose words that interrupt the main thought of a sentence, usually to explain or add to it. Also use parentheses when referring to page numbers, chapters, or dates.

Your letter **(all five pages of it)** arrived today.
Edward Lear **(1812-1888)** popularized the limerick **(see page 23)**.

Apostrophe You have already learned that apostrophes are used with possessive nouns and contractions. They are also used to form plurals of letters, numbers, symbols, and words used as words, if the plurals would be confusing to read otherwise.

Dot your *i*'s. Your *7*'s look like *9*'s.
Don't use *&*'s for *and*'s.

Exercise A
Add any needed punctuation to each sentence.

Example: Alexander Graham Bell 1847-1922 was an inventor.
Answer: Alexander Graham Bell (1847-1922) was an inventor.

1. The word telephone has three e's
2. Last Monday no it was Tuesday I called my brother
3. Did you know that he and my sister in law live in Hollywood
4. I sent them a copy of Dr. A. N. Nau's book, Eating Well
5. Dr. Nau 1938–1984 emphasized a low salt diet see pages 80–88
6. He died, though, when he was only fifty six
7. I printed ten 35s and the word Congratulations on the inside cover of the book as a birthday greeting
8. How surprised my roly poly brother was
9. He complained actually he screamed at me about my humor
10. The book Middle aged Men Shouldn't Eat at All is his next gift.

VOCABULARY ANSWER KEY

Lesson 1
Context
EXERCISE
1. prove innocent
2. job; duty
3. charges; accusations
4. test
5. extra

Lesson 2
Direct and Indirect Context Clues
EXERCISE
1. b
2. b
3. c
4. a
5. b
6. b

Lesson 3
More Context Clues
EXERCISE
1. b
2. c
3. a
4. c
5. a

Lesson 4
Clues in Longer Contexts
EXERCISE A
1. b
2. c
3. b
4. a
5. a, c
6. b
7. c
8. a
9. a
10. b

EXERCISE B
1. g
2. d
3. f
4. b
5. e

Lesson 5
Using Your Common Sense
EXERCISE A
1. c
2. a
3. c

EXERCISE B
1. b, d
2. b, e
3. a, d
4. b, e
5. b, d

Lesson 6
Understanding Word Structure
EXERCISE A
1. dis / prove
2. mask / like
3. like / able
4. un / usual
5. sorrow / ful

EXERCISE B
irregular
backyards
herbicide
nutritional
saladlike
caffeine-free

Lesson 7
Compound Words
EXERCISE
1. a
2. b
3. a
4. b
5. b
6. b
7. a
8. a
9. b
10. b

Lesson 8
Recognizing Root Words
EXERCISE A
1. reader
2. unread
3. readable
4. reread

EXERCISE B
1. friend
2. drain
3. visit
4. view
5. marine
6. mouth
7. damp
8. print
9. state
10. beat

EXERCISE C
1. d
2. b
3. d
4. b
5. c
6. a
7. d
8. a
9. c
10. a

EXERCISE D
1. imagine
2. personal
3. disharmony
4. refinish
5. measurement
6. journey
7. careless
8. superfine
9. regularize
10. cheer

Grade Eight SkillBook, Vocabulary Answer Key

Lesson 9
Using Prefixes
EXERCISE A
1. re
2. dis
3. sub
4. un
5. semi
6. anti
7. pre
8. mis
9. inter
10. trans

EXERCISE B
Answers will vary.

Lesson 10
Negative Prefixes
EXERCISE A
1. <u>mis</u>trust
2. <u>il</u>logical
3. <u>im</u>perfect
4. <u>mis</u>matched
5. <u>im</u>possible

EXERCISE B
Answers will vary.

Lesson 11
More About Prefixes
EXERCISE
1. b
2. c
3. b
4. c
5. b

Lesson 12
Using Suffixes
EXERCISE A
1. the endings
2. adventur<u>ous</u>, happi<u>ly</u>, sail<u>or</u>, depart<u>ure</u>, peace<u>ful</u>, storm<u>y</u>, danger<u>ous</u>, ribbon<u>like</u>
3. adventurous, happily

EXERCISE B
1. darken
2. darkness
3. carelessness
4. carelessly

EXERCISE C
1. careful
2. irritation
3. educational
4. enjoyable
5. legislation

READING ANSWER KEY

Lesson 1
Adjusting Reading Rate and Method to Purpose
EXERCISE A
1. "The Sound of Wedding Bells"
2. Answers will vary.
3. Answers will vary.
4. situation three
5. situation one

EXERCISE B
A. Trevino's grandfather
B. He entered the U.S. Open.

EXERCISE C
1. c
2. b
3. a
4. c
5. b

Lesson 2
Using Patterns to Help You Read
EXERCISE A
1. c
2. a
3. e
4. d

EXERCISE B
1. As a result
2. Because
3. furniture, clothing, weapons, food, gold, valuables
4. time order (also comparison-contrast)
5. cause-effect (also listing)

Lesson 3
Making a Survey
EXERCISE
1. time order
2. Answers will vary.
3. Answers will vary.

Lesson 4
Intensive Reading
EXERCISE A
1. The kind of houses settlers built on the frontier.
2. time order
3. Answers will vary.
4. Answers will vary.

EXERCISE B
1. protection from weather and enemies
2. snow; thatches
3. stone; wood
4. clay and straw
5. rocks; wood; clay; adobe
6. thick prairie soil matted with grass roots
7. time order
8. cool in summer; warm in winter; kept out wind and rain; did not burn
9. It was dark and it leaked.
10. Trains brought building materials.

EXERCISE C
1. caves; igloos; huts; stone, wood, and adobe houses
2. the Great Plains
3. turned over rows of prairie soil with plows; cut rows into blocks of sod 1 to 3 feet wide; placed these pieces of sod side by side on the ground to form outline of house; piled hunks of sod up; left spaces for doors and windows; cut poles for roof supports
4. Advantages: cool in summer; warm in winter; kept out wind and rain. Disadvantages: dark; wet.
5. railroad

Lesson 5
Putting Your Reading Skills to Work
EXERCISE
Questions will vary but should relate to article title or subheads.
1. to demonstrate the air-worthiness of dirigibles
2. Germany and the U.S.
3. They were 100 ft. longer and carried five small scout planes.
4. It burst into flames while landing and crashed.
5. It signaled the end of their development.

Lesson 6
What Is Imagery?
EXERCISE A
1. b
2. wet, sucking noises
3. a cold, sharp wind
4. salt-sea
5. The setting sun behind us cast long shadows.

EXERCISE B
Answers will vary but imagery should be evident in students' writing.

Lesson 7
Recognizing Imagery
EXERCISE A
1. sound, sight
2. feeling, sight
3. sight, taste
4. sound, sight
5. feeling

EXERCISE B
1. a
2. b
3. b
4. a
5. b

EXERCISE C
The haunted house was half in the shadows of the clump of elms in which it stood. The elms were almost bare now, and the ground around the house was yellow with damp leaves. The late afternoon light had a greenish cast which the blank windows reflected in a sinister way. An unhinged shutter thumped. Something else creaked. Meg did not wonder that the house had a reputation for being haunted.

A board was nailed across the front door, but Charles Wallace led the way around to the back. The door there appeared to be nailed shut, too, but Charles Wallace knocked, and the door swung slowly outward, creaking on rusty hinges. Up in one of the elms an old black crow gave its raucous cry, and a woodpecker went into a wild ratatattat. A large gray rat scuttled around the corner of the house and Meg let out a stifled shriek.

Lesson 8
Responding to Imagery
EXERCISE A
1. a deep rumble
2. their houses began to shake
3. The earth was churning, crumbling, and sinking.
4. cracking into huge, tilted blocks
5. trees fell; houses were ripped in two or upended

EXERCISE B
1. c
2. c
3. buildings fell; land opened; highways buckled; railroad tracks twisted; avalanches swept down the mountains
4. c
5. c

Lesson 9
Visualizing What Happens
EXERCISE A
1.
2.

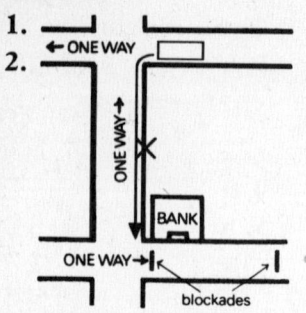 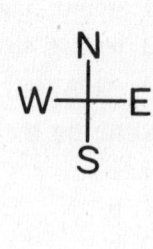

3. a hot dog stand was a familiar sight in the neighborhood
4. b, d
5. d

EXERCISE B
1. south
2. tall; broad shoulders; wearing a battered hat over tough, hard face; long, pointy nose; scar above right eye
3. b
4. south
5. bundle of old newspapers

Lesson 10
Reviewing the Use of Imagery
EXERCISE
1. Answers will vary.
2. Answers will vary.
3. c
4. the library; first, the odor of books, then, the scent of books
5. Y a. old-fashioned tables and chairs
   N b. computerized card catalog system
   N c. lace curtains at the windows
   N d. Calvin's bored expression
   Y e. shelves of books of various sizes and colors
   Y f. rose petals that have fallen on the desk

Lesson 11
What Is Figurative Language?
EXERCISE A
1. b
2. a
3. b
4. a
5. b

EXERCISE B
1. L   6. L   11. L
2. F   7. L   12. F
3. L   8. F   13. F
4. F   9. F   14. F
5. F   10. L 15. L

EXERCISE C
Answers will vary.

EXERCISE D
Answers will vary.

Lesson 12
Making Sense of Figurative Language
EXERCISE
1. a   5. b   9. c
2. b   6. b   10. c
3. a   7. c
4. c   8. b

Lesson 13
Understanding Figurative Comparisons
EXERCISE A
1. b   4. c
2. a   5. a
3. b

EXERCISE B
1. c
2. shiny black
3. Both leave tracks.
4. c
5. lights of the car's headlights

EXERCISE C
1. A spade is not a useful tool for gathering leaves.
2. Leaves are heavier than the air that fills balloons.
3. All make a rustling sound with leaves.
4. by comparing them to mountains
5. Unlike a crop, the leaves have no further use.

EXERCISE D
Answers will vary.

Lesson 14
Reviewing Figurative Language
EXERCISE
1. b
2. a

3. b
4. a snowstorm—both are white
5. seashells—both are yellowish and hard
6-10. Answers will vary but should show an understanding of using figurative language.

Lesson 15
Making Inferences
EXERCISE
1. b
2. still, doorsto[p], cookie-j[ar], cuspid, interesting
3. b
4. as I do not want to bother Aunt Carrie
5. Christmas I notice

Lesson 16
Identifying Clues
EXERCISE A
1. He saw a large car in the middle of the road.
2. He drove over tacks.
3. I was just robbed down the road. I'd appreciate it if you'd call a garage to get me a new set of tires. And then call the sheriff.
4. bring a set of VW tires
5. He had not mentioned what kind of car he was driving.

EXERCISE B
1. radio ahead, on board, passengers, cockpit, pilot
2. locate my bag, diagnosis of food poisoning, attending to
3. in the cockpit, instructions to see the passengers are calm
4. Baird's question; Janet's expression
5. immense and overpowering fear

Lesson 17
Inferences About Time and Place
EXERCISE
1. c
2. b
3. evening
4. a
5. b

Lesson 18
Inferences About Characters
EXERCISE A
1. F
2. CT
3. F
4. T
5. T

EXERCISE B
1. T
2. T
3. F
4. T
5. T
6. CT
7. T
8. F
9. F
10. T

EXERCISE C
1. T
2. F
3. F
4. T

Lesson 19
Inferences About Fantasy
EXERCISE
1. She disappeared into the future for only a brief instant.
2. She was given a choice whether to remember or not.
3. She chose not to remember the future.
4. Answers will vary.
5. Williams went into the future; she hardly flickered; she might spend several years away; "I was given the choice whether I should remember it or not after I got back"

Lesson 20
Reviewing Inferences
EXERCISE
1. a frozen sea
2. They were in an airplane crash and haven't been rescued.
3. in the present
4. the fire, the stone wall at the back of the hut, the snares, the SOS made with branches
5. not a fantasy—no impossible or improbable events

Lesson 21
Finding the Direct Statement of Main Idea
EXERCISE
1. c
2. c
3. Yes
4. c
5. d
6. Prestwich has found that most of these termite weapons owe more to chemistry than to muscle power.

7. soldier Rhinotermes or paintbrush termites
8. This paintbrush defense system is another very effective and complex form of chemical warfare.
9. b
10. Prestwich's termites are more interested in keeping their enemies at bay than doing battle with homeowners and farmers.

Lesson 22
Identifying the Implied Main Idea
EXERCISE A
1. d
2. b

EXERCISE B
1. a
2. b

Lesson 23
Evaluating Details
EXERCISE
1. a
2. b, d
3. c
4. b, c, e
5. b

Lesson 24
Reviewing Main Idea
EXERCISE
1. The boys want to make certain all the ingredients for dinner are on hand.
2. Answers will vary. Sample: The boys are responsible for making dinner for the family 2 nights a week.
3. The two Yeagers are old hands in the kitchen.
4. Answers will vary. Sample: The boys began helping in the kitchen and were taught to shop wisely at an early age.
5. Answers will vary.
6. The boys know they are helping out.
7. Answers will vary. Sample: The boys will already know how to cook when they move out on their own.
8. Answers will vary.

Lesson 25
What Are Judgments?
EXERCISE
1. <u>good judgment</u> / bad judgment
   competing in five contests
2. <u>good judgment</u> / bad judgment
   matching color for slacks; shopped for best price
3. <u>good judgment</u> / bad judgment
   the restaurant serves something each likes
4. good judgment / <u>bad judgment</u>
   ticket is expensive but seat is in the back
5. good judgment / <u>bad judgment</u>
   small apartment and can't play stereo very loud
6. good judgment / <u>bad judgment</u>
   saltwater fish need special food
7. good judgment / <u>bad judgment</u>
   if computer has problems, won't be able to get parts
8. <u>good judgment</u> / bad judgment
   saved money by getting up early

Lesson 26
Fact and Opinion
EXERCISE
1. F
2. O
3. F
4. O
5. F
6. F
7. O
8. F
9. F
10. O

Lesson 27
Mixed Statements
EXERCISE
1. M An example of a devoted athlete is Mandeva Jackson, <u>who runs six miles every day for practice.</u>
2. O You will find Mandeva on the track every day at 5 A.M.
3. F Alice Hagan practices gymnastics for three to four hours every day, six days a week, eight months a year.
4. M <u>Alice has been practicing for eight years,</u> but the daily routine of exercise is still not easy.
5. F These and other young athletes prepare for such sports as track, gymnastics, swimming, and judo.
6. F As part of their preparation, they attend several weekend competitions throughout the year.
7. F The athletes also participate in activities to raise money for travel expenses.
8. M One hard-working swim club used imaginative ways to raise money; <u>they sold doughnuts, held paper drives, and had a swim marathon.</u>
9. O These young athletes work harder than other teenagers to meet their goals.

Grade Eight SkillBook, Reading Answer Key

10. M As the best reward possible for all their hard work, athletes aged eight to eighteen compete in the Junior Olympics.
11. M They enjoy competing, even if they don't win, and they enjoy meeting the other athletes, who come from all parts of the country.
12. M Competitions are held for several weeks, giving athletes a chance to meet exciting new friends.
13. F Gold, silver, and bronze medals are awarded in each event.
14. F Sometimes only a fraction of second or point marks the difference between first place and second place.
15. M Only a small fraction of the population will ever compete in the Olympics—those athletes are very special people.

Lesson 28
Valid and Objective Opinions
EXERCISE
1. √
2. √
3. √
4.
5.

Lesson 29
Words with Emotional Effect
EXERCISE A
1. a
2. a
3. b
4. a
5. b

EXERCISE B
1. We can no longer allow other countries to fish in our waters. These greedy foreigners are stealing our food. Giving them fishing rights is a surrender of our own rights. (negative attitude toward foreign fishing boats)
2. Cats are terrible pets. They cry and cry when they are hungry. We feed them and what do we get? They give us unfriendly stares and scratched furniture. (negative attitude toward cats)
3. Calculators and electronic games are wonderful aids for studying mathematics. They make math fun and exciting. Students can easily learn to master complex problems with them. (positive attitude toward calculators and electronic games)
4. A strict curfew is needed to protect us from unruly teenagers. They roar up and down our streets at night, and they deafen us with their music. They hang out at the shopping center, looking for trouble. (negative attitude toward teenagers)
5. The planned urban renewal project is a must. Our downtown area will come alive again. Think of gleaming office buildings, dazzling cultural events, and appealing shops along a mall with no cars. (positive attitude toward the renewal project)

Lesson 30
Appeal in Advertising
EXERCISE A
1. $10,000
2. no; $15,000

EXERCISE B
1. none
2. the stereo costs $89.95; there is an installation charge.
3. The pizza has sauce and cheese on Italian bread.
4. none
5. The notebook has tabs, divider sheets, and pockets.

WRITING ANSWER KEY

Lesson 1
Main Idea in a Paragraph
EXERCISE A
1. silver veil, web shimmered, white thread, lovely tune
2. spider racing, encasing victim

EXERCISE B
Answers will vary.

EXERCISE C
Sentences that do not support the main idea are underlined. Revised paragraphs will eliminate those sentences.

    Chaos struck our house one morning. As I tried to brush my teeth, the faucet just groaned; no water came out. I couldn't wash my hair, so Dad used my hair dryer to heat the pipes. I had just bought the dryer at Kimbol's on sale. We couldn't have our usual breakfast of poached eggs, so we had cornflakes instead. My brother finished his homework upstairs. Finally, the pipes gurgled and water came out of the faucet. We gave Dad a cheer for restoring order to the house.

EXERCISE D
Answers will vary.

Lesson 2
Topic Sentences
EXERCISE A
1. The narrator met many lonely, homesick people.
2. a

EXERCISE B
1. b. A cat is an ideal pet, since it can keep you company and is generally content with food, water, and a warm spot for sleeping.
Topic sentence should be last sentence in paragraph.
2. c. Early in the nineteenth century, the dream of freedom had begun spreading through the slave cabins on all the plantations.
Topic sentence should be first sentence in paragraph.

Lesson 3
Writing a Narrative Paragraph
EXERCISE A
Answers will vary, but students should add transitions and details.

EXERCISE B
Unnecessary details are underlined; numbers show correct order.

Details: Boat drifts toward rocks 3
Helicopter is on its way 5
High winds blow up 1
Pilot acts quickly 6
Helicopter arrives in nick of time
Sailor radios for help 4
Sailor lowers sails 2
Sailor is relieved
Boat drifts away from rocks 8
Sailor is safe
Helicopter blades create wind 7

Lesson 4
Plot
EXERCISE A
1. The boy confuses Celsius and Fahrenheit.
2. The boy assumes he is dying but doesn't tell his father his fears.
3. Answers will vary. Sample: Boy asks when he is going to die.
4. The father explains the difference between Celsius and Fahrenheit.
5. Answers will vary.

EXERCISE B
Plot summaries will vary but should clearly identify the conflict, climax, and resolution.

Lesson 5
Character and Dialogue
EXERCISE A
1. It is a warm, respectful relationship.
2. Joby has been in the army for three weeks; he probably ran away from home; he's very young; he's been crying.

EXERCISE B
Answers will vary but should include details about appearance, actions, thoughts, and feelings.

Lesson 6
Classifying
EXERCISE A
1. frail
2. jammed
3. silly
4. stone
5. normal
6. joy
7. stand
8. neglect
9. die
10. blue

EXERCISE B
1. sounds
2. colors; purple-based
3. rhymes
4. social sciences, end in -*ology*
5. countries
6. occupations, end in -*er*, begin with *f*
7. dances
8. synonyms
9. flowers, begin with *d*
10. states
11. fabrics; natural, not man-made
12. liquids
13. sources of light
14. expressions, begin with *s*
15. bodies of water
16. cord materials
17. containers; used to hold liquids
18. musical instruments
19. tools
20. vegetables; used in salads

Lesson 7
Arranging Details in Spatial Order
EXERCISE A
1. outside, then inside the hut
2. right to left

EXERCISE B
1. near to far
2. alongside the ship, near the shore, through forests of, in the distance
3. on the deck of the ship

Lesson 8
Writing a Descriptive Paragraph
EXERCISE A
Details will vary but should include be specific and logically classified.

EXERCISE B
 That's why he loved his room—if you could call it that—because he could be alone yet not too alone. It wasn't even a real room. It used to be the kitchen pantry—a long, deep, dark closet that you walked into, which had a lot of shelves <u>along the wall</u> to store canned food. He and Mama had removed the shelves, except for the ones high up, <u>near the ceiling</u>, where he now kept his personal belongings. With the wooden shelves gone, there was just enough space to stick in a comfortable cot <u>against the wall</u> and a bureau and mirror <u>at the rear</u> of the tiny box-like space. Since there wasn't any electric outlet in the former closet, Mama and Gaucho had removed the heavy door, which led to the kitchen, and replaced it with a thin, almost transparent floral drapery that allowed the kitchen light to filter in and make the room glow softly. The curtain also assured Gaucho of privacy. He and Mama had a silent understanding that when the curtain was drawn <u>across the doorway</u>, she would knock <u>on the nearby wall</u> or call out to him before entering.
—from **GAUCHO** by Gloria Gonzalez
1. Details may vary.
2. Answers are underlined.

Lesson 9
Comparing and Contrasting
EXERCISE A
1. Answers will vary.
2. Answers will vary.
3. share; very different; as; on the contrary

EXERCISE B

Color of fruit	Taste
green	sweet
orange	sweet

EXERCISE C
Answers will vary.

Lesson 10
Writing a Compare/Contrast Description
EXERCISE A
Possible common details: atmosphere, access, shape of room.

EXERCISE B
Answers will vary but should reflect an understanding of comparison and contrast.

Lesson 11
Writing an Explanatory Paragraph
EXERCISE A
 <u>Mountain climbing, especially that done on rocks, is a challenging sport.</u> Rock climbers pull themselves up steep rock faces; <u><u>therefore</u></u>, they use special shoes, rope, and steel spikes. Ice climbers, <u><u>however</u></u>, face additional difficulties. To climb over ice and snow, they use ice axes and boot spikes, called crampons, to gain footing. <u><u>In addition</u></u>, they build rest spots at several points during their ascent. Mountain climbing—on rock or ice—is a sport that requires both skill and daring. <u><u>Nevertheless</u></u>, it attracts many enthusiasts.
 <u><u>While</u></u> the water was beginning to boil, SoodaWa made tea. She always made the tea <u><u>first</u></u>. <u><u>Then while</u></u> the water boiled rapidly, she prepared the flour for making bannock bread. She kneaded a batch of dough, and <u><u>then</u></u> she greased her big frying pan with fat and spread the dough upon it very evenly. She placed the pan on a red-glowing bed of coals that she had scraped away from the fire, and she held it there <u><u>until</u></u> a wonderful aroma rose from the bread <u><u>as it</u></u> slowly browned.
—*from* **LEGEND DAYS** by Jamake Highwater
Topic sentence has a single underline; transition words, a double underline.

EXERCISE B
 You can repot a plant in the following way. <u>First</u> put pebbles in the bottom of a new flowerpot for drainage. <u>Then</u> put an inch of fresh potting soil on top of the pebbles. <u>Now</u> use a knife to loosen the soil around the plant in the old pot. Carefully empty the old pot upside down into your hand. Stand the plant in the new pot. Place the top of the roots at least one inch below the rim of the pot. <u>Finally</u>, press more potting soil around the roots and water the plant.
1. Steps in a process
2. Transitions words are underlined.

EXERCISE C
Answers will vary, but sentences should be arranged in a logical order.

Grade Eight SkillBook, Writing Answer Key

Lesson 12
Cause and Effect
EXERCISE A

Causes have a single underline; effects double.
1. Julio memorized all the assigned spelling words; therefore, he won the spelling bee.
2. I am taking my dog to the vet because she needs her shots.
3. Keiko sang the part better than anyone else, and thus she won the lead in the school musical.
4. Ice covered the road, so traffic moved slowly.

EXERCISE B
1. See sentence 1.
2. See sentences 2–4.
3. a
4. See sentences 10–12.
5. See sentence 11.

Lesson 13
Writing a Cause and Effect Paragraph
EXERCISE A
1. The first sentence.
2. All sentences except the first.
3. Since; as a result

EXERCISE B

Answers will vary but should complete the cause-and-effect relationship.

EXERCISE C

Causes have a single underline; effects double.

   Have you ever marveled at how an airplane stays aloft? The secret lies in the shape of its wings and the fact that air moves constantly. Both wings are curved on their top sides, but straight on their bottoms. When the plane begins to move it causes the wings to cut through the air. Because the air meets with the resistance of the wings, it breaks up. The air that breaks over the wing pushes down on it. The air that breaks under the wing pushes up. Since the air traveling over the wings has to travel farther than the air under the wings, it flows faster than and pushes less on the wing than does the air flowing under the wing. Therefore the air flowing over the bottom wing portion pushes the wings up. As a result the plane leaves the ground. Consequently, as long as the plane keeps moving, the wings act to lift the plane and keep it airborne.

Lesson 14
Writing a Persuasive Paragraph
EXERCISE A
1. 1
2. Sentences 5 and 7
3. 5; 7

EXERCISE B

Answers will vary.

Lesson 15
Writing a Summary Paragraph
EXERCISE A
1. Title, author, setting, Captain Winter, Rudi earning the right to make the climb.
2. Sentences 1, 4–7
3. 4
4. That Rudi has a job as a mountain guide.

EXERCISE B

1 is better; reasons will vary but should focus on guidelines.

Lesson 16
Research: Choosing a Topic
EXERCISE A

Choices may vary; suggested answers are shown. Explanations will vary.
1. Comparison/contrast
2. Cause/effect or narrative
3. Cause/effect
4. Narrative or explanatory
5. Narrative or explanatory
6. Comparison/contrast
7. Cause/effect
8. Narrative or explanatory
9. Cause/effect
10. Explanatory or narrative

EXERCISE B

Topics and questions will vary but should fit the type of report.

Lesson 17
Research: Using Reference Sources
EXERCISE A
1. atlas
2. encyclopedia
3. *Readers' Guide*

4. specialized subject dictionary
5. nonprint media
6. *Readers' Guide*
7. specialized subject dictionary
8. almanac
9. biographical reference book
10. nonprint media

EXERCISE B
Reference sources will vary but should fit the questions.

Lesson 18
Research: Taking Notes
EXERCISE A
Summaries will vary. Source information below.
1. Answers question 2. "Frontier Life," *The Encyclopedia Americana*, 1986, Volume 12, p. 118.
2. Answers question 3. Stratton, Johanna L. *Pioneer Women*, New York: Simon and Schuster, 1981, p. 160.

EXERCISE B
Be sure students have taken adequate notes for their topics.

Lesson 19
Research: Organizing Information
EXERCISE A
Answers will vary. One possible sequence is shown for each set.
1. This set is for a report on Air Pollution in Big Cities:

2	1
5	6
7	8
3	4

2. This set is for a report on Old Time Baseball and Modern Baseball:

3	4
5	2
7	6
1	8

EXERCISE B
Be sure that students have sorted their notes logically and that the sequence they have chosen is appropriate for the material.

Lesson 20
Research: Outlining
EXERCISE A
The Telephone
  I. Early . . .
     A. Invented . . .
        1. Came to . . .
        2. Teacher . . .
     B. AT&T . . .
  II. Telephone . . .
     A. Local . . .
     B. Long distance . . .
     C. Overseas . . .
        1. Reaches . . .
        2. Uses . . .
  III. Modern . . .
     A. Touch-Tone . . .
     B. Car . . .
     C. Picturephones

EXERCISE B
Students' outlines will vary, but the first and last main topics should be *Introduction* and *Conclusion*, respectively.

GRAMMAR, USAGE, AND MECHANICS ANSWER KEY

Lesson 1
Kinds of Sentences
EXERCISE A
1. Who will take the minutes?
2. How quickly this vote came!
3. Please raise your hands for the vote. Clearly, the ayes have it.
   imperative, declarative

EXERCISE B
1. declarative
2. imperative
3. interrogative
4. interrogative
5. declarative
6. declarative
7. exclamatory
8. imperative
9. declarative
10. interrogative

EXERCISE C
Answers will vary.

Lesson 2
Subjects and Predicates
EXERCISE A
1. Tiny <u>fish</u> in schools | <u>dart</u> back and forth in the shadows.
2. <u>Bullfrogs</u> and <u>crickets</u> | <u>fill</u> the air with their commotion.

EXERCISE B
1. People from many countries | gather for the helium-inflated balloon's liftoff.
2. The lone balloonist | prepares her craft for the flight.
3. She | will navigate her balloon across the Atlantic.
4. The happy balloonist | jumps into the gondola.
5. The crew on the ground | releases the moorings.
6. The large and colorful monster | floats upward into the wind.
7. The strong, gusty wind | propels it over the water.
8. A noisy crowd of well-wishers | cheers at the impressive sight.
9. The balloon | will rise during the day and dip in the evening.
10. Favorable winds and good weather | should carry the craft more than two thousand miles.

EXERCISE C
11. This small <u>creature</u> | <u>was called</u> the dawn horse, or eohippus.
12. The four-toed <u>eohippus</u> | <u>could run</u> on tiptoe.
13. Its <u>toes</u> | <u>changed</u> and <u>developed</u> over thousands of years.
14. The <u>result</u> of the changes | <u>was</u> the modern horse's hoof.
15. <u>Ponies</u> of today | <u>resemble</u> another early animal, equus.
16. The primitive <u>equus</u> | <u>lived</u> and <u>thrived</u> in North America.
17. <u>Glaciers</u> and colder <u>temperatures</u> | <u>made</u> life difficult.
18. The <u>animals</u> | <u>abandoned</u> North America and <u>migrated</u> to other parts of the world.
19. Modern <u>horses</u> | <u>were brought</u> back to North America in 1537.
20. <u>They</u> | quickly <u>multiplied</u> and <u>roamed</u> the West in wild bands.

Lesson 3
Simple and Compound Sentences
EXERCISE A
compound subject and compound predicate

EXERCISE B
Subjects **S** are underlined once, and verbs, **V**, have a double underline.
1. Tulip <u>growers</u> around the world <u>import</u> these handsome flowers.
2. The <u>tulip</u> <u>originated</u> in Turkey and <u>means</u> turban in Turkish.
3. <u>Horticulturists</u> and amateur <u>gardeners</u> <u>plant</u> tulips in the fall and <u>enjoy</u> them the following spring.
4. A <u>variety</u> of shapes <u>attract</u> tulip buyers.
5. Actually, the modern <u>tulip</u> <u>is</u> a member of the lily family.
6. Unusual <u>colors</u> and <u>patterns</u> in hybrid flowers <u>require</u> years of research.
7. Either <u>bulbs</u> or <u>seeds</u> <u>may produce</u> new plants.
8. Individual <u>bulbs</u> <u>divide</u> into several bulbs and <u>yield</u> flowers sooner than seeds.
9. <u>Producers</u> <u>remove</u> diseased plants and <u>develop</u> hardier hybrids.
10. <u>Tulips</u> <u>are</u> attractive flowers and <u>remain</u> very popular.

EXERCISE C
11. compound
12. simple
13. compound
14. simple
15. simple
16. compound
17. simple
18. compound
19. simple
20. simple

Lesson 4
Sentence Fragments and Run-ons
EXERCISE A
1. Born in 1862, Edith Wharton was reluctant to become a writer because it was not considered proper for a woman.
2. Her most famous novel is *Ethan Frome*, a tale of love turned bitter.
3. Sarah Orne Jewett wrote about the difficult lives of people in rural America, particularly her native Maine.
4. Jewett's characters were vividly drawn and very realistic.
5. An example is "The Flight of Betsey Lane," a popular story.
6. Another famous writer, Willa Cather, grew up on a ranch in Nebraska and used her memories of it in her novels too.
7. She won early fame with *O Pioneers!*, but is better known for *Death Comes for the Archbishop*.
8. Katherine Anne Porter won national awards for short stories.

9. She spent twenty-two years on her only novel, *Ship of Fools*.
10. These writers portrayed women who endured hard lives.

Lesson 5

Combining Subjects, Predicates, and Sentences

EXERCISE

Some answers may vary.

1. Some proteins build muscles, and some proteins replace dead tissue.
2. Other proteins are less valuable to the body and should be avoided.
3. Protein, iron, and vitamins can be found in meat.
4. Do you have to eat meat, or can you be healthy without it?
5. Vegetarians eat fish, but they don't eat meat.
6. Many fruits, vegetables, and whole grains contain important vitamins.
7. Food experts recommend eating whole grains, and doctors agree.
8. Many people have changed their eating habits and are healthier as a result.

Lesson 6

Varying Sentence Structure

EXERCISE

Answers will vary. Here are some possibilities.

1. Deep recesses for train tracks were cut into the streets.
2. Because the train didn't run in a tunnel yet, they called it a subway.
3. Real underground trains opened in 1860 in London.
4. The tunnels resembled tubes; Londoners still call them that.
5. Boston built the first American trolley line in 1897.
6. Boston had theirs earlier, but New York soon had a larger system.
7. New York's subways travel underneath five counties and are thousands of miles long.
8. Both Paris's and Montreal's subways have rubber wheels for a quieter ride.
9. Does Tokyo have crowded subways, or are Mexico City's worse?
10. Mexico City's subways cut through ancient Aztec pyramids that look like a museum.

Lesson 7

Direct Objects and Subject Complements

EXERCISE A

1. hers (predicate pronoun)
2. ribbon (direct object)
3. game (direct object)
4. athlete (predicate noun)

EXERCISE B

1. Today we will hold a relay <u>race</u> at our school. (transitive)
2. The captain of our team is <u>Gerry</u>. (intransitive)
3. Serita and Jeffrey are team <u>members</u> too. (intransitive)
4. Jeffrey runs the first <u>leg</u> of the race. (transitive)
5. He relays the <u>baton</u> to Serita. (transitive)
6. Serita hands the <u>baton</u> to Gerry. (transitive)
7. Gerry is a faster <u>runner</u> than I. (intransitive)
8. The other teams are not <u>local</u>. (intransitive)
9. Our coach cheers <u>us</u> on eagerly. (transitive)
10. I am still <u>nervous</u> during a race. (intransitive)
11. The race was a huge <u>success</u>. (intransitive)
12. Our coach congratulated <u>us</u> and the other <u>team</u>. (transitive)

EXERCISE C

13. expert (SC—predicate noun)
14. club (DO)
15. president (SC—predicate noun)
16. she (SC—predicate pronoun), Tom Vaar (SC—predicate noun)
17. club (DO)
18. collectors (SC—predicate noun)
19. shop (DO)
20. club (DO)
21. popular (SC—predicate adjective)
22. collector (SC—predicate noun)

Lesson 8

Indirect Objects

EXERCISE A

1. Jane (indirect object)
2. her (indirect object)
3. her (object of preposition)
4. her (object of preposition)
5. Mother (indirect object)
6. Lester (object of preposition)
7. Stan (indirect object)

EXERCISE B
1. Lincoln
2. It
3. dog
4. Bouncer
5. him
6. Lincoln
7. Bouncer
8. Bouncer
9. Lincoln's little brother
10. Uncle Denis

EXERCISE C
11. Bill painted his mother a picture.
12. He built his father a pipe rack.
13. Myron gave his sister a gift certificate.
14. Tanya wove her cousin a scarf.
15. Tanya's cousin sent her some earrings.

Lesson 9
Independent and Dependent Clauses
Exercise A
1. I didn't meet the man who bought Mom's car.
2. When I got home, he had already left.
3. The car was old, but Mom got a good price for it.
4. She wants a new car that will seat more than two.
5. We will enjoy the new car, but we will miss the old one.

EXERCISE B
6. There were three candidates in the election that I lost.
7. Bobbette DeBow was the one who got the most votes.
8. After the votes were counted, I congratulated her.
9. This is the second time that I have run for class president.
10. I might run in the science-club election, which will be held next month.
11. I am interested in going into politics when I finish college.
12. If I do, my parents will probably be disappointed.
13. They point to my uncle, who has run for mayor three times and lost each time.
14. Before I decide on a political career, I'll talk it over with my parents.
15. I might change my mind, though I doubt it.

Lesson 10
Complex Sentences
EXERCISE A
1. Until the rain started, we had been planning a picnic.
2. One boy that we knew waited an hour before he left the park.

EXERCISE B
Answers will vary. Each sentence should contain a dependent clause introduced by the word in parentheses.

EXERCISE C
7. The Egyptian astronomer Ptolemy, who learned a great deal about star groups, is known for his maps of the night sky.
8. His studies, which were conducted in the second century A.D., described the motion of the planets.
9. Ancient Greeks described stars, but they had no telescopes.
10. Hans Lippershey, who invented the telescope in 1608, contributed to the study of astronomy.
11. The scientist who made the first really effective telescope was Galileo.
12. The stars appear motionless, but they are all moving.
13. Centuries ago, the North Star that you see guided sailors who did not have today's modern equipment.
14. This star, which is also called Polaris, is seen in the Northern Hemisphere.
15. When you see the Big Dipper, you are looking at the most easily identifiable group of stars.
16. The Little Dipper is called Ursa Minor, and this star group is made up of seven bright stars.
17. Most people who study the skies have observed these star groups, which often can be seen without a telescope.

Lesson 11
Compound-Complex Sentences
EXERCISE A
1. complex
2. compound-complex

EXERCISE B
1. complex
2. complex
3. complex
4. compound-complex

5. complex
6. compound-complex
7. compound-complex
8. compound-complex

EXERCISE C
Answers will vary. Compound sentences should include one or more dependent clauses added to form compound-complex sentences.

Lesson 12
Adjective and Adverb Clauses
EXERCISE A
1. <u>Before he left</u>, Tom closed and locked the window.
2. Leonard, <u>who was with him</u>, helped with the upstairs windows.

EXERCISE B
1. Kenji hurried <u>because he was late</u>. (adverb)
2. <u>As he approached the cemetery</u>, someone called his name. (adverb)
3. He could think of no one <u>who might also be out this early</u>. (adjective)
4. He peered into the shadows <u>that were cast by the tall trees</u>. (adjective)
5. <u>Since he could see no one</u>, he continued on his way. (adverb)
6. Suddenly a person <u>whom he recognized</u> came into view. (adjective)
7. Kenji felt relieved <u>when he saw Martin</u>. (adverb)
8. The two, <u>who were good friends</u>, walked along together. (adjective)
9. They were going to band practice, <u>which was early today</u>. (adjective)
10. <u>Before practice began</u>, the director handed out some new music. (adverb)

EXERCISE C
Answers will vary.

Lesson 13
Combining Sentences with Clauses
EXERCISE A
The position of some clauses may vary.
1. The word *utopia*, which now means "ideal place," comes from Greek words meaning "no place."
2. An ancient Greek book, whose author was Plato, may have been the first tale of a utopia.
3. Not all the people appreciated Plato's book, which he wrote for their improvement.
4. He wanted a land ruled by a king who was a philosopher.
5. Other books that described utopias were written by Sir Thomas More and Voltaire.

EXERCISE B
The position of some clauses may vary.
6. We all wanted to go though we couldn't agree on where.
7. Tony wanted to go to California because he wanted to try surfing.
8. Since Allie doesn't like water, she was against the idea.
9. No one else was very enthusiastic about a historic tour although Mom was all for it.
10. We argued and argued until Dad got annoyed.

Lesson 14
Improving Sentences
EXERCISE A
Some possible changes are shown.
1. There was frozen food at the picnic.
2. The food and drinks were free.
3. The day was sunny, hot, and humid.
4. Some people sat in the shade and chatted.
5. While eating dessert, the children and adults planned to play football.
6. A four-piece band played loudly and energetically.
7. Under a tree I found a sheet of music that had been written by John Lennon.
8. The clowns were nimble, silly, and amusing.
9. People from all over attended the picnic.
10. The picnic is an annual event.

EXERCISE B
Answers will vary.
The actor was tall, red-haired, and homely. His speaking voice was deep and low. He wore a bright costume. While reciting, he used several props. His character, who had a French accent, had an effect on the audience. The character was boring, sarcastic, and grouchy. He bossed other characters around. Most of them spoke softly, hesitatingly, and fearfully. When the play ended, the audience gave the cast a standing ovation.

Lesson 15
Expanding Sentences
EXERCISE A
Answers will vary. Possible answers are shown.
1. The noisy spectators cheered continuously.
2. A tall player angrily protested.
3. The young guard then hesitated.

4. Some energetic cheerleaders shouted enthusiastically.
5. The umpire's whistle blew loudly.

EXERCISE B
Answers will vary. Possible answers are shown.
1. Many points were scored by the captain.
2. Rushing to the bench, somebody slipped.
3. The coach, my favorite teacher, yelled.
4. A cup of cold water spilled.
5. Dribbling near the sideline, the player shot.
6. Dressed in a blue uniform, a guard dribbled.
7. The center jumped for the ball.
8. The buzzer sounded ending the first half.

Lesson 16
Appositives
EXERCISE A
1. The play is about the <u>future</u>, <u>the year 2222</u>.
2. It has two leading <u>characters</u>, <u>Melody and Charley</u>.
3. My <u>brother</u> <u>David</u> is playing a leading role.
4. Two other <u>characters</u>, <u>Zelly and Rabo</u>, are robots.
5. Zelly and Rabo live on the <u>planet</u> <u>Rion</u>.
6. The robots live in an underground <u>city</u>, <u>their home on Rion</u>.
7. They visit Charley and Melody in <u>Omaha</u>, <u>a city in Nebraska</u>.
8. They arrive in a <u>spaceship</u>, <u>a moon-powered craft</u>.
9. The robots marvel at two <u>pets</u>, <u>Sundae and Whiskers</u>.
10. Charley's <u>dog</u>, <u>a brown and white spaniel</u>, is named Sundae.

EXERCISE B
11. Coastlines are homes of a strange animal, the spiny lobster.
12. A favorite food, clams, is cracked open by the lobster's claw.
13. The lobster migration, a curious sight, occurs in the fall.
14. The lobsters travel in a parade, an odd procession.
15. Scientists have organized SLURP, the Spiny Lobsters Undersea Research Project.

Lesson 17
Identifying Nouns
EXERCISE A
1. We searched the <u>sky</u> and found a <u>rainbow</u>.
2. Its <u>appearance</u> gave the <u>children</u> great <u>pleasure</u>.
3. My little <u>sister</u> thinks that <u>elves</u> painted the <u>rainbow</u>.

EXERCISE B
1. I keep a <u>scrapbook</u> of <u>photographs</u> from my <u>travels</u>.
2. Each <u>year</u> my <u>family</u> travels to a different <u>state</u>.
3. We do <u>months</u> of <u>research</u> before we find a <u>place</u>.
4. Usually, <u>Dad</u> comes up with three or four <u>suggestions</u>.
5. By the <u>end</u> of <u>spring</u>, the <u>family</u> finds a <u>place</u> and makes <u>reservations</u>.
6. Then <u>Mom</u> writes to the <u>bureau</u> of <u>tourism</u> for <u>information</u>.
7. <u>Places</u> like <u>Arizona</u> and <u>Utah</u> always send lovely <u>brochures</u>.
8. <u>Friends</u> in some <u>states</u> have invited us to their <u>houses</u>.
9. Sometimes we pitch a <u>tent</u> at a <u>campsite</u>.
10. Two <u>summers</u> ago we rented a <u>cabin</u> along a <u>lake</u>.
11. In the previous <u>year</u>, the whole <u>family</u> got <u>salmonella</u>.
12. Last <u>summer</u> we visited our <u>aunt</u> in <u>San Francisco</u>.
13. We stayed at a large <u>hotel</u> near the <u>bay</u>.
14. My <u>room</u> looked out over the <u>city</u>.
15. The other <u>room</u> had a beautiful <u>mural</u> painted on the <u>wall</u>.
16. We toured the <u>area</u> for seven <u>days</u>.
17. My <u>family</u> saw old <u>homes</u> in interesting <u>neighborhoods</u>.
18. One <u>day</u> we rented <u>bikes</u> and rode to a <u>landmark</u> in the <u>city</u>.
19. That <u>night</u> we ate <u>dinner</u> at a <u>restaurant</u>.
20. I ate <u>shrimp</u> cooked in a delicious <u>sauce</u>.
21. Next <u>year</u> we will drive to the <u>mountains</u>.

EXERCISE C
22. disappearance, acceptance, appearance, avoidance, annoyance
23. teacher, singer, writer, player, dancer
24. sloppiness, wildness, happiness, laziness, fondness
25. investigator, detector, governor, translator, accelerator

Lesson 18
Kinds of Nouns
EXERCISE A
1. **common nouns:** plane
   proper nouns: Guam, Korea, *The Eagle*.
2. **common nouns:** goods, world
   proper nouns: India.

3. **common nouns:** languages, business.
4. **common nouns:** People, medicines
   proper nouns: Africa, Europe
5. **common nouns:** journeys
   proper nouns: Amazon River

EXERCISE B
1. **concrete nouns:** book, records
   abstract nouns: idea
2. **concrete nouns:** authors
   abstract nouns: intelligence
3. **concrete nouns:** records
   abstract nouns: belief
4. **concrete nouns:** book, facts, figures, comments
5. **concrete nouns:** readers
   abstract nouns: fascination

Lesson 19
Plural Nouns
EXERCISE A
taxes, dishes, echoes, loaves, workmen

EXERCISE B
1. donkeys
2. switches
3. car pools
4. libraries
5. tariffs
6. sheep
7. hatboxes
8. bosses
9. vetoes
10. calves
11. bases
12. stereos
13. foxes
14. stepsons
15. roofs
16. women
17. geese
18. children
19. knives
20. oxen

EXERCISE C
21. Our <u>canarys</u> sing us lovely <u>choruss</u> each morning. (canaries, choruses)
22. His <u>daughter-in-laws</u> had more <u>crisises</u> than anyone else. (daughters-in-law, crises)
23. The <u>clownes</u> with <u>umbrellaes</u> kept us in <u>stitchs</u>. (clowns, umbrellas, stitches)
24. <u>Rowes</u> of neat <u>pansys</u> stood in front of the <u>mulberrys</u>. (rows, pansies, mulberries)
25. <u>Workmans</u> opened the boat's <u>hatchs</u> and unloaded its freight. (Workmen, hatches)
26. Both designers' <u>studioes</u> were filled with dress <u>dummys</u>. (studios, dummies)

EXERCISE D
27. All generations have their heroes and ideals.
28. Statesmen and stateswomen are admired for leadership.
29. Some people envy the lifestyles of actors and actresses.
30. Television personalities and musicians have their followers.

Lesson 20
Possessive Nouns
EXERCISE
1. the student's pencils
2. the class's teacher
3. the foxes' den
4. the policemen's pants
5. an eighth grader's writing
6. my sister-in-law's visit
7. our ponies' pasture
8. Charles's life
9. the birds' song
10. our women's baseball team
11. my family's celebration
12. the girls' uniforms
13. a cat's paw
14. the victim's scream
15. the astronauts' spaceship
16. the Millers' homes
17. the neighbor's dog
18. the mayor's election
19. the crowd's reaction
20. the ships' crews
21. the rockets' glare
22. that gentleman's hat
23. the babies' playpen
24. this story's ending
25. the deer's antlers

Lesson 21
Plural or Possessive
EXERCISE A
1. plural
2. possessive
3. possessive
4. possessive
5. plural
6. possessive
7. plural
8. plural possessive
9. possessive
10. possessive
11. plural
12. possessive
13. possessive
14. plural
15. plural
16. possessive
17. possessive
18. plural possessive
19. possessive
20. plural

EXERCISE B
1. Words have fascinated people for centuries.
2. Not all words were written with letters.
3. Some words' meanings took years to understand.
4. An archaeologist's job is understanding the past.
5. Archaeologists have studied ancient Egyptians' writing.
6. The Egyptians influenced the Greeks' way of writing.
7. The shapes of letters in alphabets have changed.
8. Different languages have different alphabets.
9. Some languages do not even have alphabets.
10. Archaeologists' investigations concern other things too.

Lesson 22
Personal Pronouns
EXERCISE A
1. <u>Ana and Jean</u> decided <u>they</u> would go hiking.
2. <u>The girls</u> invited Bob to join <u>them</u>.
3. <u>Joel</u> asked, "May <u>I</u> come too?"
4. Ana packed a <u>lunch</u> and brought <u>it</u> along.
5. <u>Dom and I</u> met the <u>group</u> and asked if <u>we</u> could accompany <u>them</u>.

EXERCISE B
1. I spoke up, "José, I will drive!"
2. José insisted that he would drive.
3. We tossed a coin to decide.
4. He won and got behind the wheel.
5. We met two pals and invited them along.
6. The boys said they would help polish.
7. José and I were glad they could help us.
8. Then we decided to wax the car.
9. Our pals groaned as they worked.
10. "You know, we should have walked."

EXERCISE C
11. Manny and Liz
12. My friends and I
13. The race
14. Bill and Jim
15. riders
16. Rick
17. mother
18. Students
19. principal
20. students

Lesson 23
Possessive Pronouns
EXERCISE A
1. Walter thought that <u>his</u> teacher was remarkable.
2. <u>My</u> teacher and <u>his</u> is Mr. Griffin, a professional weight lifter.
3. <u>Our</u> workouts are held in the basement of <u>his</u> family's house.
4. The weights are <u>mine</u>, but the basement is <u>theirs</u>.
5. What are some of <u>your</u> hobbies?

EXERCISE B
6. It is his folder. The folder is his.
7. It is her fancy red notebook. The fancy red notebook is hers.
8. They are our new yellow pencils. The new yellow pencils are ours.
9. The erasers are yours. Yours are the erasers.
10. The new book bags are theirs. Theirs are the new book bags.

EXERCISE C
11. The sports shop was crowded. Its customers had to wait.
12. We took a number. Our number was finally called.
13. Sally needs a new ski jacket. Hers is worn out.
14. May had lent me some skis. But her skis were way too short for me.
15. Skis should be the right height. Are your skis right for you?
16. The clerk showed me some skis. They were just my height.
17. My boots fit well. Do yours?
18. Sally and Joe bought matching jackets. Theirs are bright red.
19. They have blue hats and mittens. Their outfits are colorful.
20. The season starts soon. Our equipment is ready.

Lesson 24
Interrogative, Relative and Demonstrative Pronouns
EXERCISE A
1. <u>Who</u> gave you <u>that</u>?
2. <u>Which</u> of the vendors sold you <u>these</u>?
3. Any store <u>that</u> stocks <u>this</u> shouldn't be trusted.
4. <u>These</u> are too expensive for me.
5. I need a bike <u>that</u> is more in my price range.
6. To <u>whom</u> should I speak about my problem?

EXERCISE B
1. interrogative
2. relative
3. relative
4. relative
5. interrogative, relative
6. interrogative
7. interrogative
8. relative
9. interrogative
10. relative

EXERCISE C
11. <u>This</u> is very soft and delicate for an oil painting. (demonstrative)
12. For <u>whom</u> are you buying the sketch? (interrogative)
13. Here is the canvas <u>that</u> won first prize. (relative)
14. <u>Who</u> painted the portraits of the royal family? (interrogative)
15. The artist <u>who</u> painted them does not want to sell. (relative)
16. <u>Whose</u> is the ink sketch of a sailboat? (interrogative)
17. <u>Which</u> do you think my sister would like? (interrogative)
18. <u>Those</u> are all made of fabric and string. (demonstrative)
19. Have you looked at the drawings <u>that</u> are hanging upstairs? (relative)
20. <u>What</u> is the title of the large pastel drawing? (interrogative)

Lesson 25
Reflexive and Intensive Pronouns
EXERCISE A
1. reflexive
2. intensive
3. reflexive
4. reflexive
5. reflexive
6. reflexive
7. intensive
8. reflexive
9. intensive
10. intensive

EXERCISE B
1. He had designed the bracelet himself.
2. Tom and I gave it to the cat.
3. The cat chewed it up before cleaning itself.
4. We couldn't forgive ourselves for letting that happen.
5. Jack said he himself would repair the bracelet.
6. He told Tom and me that the accident was our fault.
7. We promised ourselves to be more careful.
8. We would make Tom a present ourselves.
9. I asked myself what we could make for him.
10. Finally, Tom himself said he would like a new keychain.

Lesson 26
Indefinite Pronouns
EXERCISE A
1. <u>Antiques</u> sell fast. <u>Several</u> are very expensive.
2. Old comic <u>books</u> are hot items too. <u>Few</u> are left.
3. I bought two <u>books</u> and enjoyed <u>both</u>.
4. My <u>parents</u> bought a vase, but <u>neither</u> really liked it.
5. <u>Kevin</u> and <u>George</u> found an old phonograph. <u>Both</u> wanted it.
6. Two more <u>phonographs</u> were there. <u>Neither</u> worked very well.
7. The <u>buyers</u> were anxious. <u>All</u> of them were looking around.
8. Kevin found two <u>dictionaries</u>. <u>Each</u> of them was very old.
9. Six <u>books</u> were nearly falling apart. <u>Others</u>, though, were new.
10. The new <u>books</u> were in boxes. <u>Several</u> were best sellers.
11. I bought two <u>books</u>. <u>Both</u> should be quite interesting.
12. I found a <u>bookmark</u> in a book. <u>Something</u> like that is priceless.
13. My <u>friends</u> are attending this show next week. <u>Everyone</u> is excited about all the antiques.
14. There is always a large <u>crowd</u> there, but <u>everybody</u> always sees a familiar face.
15. The <u>variety</u> is amazing. <u>Everything</u> looks interesting to me.
16. My mother looked at the <u>teacups</u>. She could buy only <u>one</u>.
17. She looked at the <u>cups</u> again. <u>Many</u> of them were beautiful.
18. I looked at the <u>candlesticks</u>. <u>Few</u> of them were what I wanted.
19. One booth sold antique <u>radios</u>. I found <u>many</u> that were more than fifty years old.
20. Depression glass <u>plates</u> are lovely. I bought <u>several</u>.

EXERCISE B
1. <u>Several</u> of the booths are open. (plural)
2. <u>Everyone</u> comes early for bargains. (singular)
3. <u>Anybody</u> who is in school is welcome. (singular)
4. <u>Each</u> of the sellers has marked-down items. (singular)
5. <u>Many</u> of the buyers appreciate a bargain. (plural)

Lesson 27
Subject and Object Pronouns
EXERCISE A
1. Sue and (<u>I</u>, me) are reporters.
2. We asked Tom and (they, <u>them</u>) about their plans.
3. We get our news from the neighbors and (they, <u>them</u>).

Grade Eight SkillBook, Grammar, Usage, and Mechanics Answer Key

4. (She, Her) and Li will edit the paper.
5. (We, Us) and Kiku will get the paper typed and copied.
6. The advertising will be handled by Li and (we, us).
7. You can send classified ads to Sam and (she, her).
8. The editorials will be written by Kiku and (I, me).
9. We put Herb and (he, him) in charge of photography.
10. (She, Her) and Pat can write the headlines.
11. (He, Him) and Tom will deliver the papers.
12. (They, Them) and the neighbors have hopes for our success.
13. Send your advertising to (he, him) by the tenth of the month.
14. Design will be handled by my brother and (she, her).
15. (They, them) have already designed a sample copy.
16. We know we can trust (they, them) with the design.
17. I have never designed a paper, but (they, them) have.
18. Because I have reported before, you can trust (I, me) with that.
19. Some neighbors have said they would support (we, us).
20. We will not disappoint (they, them).

EXERCISE B
1. The Brands and (we, us) are going on vacation together.
2. It will be a lot of fun for (they, them) and (we, us).
3. (We, Us) and (they, them) enjoy doing things together.
4. Their son Tony and (I, me) are good friends.
5. (He, Him) and (I, me) will be the navigators.
6. New York City will be a new experience for (he, him) and (I, me).
7. Mom will take my sister and (I, me) to the art museum with Mrs. Brand and (she, her).
8. (She, Her) and my sister Gen are both painters.
9. I sometimes paint with Gen and (she, her).
10. (She, Her) and Mr. Brand also want to go to Philadelphia.
11. We'll go to Independence Hall and the Betsy Ross House with Tony and (they, them).
12. (They, Them) and (I, me) like to visit historical places.
13. (We, Us) look for historical places wherever we are.

14. Last year Dad took Gen and (I, me) to Plymouth Rock.
15. (He, him) showed us the Puritan village there too.

Lesson 28
Pronouns as Subject Complements
EXERCISE A
1. It was she who won the contest.
2. It was I who came in second.
3. They congratulated Vinnie and me.
4. It was they who congratulated us.
5. Then we all sang a victory song beginning with the words "We are champions, champions are we."

EXERCISE B
1. OWNER: Did my greedy nephew steal the jewels?
   HOLMES: It was not he.
2. OWNER: Did the butler steal them?
   HOLMES: It couldn't have been he.
3. OWNER: Did the maids steal them?
   HOLMES: It was definitely not they.
4. OWNER: Did the detectives from your department steal them?
   HOLMES: It certainly wasn't they.
5. OWNER: Did you steal them for the insurance money?
   HOLMES: I confess; it was I.

EXERCISE C
6. Albert invited Jack and (I, me) to the party at the farm.
7. It was (he, him) who thought of having the party there.
8. (He, Him) and his friends prepared most of the food.
9. The best cooks were Jack and (I, me).
10. It was (we, us) who made the salad and baked beans.
11. Albert took Jack and (I, me) horseback riding.
12. The first one to ride was (I, me).
13. Albert and (I, me) did just fine, but not Jack.
14. It was (he, him) who said not to be afraid.
15. Jack told (we, us) that horseback riding was easy.
16. It was (he, him) who claimed the horses were safe to ride.
17. It was (we, us) who had the frisky horses, not Jack.
18. Yet it was (he, him) who fell off the horse.

19. The luckiest of the riders was (I, me).
20. The sorest and most bruised was (he, him).
21. There (he, him) was, rubbing his wrist.
22. It must have hurt (he, him) very much.
23. "(I, me) am not as great a rider as you are," he said.
24. "The horse threw (I, me) before I knew what had happened."
25. "It was (I, me) who learned a lesson today!"

Lesson 29
Pronouns in Comparisons
EXERCISE A
1. Sasha helped José more than I helped José.
2. Sasha helped José more than he helped me.
3. Fran is as good a dancer as he is a dancer.
4. Lee annoyed Pat as much as he annoyed us.

EXERCISE B
1. The high-school swim club practices as much as (they, them).
2. Coach Penn works more with Crista than with (I, me).
3. After swimming fifty laps, Jay was more tired than (we, us).
4. Sid will have to swim as fast as (he, him).
5. Sharon likes to dive more than (I, me).
6. Joe thinks that everyone is a better swimmer than (he, him).
7. More points were awarded to Nona than (she, her).
8. Ian has a much stronger stroke than (he, him).
9. Everyone wants to swim against Jessie rather than (she, her).
10. Do the junior swimmers get more practice time than (we, us)?

EXERCISE C
11. I got more birthday cards than he. (correct)
12. Jerry likes to write letters more than I. (correct)
13. My sister Diana makes more telephone calls than I.
14. She talks on the telephone as much as he.
15. I don't talk as long as she.

Lesson 30
Using *who* and *whom*
EXERCISE A
1. object of preposition
2. subject of clause
3. subject
4. direct object

EXERCISE B
1. correct
2. With whom did you play softball?
3. correct
4. correct
5. Who is coming to the meeting?

EXERCISE C
6. With whom did you go to the music awards? object of preposition
7. Who, in your judgment, was the best singer? subject
8. Davey Sanchez, who wrote "Ballad for L. A.," was best. subject
9. Wilma preferred Karen Ching, who sang "My Side." subject
10. To whom was the prize for best song awarded? object of preposition
11. I also liked Jay King, whom Wilma praised. direct object
12. His songs are often sung by the Valdez Brothers, who are young Mexican-Americans from Fresno. subject
13. Whom did most people like best? direct object
14. Who sings better than Vera and Jay King? subject
15. Aren't they the ones who won the most awards last year? subject
16. Jay gave his gold records to his parents, who are delighted. subject
17. Who can blame them for being pleased? subject
18. Whom did you really prefer? direct object
19. I agreed with the judges, with whom I usually disagree. direct object
20. He was the one whom I would vote for too. object of preposition

Lesson 31
Pronoun Agreement
EXERCISE A
1. Authors want (his, their) works to be widely read.
2. Michele Sim wants (her, their) client's work published.
3. Publishers produce books (he, they) can sell.
4. Kristy Lee often helps publicize (her, their) own books.
5. Each reader knows what books (he or she, they) will enjoy.
6. Librarians buy books (his, their) towns will read.
7. Neither of the boys brought (his, their) own book to read.
8. Did either of the students write (his or her, their) own story?

9. Several of the women wrote (his, <u>their</u>) autobiographies.
10. Not one of the boys had finished (<u>his</u>, their) story.

EXERCISE B
1. Neither of the girls wants <u>her</u> picture taken.
2. When everyone arrived, <u>he or she</u> began work on the mural.
3. correct
4. Each typist was rated on his or her speed and accuracy.
5. correct

Lesson 32
Identifying Verbs
EXERCISE A
1. Ned <u>bought</u> tickets for the baseball game. (action)
2. He <u>was</u> a fan of the Jersey Jaguars. (linking)
3. The Jaguars <u>won</u> all their games last year. (action)
4. Now they <u>appeared</u> ready for another successful season. (linking)

EXERCISE B
1. A year ago he <u>ran</u> last in his division. (physical)
2. He <u>thought</u> about his goal for this year. (mental)
3. During the summer he <u>jogged</u> every day. (physical)
4. He <u>remembered</u> his poor physical condition last year. (mental)
5. He and his teammates <u>participated</u> in daily workouts. (physical)
6. Sometimes they <u>swam</u> as a part of their conditioning. (physical)
7. Soon Henry <u>noticed</u> an improvement in his speed. (mental)
8. He <u>cut</u> several seconds off last year's time. (physical)
9. The coach <u>marveled</u> at Henry's improvement. (mental)
10. This fall the team <u>raced</u> against some stiff competition. (physical)

EXERCISE C
11. Its hero Odysseus <u>started</u> on his voyage home from Troy.
12. He <u>was</u> also a great Greek warrior like Achilles.
13. Odysseus's voyage home to Greece <u>seemed</u> simple enough.
14. In the end, Odysseus <u>journeyed</u> over twenty years.
15. Some of Odysseus's adventures <u>were</u> dreadful.
16. One time, he <u>endured</u> the unearthly screams of the Sirens.
17. Their irresistible cries almost <u>drove</u> him mad.
18. His men <u>tied</u> him to the mast of the boat for his own sake.
19. Another time, his party <u>wandered</u> into the giant Cyclops's cave.
20. The eye in the middle of the giant's head <u>looked</u> monstrous.
21. He <u>trapped</u> the men with a boulder in the cave's entrance.
22. Then he hungrily <u>devoured</u> two of the men.
23. The rest of the crew <u>were</u> afraid for their lives.
24. However, the clever Odysseus <u>was</u> calm as always.
25. He quickly <u>thought</u> of a clever escape.
26. Odysseus <u>tricked</u> the Cyclops with a powerful liquid.
27. Within a short time, the Cyclops <u>felt</u> sleepy.
28. Then they <u>blinded</u> the sleeping giant with a fiery stake.
29. The furious Cyclops <u>searched</u> in vain for the men.
30. The next day, Odysseus and his men <u>escaped</u> to their ship.

Lesson 33
Action or Linking Verb
EXERCISE A
1. Ann <u>looked</u> ill. (linking verb)
2. She <u>felt</u> a pain in her side. (action verb)
3. Ann's mother <u>looked</u> at her. (action verb)
4. Ann <u>appeared</u> pale. (linking verb)
5. Ann <u>smelled</u> the medicine. (action verb)
6. It <u>smelled</u> strange. (linking verb)
7. She <u>tasted</u> it cautiously. (action verb)
8. Soon Ann <u>felt</u> better. (linking verb)

EXERCISE B
1. This probably <u>sounds</u> a little strange. (linking verb)
2. I never <u>feel</u> lazy about one kind of errand. (linking verb)
3. One time my mother <u>felt</u> too busy for a visit to the bakery. (linking verb)
4. This errand <u>remains</u> my favorite. (linking verb)
5. The aroma of freshly baked bread <u>smells</u> wonderful to me. (linking verb)
6. I even <u>smelled</u> it blocks away from the bakery. (action verb)
7. I <u>grew</u> more ravenous by the minute. (linking verb)
8. Soon I <u>felt</u> hunger pangs in my stomach. (action verb)

9. Finally, I <u>appeared</u> in front of the shop. (action verb)
10. It <u>looked</u> busier than usual. (linking verb)
11. I <u>remained</u> calm nevertheless. (linking verb)
12. I <u>looked</u> for some standing room near the counter. (action verb)
13. I <u>remained</u> close to the door with my number in my hand. (action verb)
14. My anticipation <u>grew</u> because of the long wait. (action verb)
15. Finally, my number <u>sounded</u> above the noisy voices. (action verb)
16. The clerk <u>looked</u> at me curiously. (action verb)
17. She <u>appeared</u> very friendly, however. (linking verb)
18. I <u>felt</u> in my pocket for my money. (action verb)
19. I <u>remained</u> there long enough for my order. (action verb)
20. Once outside the door, I <u>looked</u> into my bag. (linking verb)
21. The rolls still <u>felt</u> warm from the oven. (linking verb)
22. They <u>smelled</u> delicious. (linking verb)
23. I <u>tasted</u> one with a buttery crust. (action verb)
24. It <u>tasted</u> moist and rich. (linking verb)
25. I <u>looked</u> into the bag often. (linking verb)
26. The rolls <u>looked</u> better with each step. (linking verb)

Lesson 34

Verb Phrases

EXERCISE A

1. Al <u>had climbed</u> that mountain before.
2. Al <u>has been climbing</u> for four years.
3. He <u>will</u> soon <u>climb</u> a new mountain.

EXERCISE B

1. Our class <u>will</u> soon <u>be going</u> on a nature walk.
2. We <u>may hike</u> through Jensen Nature Preserve this time.
3. Several teachers <u>might lead</u> us.
4. Mr. Hilton <u>has been</u> a well-known naturalist for many years.
5. His nature tours <u>should interest</u> us.
6. <u>Can</u> we <u>join</u> his group?
7. Bird watchers <u>should have registered</u> with Ms. Dee's tour.
8. <u>Does</u> she <u>know</u> all of the nesting areas?
9. Many rare birds <u>have been seen</u> on her tour.
10. <u>Would</u> you <u>bring</u> your field glasses with you?
11. Fiona McGee <u>is lecturing</u> on wildflowers again.
12. Her lecture <u>will take</u> about thirty minutes.

EXERCISE C

13. Mountaineering <u>could</u> eventually <u>grow</u> in popularity.
14. The conquest of Mt. Everest in 1953 <u>may</u> well <u>have increased</u> interest in the sport.
15. Climbers <u>have</u> now <u>reached</u> the summit dozens of times.
16. The Nabisco Wall <u>has</u> always <u>been regarded</u> as Mt. Everest's most difficult face.
17. Bad weather <u>has</u> often <u>caused</u> trouble for climbers.
18. They <u>must</u> surely <u>be conditioned</u> properly for the task.
19. One man <u>had</u> actually <u>fallen</u> over one mile without injury!
20. Climbers <u>should</u> always <u>use</u> the best gear available.
21. Experts <u>would</u> never <u>climb</u> alone either.
22. <u>Did</u> you <u>hear</u> about the Mt. Everest skier?
23. Luckily for him, he <u>did</u> not <u>kill</u> himself!
24. Most people <u>can</u> hardly <u>imagine</u> a five-mile-high mountain.
25. Someone <u>might</u> possibly <u>be climbing</u> it right now.

Lesson 35

Simple Tenses

EXERCISE A

1. Dana and Sean <u>are</u> junior mountain climbers from our school. (present)
2. They <u>climb</u> Mt. Baldy at least once every year. (present)
3. Last summer they <u>climbed</u> it twice. (past)
4. They and their group <u>will scale</u> it again tomorrow. (future)
5. Francis, their guide, <u>trained</u> the whole group well. (past)
6. He <u>instructed</u> them in the latest rescue techniques. (past)
7. Dana <u>excelled</u> as a group leader. (past)
8. Sean <u>completes</u> his last lesson with Francis today. (present)
9. All group members <u>conditioned</u> themselves for instructions. (past)
10. Some of the group <u>departed</u> at four o'clock this morning. (past)
11. They <u>left</u> early to set up their base camp. (past)
12. They <u>have</u> the first-aid supplies also. (present)
13. They <u>will wait</u> there until the others arrive. (future)

14. The second group brought all the food. (past)
15. They shopped for all the food last night. (past)

EXERCISE B
1. studied
2. need
3. will sing
4. will accompany
5. hope
6. stopped
7. will be
8. appeared

Lesson 36
Principal Parts of Verbs
EXERCISE A
1. We vacationed in Wisconsin. vacation, (are) vacationing, vacationed, (have) vacationed
2. Mother visits there often. visit, (is) visiting, visited, (have) visited
3. My uncle lives on an island. live, (is) living, lived, (have) lived
4. He stays there all year. stay, (is) staying, stayed, (have) stayed
5. Our family likes tours. like, (is) liking, liked, (have) liked
6. Some hurry to the beaches. hurry, (is) hurrying, hurried, (have) hurried
7. They skip in the sand. skip, (is) skipping, skipped, (have) skipped
8. They fish in the lake. fish, (is) fishing, fished, (have) fished
9. They pack picnic lunches. pack, (is) packing, packed, (have) packed
10. Everyone loves it there. love, (is) loving, loved, (have) loved

EXERCISE B
1. Who has asked you?
2. Which ones had baked bread?
3. What has started the fire?
4. Who has consulted you?
5. Which one had seemed sleepy?
6. Who has answered the phone?
7. Who has patched this coat?
8. Which stars have appeared?
9. Who has watched the play?
10. Which ones had acted in it?

EXERCISE C
11. Donna cares for someone. present
12. Tom had mixed the paint. past participle
13. They have used their brains. past participle
14. Sam showed his medals. past

15. Meg is laughing out loud. present participle
16. Amy has fixed the stove. past participle
17. My pay included a bonus. past
18. She is starting a trend. present participle
19. He operates a tractor. present
20. Who is playing the piano? present participle

Lesson 37
Perfect Tense
EXERCISE A
1. Have you heard of the lost city of Atlantis? (present perfect)
2. I had not thought about it for years. (past perfect)
3. Soon I will have read almost everything on the subject. (future perfect)
4. They say that Atlantis had been a rival of Athens. (past perfect)
5. There have been many references to this strange place in myths. (present perfect)
6. Perhaps Atlantis had sunk during an earthquake. (past perfect)
7. Since then, many adventurers and scholars have looked for it. (present perfect)
8. By now, they will have searched both seas and oceans. (future perfect)
9. They will have discovered many lost cities in the process. (future perfect)
10. No one has ever found any evidence of Atlantis's existence. (present perfect)

EXERCISE B
Sentences will vary.

EXERCISE C
16. I had planned to attend a concert this year.
17. My family has decided on plans for vacation.
18. I will have finished sixty books by my sixteenth birthday.
19. I have tried skydiving.
20. I have studied for my science exam.

Lesson 38
Transitive and Intransitive Verbs
EXERCISE A
1. transitive
2. transitive
3. intransitive
4. transitive
5. intransitive

EXERCISE B
1. Juanita plays field hockey on a team in her neighborhood.

2. She <u>plays</u> a forward <u>position</u>.
3. Her team <u>beat</u> <u>Overton</u> in the semifinals last week.
4. Overton <u>lost</u> the <u>game</u> in the last two minutes.
5. Juanita <u>scored</u> two important <u>goals</u> for her team.
6. She and her teammates <u>play</u> <u>Clifton</u> in the finals on Friday.
7. Clifton <u>won</u> the <u>championship</u> last year.
8. As a result, their games always <u>attract</u> a <u>crowd</u>.
9. Two coaches <u>accompany</u> Clifton's <u>team</u> to the playing field.
10. The better team <u>will win</u> the <u>match</u>.

EXERCISE C
11. Expert swimmers <u>helped</u> <u>them</u> with their lessons. (transitive)
12. intransitive
13. intransitive
14. intransitive
15. A guard <u>helped</u> <u>Inez</u> with the motions. (transitive)
16. intransitive
17. intransitive
18. Once she <u>kicked</u> the <u>wall</u> of the pool by mistake. (transitive)
19. She finally <u>learned</u> the correct <u>movements</u> for the dog paddle. (transitive)
20. intransitive
21. The guard <u>had complimented</u> <u>her</u> on her abilities. (transitive)
22. intransitive
23. She <u>might teach</u> <u>others</u> about techniques and movements in a pool. (transitive)

Lesson 39
Principal Parts of Irregular Verbs
EXERCISE A
1. begin, began, begun
2. draw, drew, drawn
3. know, knew, known
4. drive, drove, driven
5. become, became, become

EXERCISE B
1. Rehearsal time for the performance has (flew, <u>flown</u>).
2. All of the students have (grew, <u>grown</u>) in their acting abilities.
3. Tess (<u>wore</u>, worn) her costume to school.
4. On stage Russ (freezed, <u>froze</u>).
5. A stagehand (speaked, <u>spoke</u>) the cue for his next line.
6. The actors have (took, <u>taken</u>) many curtain calls.
7. The "acting bug" has (stang, <u>stung</u>) Carrie and Tess.
8. Some students have (chose, <u>chosen</u>) their favorite activity.
9. Everyone (rid, <u>rode</u>) home after the play.
10. A local critic has (wrote, <u>written</u>) of the play's success.

EXERCISE C
11. put
12. hit
13. shrank (or shrunk)
14. seen
15. fell
16. stole
17. ate
18. swung
19. lost
20. brought

Lesson 40
Forms of *be, have,* and *do*
EXERCISE A
1. Marjorie Kinnan Rawlings is the author of *The Yearling*.
2. Her home in Florida has been preserved.
3. She and her husband were farmers.
4. Her first success as a writer was the story of a boy.
5. The book, *The Yearling*, has been read worldwide.
6. Frank isn't planning to read this book.
7. I told him he is being silly.
8. "I am not interested in her books," he said.
9. "You were never interested in reading anything," I said.

EXERCISE B
(1) I had begun to wish that I knew more about other lands. (2) Most people have little knowledge about other countries. (3) My friends and I have started to learn more. (4) We should have learned about large and small countries long ago. (5) Some small, independent countries have names I have never heard before. (6) Have you heard of Nauru or Liechtenstein? (7) Liechtenstein is a tiny country and has no army. (8) Jody has decided to go there someday.

EXERCISE C
9. The interviewer said, "What kind of work have you done?"

10. I said that I like to do some kind of work each summer.
11. "What did you do last summer, for instance?" she asked.
12. "I don't remember all the jobs that I did then," I said.
13. "Why don't you?" the interviewer asked.
14. "It doesn't matter because I like many kinds of jobs."
15. "Don't you remember the odd job you liked best?" she asked.
16. "Rescuing a cat is the most interesting thing I have done so far."

Lesson 41
Troublesome Verb Pairs
EXERCISE A
1. a. Lay the book on the table. b. Lie on the couch.
2. a. Sit down over there. b. Set it down over there.
3. a. Let me go home. b. Leave the room at once.
4. a. Please lend me the book. b. Borrow it from him.
5. a. I'll learn my lesson later. b. Can you teach me to dance?
6. a. Take him away from here. b. Bring your game here.
7. a. Please raise the window. b. Watch the temperature rise.

EXERCISE B
1. Yesterday the workers (laid, lay) all the tools on the bench.
2. I have (learned, taught) you everything I know.
3. (Let, Leave) me show you the way out.
4. He (laid, lay) down to rest before the game.
5. Paul (brought, took) his bike here with him.
6. The student (raised, rose) his hand in class.
7. I think I'll (set, sit) down here in this chair.
8. She (rose, raised) to her feet before speaking.
9. We shall (let, leave) for our vacation next week.

EXERCISE C
10. I (lent, borrowed) her that book last Tuesday.
11. Will your mother (leave, let) you go?
12. (Sit, Set) your packages in the corner.
13. She (lent, borrowed) the skirt from me.
14. (Take, Bring) this with you when you go.
15. Maggie (has lain, has laid) on that rug for hours.
16. Why don't you (lay, lie) in the shade?
17. Jane taught her parakeet to (set, sit) on her head.
18. (Leave, Let) him buy his own ticket.

19. I have to (bring, take) this trash out to the incinerator.
20. Mom (learned, taught) us how to make hollyhock dolls.
21. Mrs. Suarez asked me to (bring, take) her cake to the bake sale.

EXERCISE D.
22. (Lie, Lay) down and be quiet.
23. Did the doctor say that you could (set, sit) up?
24. As soon as the company left, Mother (laid, lay) down again.
25. Someone with muddy shoes had (laid, lain) on the sofa.
26. Someone had (laid, lain) a muddy shoe on the sofa.
27. Pat (lie, lay) awake for hours, worrying about the test.
28. Where should I (set, sit) this orange crate?
29. I won't (borrow, lend) him my skates again.
30. Please (raise, rise) the window shade all the way up.
31. He wanted the bread to (raise, rise) for one more hour.
32. Once it (raised, rose) he put it in the oven.
33. He (laid, lay) there for at least ten minutes.
34. Mr. McPherson (raised, rose) all our salaries.
35. His temperature (raised, rose) too.
36. Please (leave, let) the light on for me.
37. Don't let the cat (lay, lie) on the bed.
38. Will you (bring, take) these clothes over to the rummage sale?
39. Please don't (bring, take) any other used items back home.

EXERCISE E
40. Just as she lay down, the telephone rang.
41. Did Ronnie remember to take his watch to the jeweler?
42. The temperature has risen ten degrees in one hour.
43. Do you think that I could teach my dog to sit up and beg?
44. My friend taught his dog to lie down and roll over.
45. After I take my book back to the library, I'll lie down and take a nap.
46. I'll let you borrow my ax if you'll lend me your saw.
47. Mother was furious when she found out that I had lain around the house all day.

Lesson 42
Active and Passive Verbs
EXERCISE A
1. active
2. active
3. passive
4. passive
5. passive
6. passive
7. active

EXERCISE B
1. My brother Hank <u>cooks</u> like a pro. (active)
2. Pies and cakes <u>are prepared</u> at our place for any occasion. (passive)
3. Yesterday he <u>made</u> "Cheesecake à la Hank" for Mrs. Elroy. (active)
4. Eggs <u>were beaten</u> by him. (passive)
5. Flour <u>was sifted</u> before he began. (passive)
6. Graham crackers <u>were crushed</u> by hand. (passive)
7. Hank <u>slaved</u> away in the kitchen for hours. (active)
8. Finally, the cake <u>was delivered</u> to Mrs. Elroy. (passive)
9. Mrs. Elroy <u>remarked</u>, "How nice of your mother!" (active)
10. Poor Hank <u>didn't</u> even <u>correct</u> her. (active)

EXERCISE C
11. The theater advertised the movie as a kiddie matinee.
12. Their parents had taken the children to the movie.
13. The children bought popcorn and candy in abundance.
14. The ushers showed the boys and girls to their seats.
15. The owner darkened the theater lights.
16. The projectionist showed the movie.
17. Some audience members screamed high-pitched cries.
18. Others shrieked piercing yelps.

Lesson 43
Consistent Verb Tenses
EXERCISE A
1. Miranda takes off her hat and <u>bows</u> deeply to the audience.
2. She <u>lifts</u> her clubs into the air and begins juggling.
3. The clubs <u>fly</u> through the air; they never fall.
4. But wait. Here <u>comes</u> Phil and he has another club.
5. He <u>throws</u> it in too, so now there are five.
6. She <u>is</u> doing it! Now she takes off her hat and throws it in too.
7. Phil <u>catches</u> the hat and tosses it back.

EXERCISE B
1. We knew there was some kind of carnival at the shopping center, but we didn't expect to see an elephant there.
2. The sign read "Elephant rides for $1.00." At the time it seemed a reasonable price for an unusual five-minute ride.
3. The face of the man by the sign looked as wrinkled as the elephant's face was. He assured me, "It's an experience."
4. My friends urged me to try a ride, and I got my courage up as much as I could while the elephant man began to instruct me.
5. "You were a brave young woman," the elephant man said when he led me to the stepladder for the ascent.

Lesson 44
Subject-Verb Agreement
EXERCISE A
1. Either Tim or Debbie (<u>is</u>, are) supervising the cleanup.
2. Both Rob and Fred (<u>are</u>, is) bringing trash bags.
3. Neither the students nor the counselor (understand, <u>understands</u>) how the park got so messy.
4. Both Tim and Bart (has, <u>have</u>) begun painting benches.
5. Either Lisa or Margo (<u>is</u>, are) planting flowers.
6. Barry and Pam (is, <u>are</u>) picking up cans, bottles, and papers.
7. Neither Rob nor Fred (know, <u>knows</u>) the way to the recycling center.
8. Either Mr. Malone or Tim (<u>has</u>, have) a map.
9. Both Rob and Fred (<u>want</u>, wants) to celebrate with a cookout.
10. Both the neighbors and the park department (is, <u>are</u>) pleased with the way the park looks now.

EXERCISE B
1. A debate (<u>is</u>, are) an event in a speech contest.
2. Four weeks (<u>is</u>, are) the usual time spent in preparation.
3. I (studies, <u>study</u>) the arguments for both sides.
4. Ten minutes (<u>is</u>, are) the limit for a beginning speech.
5. We (listens, <u>listen</u>) carefully to the opponent.
6. Debaters (discusses, <u>discuss</u>) all issues that arise.

7. A second speech (<u>argues</u>, argue) against an opponent's remarks.
8. Debate rules (allows, <u>allow</u>) time for a rebuttal.
9. Judges (gives, <u>give</u>) points for skill in delivery and logic.
10. Persuasive and emotional appeals (is judged, <u>are judged</u>).
11. Five hundred dollars (<u>is</u>, are) the prize.
12. *Watch Those Arguments* (<u>gives</u>, give) guidelines for debaters.
13. Smith and Sons (<u>carries</u>, carry) books on debating.

Lesson 45

Subjects Separated from Verbs
EXERCISE A

Each verb agrees in number with its subject. Subjects are underlined.

1. A <u>bundle</u> of the twins' outgrown clothes seems a good donation.
2. The <u>prices</u> of some items of clothing seem high to me.
3. The <u>table</u> with vases and knickknacks has some interesting items.
4. The <u>worker</u> behind the table with kitchen utensils looks busy.

EXERCISE B

1. That <u>man</u> (with the huge radio in his arms) <u>is</u> rude.
2. This <u>bench</u> (in the park) <u>has been</u> an island of peace for me.
3. The <u>voice</u> (of the disk jockey now) <u>jars</u> my peace.
4. The <u>radio</u> (with a thousand knobs and dials) <u>blares</u>.
5. The <u>thoughtlessness</u> (of some people) <u>makes</u> me furious.

EXERCISE C

6. The members of the most successful hockey team in the history of the school (has, <u>have</u>) thanked the coach for his help.
7. A grapefruit with brown spots probably (<u>is</u>, are) rotten.
8. The woman's story about hearing the howling of wolves (<u>sends</u>, send) shivers up my spine.
9. The moonlight on the river and on the trees (<u>makes</u>, make) everything around look snowbound.
10. That friend of my parents (<u>is</u>, are) waving at us.
11. The dog with the newborn puppies (<u>was</u>, were) protective.
12. The holidays on the calendar in my room (has, <u>have</u>) been printed in red.
13. The man with the shiny shoes and gray pants (<u>is</u>, are) singing.
14. Your plaid jacket of black, red, and yellow (<u>looks</u>, look) great with black slacks.
15. The small craft on the angry waves (bob, <u>bobs</u>) up and down.

Lesson 46

Sentences in Inverted Order
EXERCISE A

1. <u>Is</u> <u>Gerald</u> <u>coming</u> to the parade too?—agree
2. There <u>is</u> a good <u>place</u> to stand on the sidewalk.—agree
3. Here <u>comes</u> the <u>Boy Scouts</u> on the left.—do not agree
4. Down the street <u>marches</u> our <u>baton twirlers</u>.—do not agree
5. <u>Isn't</u> that <u>music</u> stirring?—agree

EXERCISE B

1. Under the old coats (<u>hides</u>, hide) the cat.
2. Among the exhibits (<u>was</u>, were) a collection of famous drawings.
3. At the bottom of the box (was, <u>were</u>) the flashcubes.
4. Then around the corner (comes, <u>come</u>) two more fire trucks.
5. After the cheerleaders and the team (comes, <u>come</u>) the floats.
6. (Is, <u>Are</u>) Matt and Miguel tennis partners for the tournament?
7. (There's, <u>There are</u>) thirty days in April.
8. Down the staircase (creeps, <u>creep</u>) the cat and kittens.
9. Here (comes, <u>come</u>) the twins.
10. Hidden in the mattress (was, <u>were</u>) three diamond rings.
11. There (isn't, <u>aren't</u>) enough potato chips.
12. (Does, <u>Do</u>) the girls sing in the play?
13. (Here's, <u>Here are</u>) the balloons for the party.
14. Where (was, <u>were</u>) your parents last night?
15. (There's, <u>There are</u>) still a few copies left.

EXERCISE C

Answers will vary.

Lesson 47

Agreement with Special Subjects
EXERCISE A

1. The team (<u>is</u>, are) playing a game of baseball.
2. At the end of every show, the audience quickly (<u>moves</u>, move) toward the exit.

3. The troop (has, have) established new rules for membership.
4. The panel (is, are) arguing heatedly with each other about the issue.
5. The crowds (stands, stand) back to let the queen pass.
6. The crew of the ocean liner (has, have) scattered to tell the guests about the storm.
7. My class (has, have) held a debate.
8. The cast of the play (has, have) performed for the mayor.
9. The jury (has, have) gone to the courthouse.
10. The rancher's family (has, have) all helped him round up the cattle.
11. The band (is, are) taking the school bus when they tour the United States this year.
12. The army (was, were) on maneuvers for several days and nights during this past month.
13. The orchestra (has, have) played each weekend in this city for over twenty years.
14. The junior high school faculty (has, have) all reported to the principal on the proposed addition to the school.

EXERCISE B
Answers will vary.

Lesson 48
Agreement with Indefinite Pronouns
EXERCISE A
1. is   2. seem   3. belongs

EXERCISE B
1. Both of my parents (has, have) interesting jobs.
2. Anyone with a mitt (is, are) welcome to be the catcher.
3. Few of the forecasters' predictions (has, have) come true.
4. Some of us with responsibilities (has, have) to work hard.
5. Several of the squirrels (has, have) moved into our attic.
6. Nobody in my family (thinks, think) the house has ghosts.
7. Everybody in my classes (likes, like) to raise questions.
8. Neither of the planes from Canada (has, have) landed yet.
9. Many of my best ideas (occurs, occur) to me before sleep.
10. Each of the stories (ends, end) happily.
11. Everyone on the teams (thinks, think) the umpire is wrong.

12. One of the paintings (was, were) damaged in the flood.
13. Many of the teachers (has, have) finished their grades.
14. All of my friends (is, are) going to the concert.
15. No one in any of my study halls (wastes, waste) time.

EXERCISE C
16. has
17. have
18. have
19. have
20. has
21. has
22. has
23. have
24. has
25. has
26. has
27. Have
28. has

Lesson 49
Identifying Adjectives
EXERCISE A
1. graceful horses
2. two small puppies
3. Shetland pony—proper
4. English setter—proper
5. few giraffes
6. that Siamese cat—proper

EXERCISE B
1. Fossils provide a record of past life forms.
2. Soft rocks, such as sandstone and shale, preserve many fossils.
3. Some coal contains the delicate outlines of extinct plants.
4. Certain dead organisms are the source of valuable fossil fuels.
5. The muddy bottoms of lost rivers eventually dried to sandstone.
6. This sedimentary rock trapped animal bones and shells.
7. Fossil hunters find whole impressions of extinct fish skeletons in the soft rock.
8. In these searches, geological maps and hammers are useful.
9. In June I found Petoskey stone on a Michigan beach.
10. For a million years, dead coral had piled up in a shallow sea.

EXERCISE C
11. We had a United Nations party at school.
12. A student from Ireland brought Irish stew and soda bread.
13. Another student prepared a colorful platter of Mexican tacos.

14. Our teacher is <u>Italian</u>, and she cooked a <u>spaghetti</u> casserole.
15. I enjoyed the <u>warm</u> <u>French</u> bread and <u>onion</u> soup.
16. <u>Another</u> classmate brought <u>Swedish</u> meatballs from home.
17. Doug taught us an <u>old</u> <u>Scandinavian</u> <u>board</u> game.
18. Kiku wore a <u>silk</u> kimono, and Carla read us <u>African</u> legends.
19. <u>Four</u> students demonstrated <u>several</u> <u>Polish</u> dances.
20. Everyone learned <u>some</u> characteristics of <u>other</u> cultures.

Lesson 50
Comparative Forms of Adjectives
EXERCISE A

1. smaller, -est
2. greener, -est
3. livelier, -iest
4. more, most humorous
5. worse, worst
6. later, -est
7. rougher, -est
8. slimmer, -est
9. larger, -est
10. better, best
11. more, most delicious
12. fatter, -est
13. prettier, -est
14. more, most curious
15. clearer, -est
16. windier, -est
17. more, most unusual
18. more, most
19. less, least
20. more, most beautiful

EXERCISE B

1. The most interesting of all stories about Niagara Falls tells about Charles Blondin.
2. Charles Blondin was the most daring of all acrobats.
3. He was more imaginative than other acrobats of his time.
4. Blondin's feats were also funnier than those of most acrobats.
5. He performed the most astonishing feats of his life in 1859.
6. He walked across Niagara Falls on a tightrope thinner than wire.
7. Each new stunt was more dangerous than the last.
8. Next he rolled a heavy wheelbarrow across the tightrope.
9. A fearful crowd watched this stunt in horror.
10. His very best stunt of all also involved Niagara Falls.
11. This time Blondin made the walk even more difficult by crossing on stilts.
12. Then he gave the crowd the worst scare of their lives by actually repeating this stunt blindfolded.

Lesson 51
Identifying Adverbs
EXERCISE A

1. Gina studied for a <u>very</u> difficult history test. (difficult)
2. She began <u>early</u> in the evening. (began)
3. <u>First</u> she listed the important events. (listed)
4. She reviewed her notes <u>carefully</u>. (reviewed)
5. She studied <u>quite</u> <u>hard</u> until eleven o'clock. (studied—hard) (hard—quite)
6. <u>Afterwards</u> she slept <u>soundly</u>. (slept)

EXERCISE B

Adverbs are underlined; modified words have a double underline.

1. The crash <u>happened</u> <u>suddenly</u>. when
2. Lights <u>flashed</u> <u>outside</u>. where
3. The police <u>came</u> <u>instantly</u>. when
4. <u>Then</u> the ambulance <u>arrived</u>. when
5. A man <u>promptly</u> <u>received</u> aid. when
6. His arm was <u>badly</u> <u>hurt</u>. how
7. The traffic <u>moved</u> <u>slowly</u>. how
8. An officer <u>soon</u> <u>fixed</u> that. when
9. Trucks <u>pulled</u> the cars <u>away</u>. where
10. <u>Finally</u> everyone <u>left</u>. when

EXERCISE C

11. <u>Almost</u> <u>all</u> clowns go to a special school. adjective
12. Making people laugh can be a <u>very</u> <u>difficult</u> job. adjective
13. Clowns <u>quite</u> <u>often</u> study acrobatics. adverb
14. Many of them are <u>rather</u> <u>good</u> actors and make-up artists. adjective
15. The work they do is <u>extremely</u> <u>precise</u> and requires discipline. adjective
16. Clowns dress <u>somewhat</u> <u>oddly</u>, but that is part of their charm. adverb

Lesson 52
Functions of Adverbs
EXERCISE A

1. intensifier, time
2. place
3. time, manner, place
4. manner

EXERCISE B

Answers will vary.

EXERCISE C

7. <u>Recently</u>, Ramona's radio show has been <u>extremely</u> popular. time, intensifier

8. She <u>cleverly</u> interviews <u>rather</u> unusual guests. manner, intensifier
9. <u>Tonight</u> her program should be <u>quite</u> informative. time, intensifier
10. An <u>extremely</u> shy star <u>finally</u> agreed to an interview. intensifier, time
11. A mayoral candidate will be <u>there</u>. place
12. Her guests <u>usually</u> answer her personal questions <u>frankly</u>. time, manner
13. <u>Next</u>, Ramona will cover some <u>really</u> important issues. time, intensifier
14. Listeners may <u>then</u> call <u>in</u> with their questions. time, place
15. <u>Later</u>, she will <u>graciously</u> thank her guests for their visit. time, manner
16. Ramona <u>never</u> disappoints her <u>very</u> loyal audience. time, intensifier

Lesson 53
Comparative Forms of Adverbs
EXERCISE A
Answers will vary.

EXERCISE B
1. Rachel shopped more carefully at the record store than Vernon.
2. She walked more slowly down each aisle than he.
3. She looked more closely for special sales than other shoppers.
4. Vernon cared less about sales than Rachel.
5. He enjoys rock and roll more than jazz.
6. Vernon likes the blues best of all.
7. Classical music interests him least of all.
8. One record quickly caught his eye as he browsed.

Lesson 54
Adjective or Adverb
EXERCISE A
1. Incorrect
2. Correct
3. Incorrect
4. Incorrect
5. Correct
6. Incorrect

EXERCISE B
1. correct
2. I've been doing poorly in science.
3. correct
4. I chose my research-paper topic carefully.
5. correct
6. He can identify most insects very quickly.
7. He has a really large collection of books about insects.
8. correct
9. One insect is surely different from another.
10. I think my report will be really excellent.

EXERCISE C
1. Cicadas, or seventeen-year locusts, grow (slow, <u>slowly</u>).
2. Their development underground is (<u>slow</u>, slowly).
3. Their time aboveground is (<u>quick</u>, quickly), though.
4. You should look (close, <u>closely</u>) at a locust sometime.
5. You can see them (clear, <u>clearly</u>) without a magnifying glass.
6. Swarms of locusts can be (real, <u>really</u>) large.
7. They damage crops (terrible, <u>terribly</u>) by feeding on them.
8. Farmers don't feel (<u>sad</u>, sadly) that cicadas are short-lived.

Lesson 55
Good, well, bad, and *badly*
EXERCISE A
Adjectives and adverbs have a single underline; modified words have a double underline.
1. Kim Lee always <u><u>bowls</u></u> (good, <u>well</u>).
2. Until he helped me with my delivery, I <u><u>bowled</u></u> pretty (bad, <u>badly</u>).
3. <u><u>I</u></u> felt (<u>bad</u>, badly) about my poor game.
4. Now I <u><u>am doing</u></u> (good, <u>well</u>).
5. <u><u>I</u></u> feel (<u>good</u>, well) when I get a strike.
6. Andy <u><u>doesn't</u></u> do too (bad, <u>badly</u>) either.
7. Our team <u><u>bowled</u></u> (good, <u>well</u>) last night.
8. Only once this season have we lost because we <u><u>bowled</u></u> (bad, <u>badly</u>).
9. Anyone who <u><u>bowls</u></u> (good, <u>well</u>) enough can join the team.
10. How (bad, <u>badly</u>) <u><u>do</u></u> you want to be on the team?
11. Since you're not (bad, <u>badly</u>) <u><u>run-down</u></u>, you can learn to bowl.

EXERCISE B
1. Lonnie plays basketball well for being so short.
2. Yesterday she got over twenty points, even though the rest of her team played badly.
3. Can Lonnie play baseball as well as she plays basketball?
4. I felt bad for Sara when she didn't make the team.
5. Our baseball team usually doesn't play well.
6. Ron and I can hit well, but we don't often hit home runs.

7. No matter how hard he tries, Fred fields badly.
8. Fred's chances of being a starter don't look too good.
9. My brother swims well enough to win almost every meet.
10. Unlike my brother, the champion, I swim badly.

Lesson 56
This, that, these, and those
EXERCISE A
1. (Them, <u>Those</u>) pans are just the right size.
2. What do I need besides (<u>this</u>, these) kind of pots?
3. (<u>Those</u>, Those there) tomatoes are ripe enough to eat now.
4. Do you like (<u>this</u>, these) sort of recipe?
5. For (<u>that</u>, that there) dish we need potatoes and onions.
6. Joyce wants (<u>that</u>, those) kind of dessert.
7. (Them, <u>Those</u>) grapes need to be washed.
8. According to (<u>this</u>, this here) recipe, honey can be used.
9. Use (<u>this</u>, these) sort of scissors to cut the celery leaves.
10. We can't use (<u>this</u>, these) kind of apples for baking.
11. When you chop (<u>these</u>, these here) onions, be ready to cry.
12. Elmer bought both of (them, <u>those</u>) kinds of berries.
13. Have you tasted (<u>that</u>, that there) fruit punch?
14. (<u>This</u>, This here) new cookbook is a big help.
15. (That, <u>Those</u>) kinds of food are very appetizing.

EXERCISE B
1. That atlas isn't as good as this one.
2. This atlas on my lap contains maps of the solar system.
3. Did you renew all of these books sitting here on the table?
4. Yes, but I forgot those two upstairs in my room.
5. On this map I have here you can see the Ohio River.
6. Turn the page and you will see that mountain I described.
7. Those lakes you mentioned are about 300 miles south of here.
8. We still enjoy living in this city.
9. How many of those islands out on the bay are inhabited?
10. How far is it to that ranger tower over there?

Lesson 57
Using Negative Words
EXERCISE A
1. I (couldn't, <u>could</u>) scarcely say no.
2. Ruth and I don't know (nothing, <u>anything</u>) about soccer rules.
3. How can you eat cold beef without (no, <u>any</u>) horseradish?
4. Didn't (neither, <u>either</u>) of the two want the job?
5. She (couldn't, <u>could</u>) barely lift that heavy suitcase.
6. There wasn't (nobody, <u>anybody</u>) collecting tickets.
7. I would have drunk some milk, but there wasn't (none, <u>any</u>).
8. Weren't there (no, <u>any</u>) guards around?
9. Dad won't let (none, <u>any</u>) of us use his new camera.
10. We didn't have (no, <u>any</u>) snow until the end of December.
11. I (can't, <u>can</u>) hardly wait for spring vacation!
12. Sam won't go (nowhere, <u>anywhere</u>) without that rabbit's foot.
13. But you haven't (never, <u>ever</u>) had the mumps!

EXERCISE B
Answers will vary.

Lesson 58
Placement of Modifiers
EXERCISE A
Underlined words should be placed at the vertical line. Number 9 has three possible placements.
1. The lion | ignored the crowd <u>that was pacing in his cage</u>.
2. | Martha opened the door of the new house <u>with a broad smile</u>.
3. Sal appointed a committee to count the ballots <u>before the voting began</u>.
4. | The explorer told about his many adventures <u>at a meeting of the Optimists Club</u>.
5. We took the bicycle wheel | to a repair shop <u>that was bent out of shape</u>.
6. | They watched the whale dive <u>through their binoculars</u>.
7. <u>After they were rounded up</u>, the cowhands branded the cows |.
8. A groundskeeper found the lucky coin | in the park <u>that Inez had lost last week</u>.
9. | The ferocious dog | barked | at the mail carrier <u>with bared teeth</u>.

10. Kenji and I put the ripe apples | into a bushel basket that had fallen off the tree.

EXERCISE B
Answers will vary.

Lesson 59
Participles and Participial Phrases
EXERCISE A
1. The <u>barking</u> <u>dog</u> alerted them. (present participle)
2. The <u>cracked</u> <u>windowpane</u> made them suspicious. (past participle)
3. They hurried into the <u>darkened</u> <u>house</u>. (past participle)
4. <u>Holding</u> their breath, <u>they</u> tiptoed from room to room. (present participle)
5. Sentence 4 *holding their breath*

EXERCISE B
1. sun
2. explorer
3. people
4. earth
5. rain
6. breezes
7. relic

EXERCISE C
8. The <u>biting</u> wind licked at his heels.
9. <u>Frozen</u> snow crunched under his feet.
10. (<u>Looking</u> alarmed), the puppy ran into an alley.
11. A siren, (<u>screeching</u> loudly), caused him to hide in a box.
12. The sound came closer to the <u>terrified</u> animal.
13. A lady (<u>taking</u> a walk) saw him.
14. (<u>Rushing</u> to him), she gathered him in her arms.
15. Her <u>comforting</u> embrace soothed his nerves.
16. A dogcatcher (<u>driving</u> a van) waved to the lady.
17. (<u>Feeling</u> secure), the puppy barked at the van.

EXERCISE D
18. <u>Motivated by the prizes</u>, <u>everyone</u> entered the contests.
19. <u>Pedro</u>, <u>carrying an egg in a spoon</u>, beat Lisa.
20. <u>Being a runner</u>, <u>she</u> expected to win.
21. The crowd cheered the <u>contestants</u> <u>hopping in the one-leg race</u>.
22. The <u>winners</u>, <u>exhausted from their efforts</u>, got their prizes.
23. <u>Looking pleased</u>, <u>Mike</u> won a ticket to the movie.
24. <u>Willa</u>, <u>soaking wet</u>, beat Ed at the loop toss.
25. <u>Resting between games</u>, <u>contestants</u> compared scores.

Lesson 60
Gerunds and Gerund Phrases
EXERCISE A
1. predicate noun
2. object of prep.
3. subject
4. direct object
5. subject
6. direct object
7. object of prep.

EXERCISE B
Answers will vary.

EXERCISE C
13. (<u>Visiting</u> museums) is educational.
14. Does <u>touring</u> appeal to you?
15. <u>Learning</u> is easier this way.
16. Do you enjoy (<u>walking</u> so much?)
17. (<u>Studying</u> exhibits) is educational.
18. The guide is an expert in <u>lecturing</u>.
19. Here are some earphones for <u>listening</u>.
20. (<u>Seeing</u> a movie) is next.
21. The museum theater is for (<u>showing</u> educational films).
22. Here is a good spot for <u>viewing</u>.
23. I hate to think of (<u>leaving</u> the museum).
24. (<u>Walking</u> slowly) helps us see more.
25. Observing the exhibits carefully is important.

EXERCISE D
Gerunds and gerund phrases are underlined.
26. The team started <u>exercising</u> early each morning. direct object
27. One of the most difficult tasks is <u>doing sit-ups</u>. predicate noun
28. Some students dislike <u>climbing up ropes</u>. direct object
29. The objective is <u>climbing to the top in less than a minute</u>. predicate noun
30. <u>Sliding down afterwards</u> is fun. subject
31. <u>Tumbling</u> makes me dizzy sometimes. subject
32. Several persons have signed up for<u> tumbling next month</u>. object of prep.
33. Some people prefer <u>lifting in the weight room</u>. direct object
34. <u>Working out regularly</u> is important. subject
35. A big mistake is <u>resting too much between exercises</u>. predicate noun
36. <u>Exercising</u> is really good for you and a lot of fun. subject

EXERCISE E
Answers will vary.

Lesson 61
Infinitives and Infinitive Phrases
EXERCISE A
1. We hoped <u>to travel this summer</u>. direct object
2. <u>To visit Alaska</u> was our first choice. subject
3. The whole family wants <u>to see Mount McKinley</u>. direct object
4. Our purpose would be <u>to photograph the highest mountain in North America</u>. predicate noun

EXERCISE B
Answers may vary. Possible answers are shown.
1. to move
2. (to) build
3. To find
4. to return
5. to shop
6. to listen
7. to live
8. (to) cut
9. to sail
10. to work
11. To write

EXERCISE C
12. Francine helped <u>raise the young gorilla Koko</u>. direct object
13. She decided <u>to teach the gorilla sign language</u>. direct object
14. <u>To teach Koko 375 signs</u> took six years. subject
15. Koko uses signs when she wants <u>to "talk."</u> direct object
16. Koko eventually learned <u>to ask questions</u>. direct object
17. She wouldn't dare <u>tell lies</u>. direct object
18. Koko has learned <u>to understand many directions</u>. direct object
19. Koko's new task is <u>to use a computer</u>. predicate noun
20. The computer helps <u>translate her thoughts</u>. direct object
21. <u>To know Koko</u> is <u>to love her</u>. subject; predicate noun

Lesson 62
Placement of Participial Phrases
EXERCISE A
Sentences may vary. Suggested responses are given.
1. Coming down the hill, we found a patch of ripe strawberries.
2. The umpire almost didn't see Rob stealing second base.
3. My uncle likes chicken livers wrapped in bacon strips.
4. Watering the plants, Rachael saw three rosebushes.

EXERCISE B
Correct sentences are underlined.
1. <u>Tied with a red ribbon, the package sat on the table.</u>
   The package sat on the table tied with a red ribbon.
2. <u>Camping out last summer, we saw a bear.</u>
   We saw a bear camping out last summer.
3. The plane startled the onlookers coming in for a landing.
   <u>Coming in for a landing, the plane startled the onlookers.</u>
4. <u>We couldn't see the birds perched on the topmost branches.</u>
   Perched on the topmost branches, we couldn't see the birds.
5. <u>Climbing in a window, Cara saw a burglar.</u>
   <u>Cara saw a burglar climbing in a window.</u>

EXERCISE C
6. Browsing through the library, Herb found a rare book.
7. Hidden in a truck, the detective watched the house.
8. Running down the stairs, Fred could hear the music.
9. Sybil found the lost shovel lying under a pile of leaves.
10. The nurse comforted the patient who was breathing with difficulty.
11. Crossing the desert, the explorers found an oasis.
12. Ira thought the sun setting over the lake looked beautiful.

Lesson 63
Prepositions and Prepositional Phrases
EXERCISE A
Some answers will vary. Possible prepositions are shown.
1. of, about
2. for, to
3. after, for
4. of
5. for, to
6. like
7. above
8. in
9. by
10. about

EXERCISE B
Prepositions have a single underline; objects double.
1. Steve is a chimney sweep and goes <u>around</u> <u><u>town</u></u> <u>in</u> a green <u><u>van</u></u>.
2. He knocks <u>on</u> <u><u>doors</u></u> and explains his work <u>to</u> <u><u>people</u></u>.

3. Until his visit many people didn't know about sweeps.
4. Steve's services sound strange to them, but in spite of their surprise they make contracts with him for work.
5. Steve arrives in his tall black hat and black clothes.
6. First, he pushes a long brush up the walls of the chimney.
7. Next he loosens the soot and ashes along the chimney walls.
8. The dirt and debris fall into the fireplace and sometimes spread across the room.
9. Steve runs his giant vacuum cleaner over the floor and rugs.
10. Then he climbs into his van and drives to his next job.

Lesson 64
Preposition, Adverb, or Infinitive
EXERCISE A
1. infinitive, preposition
2. infinitive, adverb
3. preposition
4. preposition, infinitive
5. adverb, adverb

EXERCISE B
Infinitives retain single underline; Prep. phrases are also bracketed.
1. My friend called me to talk [to someone] about her problem.
2. But I had to leave to go [to a doctor's appointment].
3. I had to hurry [to the doctor's office].
4. To join school athletic teams you need to have a physical.
5. So on the phone I said some hard words [to my friend.]
6. To tell the truth, I told her to jump in the lake.
7. I even told her that I would drive her [to the lake.]
8. Normally, I would not say that [to anyone.]
9. When I lose my patience though, I say crazy things [to people.]
10. Later on, I have to apologize [to them.]

EXERCISE C
Adverbs retain single underline; prepositions are also bold.
11. We argued **over** lunch **about** our quarrel **on** the phone.
12. She was angry **at** me **for** several reasons.
13. My friend and I waited outside **for** a few minutes.
14. Then we went in and chatted **in** the lobby.
15. Inside the restaurant, we sat down and talked some more.
16. Then my friend stood up and began pacing around.
17. She was so angry that she almost walked out **of** the restaurant.
18. **For** a long time, we talked **about** the situation.
19. When I apologized **to** her, she calmed down.
20. **After** lunch, we walked over **to** a pond **near** the restaurant.

Lesson 65
Adjective and Adverb Prepositional Phrases
EXERCISE A
1. The Colorado River flows through the gorge.—V
2. Forests grow along the canyon's rims.—V
3. The rocks in the canyon are more than a million years old.—N
4. Over the years, the river has cut a deep gorge.—V
5. Thousands of mule deer range throughout the canyon.—N; V
6. The waters of the river swarm with trout.—N; V
7. Preservation of the canyon's natural beauty is the responsibility of the National Park Service.—N; N
8. Some brave tourists raft through the rapids.—V
9. Visitors can tour on a boat or travel by mule.—V; V
10. Rock carvings by ancient Indians sometimes remain on the canyon walls.—N; V
11. Many people worry about the area's future.—V
12. Pollution and erosion concern thousands of park visitors.—N

EXERCISE B
Adjective phrases have single underline; adverb phrases double.
1. During the spring, ducks and geese arrive in large numbers at our local park.
2. The small pond inside the park becomes their haven in the city.
3. People in the blocks around the park enjoy their aerial antics.
4. With great concentration, imagine a nearby pair of ducks.
5. One lost mallard stands outside a hamburger stand and begs for food.

6. <u>For its own sake</u>, I shoo it back <u>toward the park</u>.
7. <u>Within a minute</u>, the duck is flying <u>over the buildings</u>.
8. Fortunately, the keepers <u>at the nearby zoo</u> feed the ducks and geese <u>during the warm months</u>.
9. <u>Throughout the summer</u>, residents of the neighborhood enjoy the adorable ducklings and goslings.
10. <u>By autumn</u>, they will migrate like their parents <u>to some other pond</u>.

EXERCISE C
Answers will vary.

Lesson 66
Two Kinds of Conjunctions
EXERCISE A
1. I go to <u>either</u> matinees <u>or</u> early evening shows to avoid crowds. correlative
2. <u>Both</u> Roger <u>and</u> Gene liked this movie, <u>so</u> I know I will too. correlative; coordinating
3. The movie was humorous <u>yet</u> suspenseful. coordinating
4. I couldn't guess the ending, <u>nor</u> could my friend. coordinating
5. He thought the music was loud <u>and</u> distracting, <u>but</u> I didn't. coordinating; coordinating
6. I enjoyed <u>both</u> the acting <u>and</u> the special effects. correlative
7. <u>Neither</u> the long wait for tickets <u>nor</u> the noisy little children could spoil the movie for me. correlative
8. I see almost every movie, <u>for</u> I plan to be a film critic. coordinating

EXERCISE B
Suggested conjunctions are given.
1. and
2. neither . . . nor
3. both . . . and *or* either . . . or
4. so
5. both . . . and
6. either . . . or *or* both . . . and
7. but
8. for
9. so
10. nor

Lesson 67
Identifying Interjections
EXERCISE A
1. Ah
2. Phew
3. Oh
4. Oops
5. Shh!
6. Psst
7. Ugh
8. Wow
9. My
10. Alas
11. Whee
12. Wow
13. Super!
14. Ugh
15. Hey

Lesson 68
Combining Sentences with Modifiers
EXERCISE
Answers may vary. Possible answers are shown.
1. She was young, intelligent, and well-educated.
2. Under the name Nellie Bly, she wrote about factory workers for the *Pittsburgh Dispatch*.
3. She wrote honestly and sympathetically.
4. Then she moved from Pittsburgh to New York.
5. Her first assignment for the *New York World* was difficult, dangerous, and exciting.
6. Her story proved that mental patients were treated cruelly, unfairly, and thoughtlessly.
7. To get the story, she lived in the mental hospital among the patients.
8. Her most famous and enjoyable adventure was a trip around the world.
9. She traveled by ship and by special train.
10. People bought the *World* to read her light, informative, and entertaining stories.

Lesson 69
Capitalizing Proper Nouns and Adjectives
EXERCISE A
1. This spring <u>carver</u> <u>school</u> will host <u>sportarama</u>, a national sport competition.
2. It will begin on <u>monday</u>, <u>march</u> 17, which is <u>st. patrick's</u> <u>day</u>.
3. There will be teams from such states as <u>west virginia</u>, <u>nevada</u>, <u>florida</u>, and <u>new hampshire</u>, as well as <u>jamaican</u> and <u>puerto rican</u> teams.
4. One team is coming from as far north as <u>winnepeg</u>, <u>canada</u>.
5. They will fly into <u>montclare</u> <u>airport</u> on a <u>boeing</u> 727.

334   Grade Eight SkillBook, Grammar, Usage, and Mechanics Answer Key

6. My cousin, hans jorgen, is here as a german exchange student.
7. My school asked cousin hans to be on our soccer team.
8. Because he was so happy, he went to bennet's department store and bought a special pair of whoopee soccer shoes.
9. A committee is planning entertainment, which will include a performance by a group of irish dancers at the agora theater.
10. If we can get enough tickets, mom, dad, and my sister patti all plan to go.
11. My older brother frank won't be able to attend sportarama.
12. He is going to be at a reunion of his graduating class at the university of vermont.
13. Mom says frank is one of several vermont alumni trying to locate members of the class who graduated in 1990.
14. Frank says members of his class have gone in all directions—north, south, east, and west—since they left vermont.
15. I know it's true because I've seen his list with addresses from anchorage, alaska; coral gables, florida; and several towns from the midwest and southeast.
16. One of the envelopes went to a woman who works at a mount rushmore souvenir shop in south dakota.
17. Frank's best friend in college is now stationed at fort benning, georgia.
18. A girl frank used to date ran st. rita's orphanage in southeast asia.
19. His old roommate, rafael santana, now is an atlanta executive for creighton industries, where he designs all the ads for olympia tractors.
20. Frank can hardly wait to go to new england in march to see all his old friends.

EXERCISE B
1. a. American Revolution
   b. American history
2. a. English countryside
   b. English Channel
3. a. Kentucky Derby
   b. Kentucky natives
4. a. Roman Empire
   b. Roman architecture
5. a. Irish setter
   b. Irish Sea
6. a. Indian food
   b. Indian Ocean

7. a. Mississippi River
   b. Mississippi tributary
8. a. Ferris Avenue
   b. Ferris wheel

Lesson 70
Capitalizing Titles
EXERCISE A
1. *Joan of Arc*
2. *Roughing It*
3. "Woman with Flower"
4. *Sixty Minutes*
5. *Reader's Digest*
6. *I Am the Cheese*
7. *Evanston Review*
8. *The Gilded Age*
9. *Christina's World*
10. *The Adventures of Tom Sawyer*
11. "A Man Who Had No Eyes"
12. "The Day the Sun Came Out"
13. "This Land Is Your Land"
14. "President Cleveland, Where Are You?"
15. *The Prince and the Pauper*
16. *A Connecticut Yankee in King Arthur's Court*

EXERCISE B
1. The president planned a reception at the White House.
2. The reception was in honor of prince Charles.
3. Unfortunately, the guest of honor caught a bad cold.
4. His doctor advised him to stay in bed.
5. "I will follow your orders, doctor," Charles said.
6. The secretary of state came to see how he was.
7. The vice president also dropped by.
8. Charles's mother, queen Elizabeth, heard that he was ill.
9. The queen called long distance and spoke to dr. Longford.
10. "Your majesty, it's just a cold," the doctor reassured her.
11. princess Anne and prince William cheered him up.
12. Even mrs. Longford sent him some chicken soup.

Lesson 71
Commas in Sentences
EXERCISE
1. Baseball, basketball, and ice hockey are my favorite sports.

Grade Eight SkillBook, Grammar, Usage, and Mechanics Answer Key

2. Personally, I prefer swimming, the greatest sport of all.
3. Ellen, do you still run, or do you prefer some other activity?
4. Jogging, in my opinion, is still the way to stay fit.
5. After Tim, Gene, and I took up yoga, I felt so relaxed and limber.
6. Believe it or not, I used to do calisthenics every day, but now I ride a bike instead.
7. Ms. Cusick, our English teacher, and Mrs. Lane, the principal's secretary, walk three miles together every morning.
8. Though he gets no exercise, Jerry looks better than any of us.
9. What's your secret, old pal?
10. I eat balanced meals, take vitamins, and get enough sleep.
11. Will you help us, Glen, to set up an exercise program?
12. It should contain simple, average, and challenging activities.
13. You don't really need a rigid program, but I'll help you anyway.
14. Sy's health club, by the way, has a new program for teenagers.
15. It's inexpensive and it looks like fun.
16. Lisa, Karen, and Karen's little brother went to a baseball game.
17. They sat in the bleachers, ate popcorn, and cheered.
18. Frank, Karen's little brother's friend, sat five rows away.
19. At the end of the third inning, the two boys noticed each other.
20. Luckily, they saw a few empty seats, so they got closer together.

Lesson 72
Other uses of Commas
EXERCISE A
1. Incorrect
   Mary and Diane attend a college in Boise, Idaho.
2. Incorrect
   Their car has over 80,000 miles on the odometer.
3. Correct
4. Incorrect
   Mary will graduate on May 26, 1996, in an outdoor ceremony.
5. Incorrect
   She will live at 23 Oak Road, Provo, Utah, after graduation.

EXERCISE B
47 Fifth Avenue
New York, NY 10003

March 27, 1999

Dear Glenda,
   I finally received your letter dated Friday, December 1. We have moved from Hoosick Falls, New York, to New York City. Dad is now working at 850 Park Avenue, his company's main office.
   As you can imagine, I wasn't too happy about moving. I knew I would miss Tanya, Dave, Shirley, and my other good friends. I miss them, but I am having an exciting time here. Come visit me this summer. I'll show you the Statue of Liberty, the Empire State Building, and the World Trade Center. We can ride bikes, row on the pond, and visit the zoo. Write soon, Glenda, so we can make plans.

Your friend,

Lesson 73
Semicolons and Colons
EXERCISE A
1. This was the heaviest snowfall in years; it broke all records.
2. People couldn't get to work; however, no on complained.
3. Some went skiing on Main Street; others rode on sleds.
4. Snow stood in ten-foot drifts; it amazed everyone.
5. The children grew fidgety; the parents grew impatient.

EXERCISE B
1. This letter confirms your reservation for 8:30 on June 14.
2. I love tennis; in fact, I play four times a week.
3. Branch offices are located in San Francisco, Los Angeles, and Oakland, California; Dallas and Houston, Texas; and Springfield and Chicago, Illinois.
4. Lee, rake the yard; Al, wash the car; Fritz, clean the basement.
5. One week he travels on Monday, Wednesday, and Friday; and the next week he travels on Tuesday, Thursday, and Saturday.
6. Add these things to your list: soap, flour, and bread; and come back as quickly as you can.

Lesson 74

Quotation Marks

EXERCISE A

1. Correct
2. "Look," Mike said, "Ace Sporting Goods is having a super sale."
3. "Jogging shoes are marked down fifty percent," he continued.
4. Correct
5. "I could use a new pair of shoes," Emmy Lou admitted.

EXERCISE B

1. Ben Franklin whistled "Yankee Doodle" as he emerged from his time machine, saw a woman, and asked, "Can you help me?"
2. He said, "Franklin's the name. Can you tell me what that is?"
3. "That," the woman replied, "is an electric light."
4. "But there's no storm," he said. "Also we have no kite."
5. "You have an uncanny resemblance," she said, "to someone."
6. She asked, "Have you ever appeared on late-night TV?"
7. "I don't know what TV is," he exclaimed, "but I believe in going to bed early."
8. Franklin continued, "Is that a stove?"

10. The book *Middle-aged Men Shouldn't Eat at All* is his next gift.

Lesson 75

Other Punctuation Marks

EXERCISE A

1. The word telephone has three *e*'s.
2. Last Monday—no it was Tuesday—I called my brother.
3. Did you know that he and my sister-in-law live in Hollywood?
4. I sent them a copy of Dr. A. N. Nau's book, *Eating Well*.
5. Dr. Nau (1938–1984) emphasized a low-salt diet (see page 80–88).
6. He died, though, when he was only fifty-six.
7. I printed ten *35*'s and the word *Congratulations* on the inside cover of the book as a birthday greeting.
8. How surprised my roly-poly brother was!
9. He complained—actually he screamed at me—about my humor.
or He complained (actually he screamed at me) about my humor.